Automated Testing Ur

Automated Testing Engineering Fundamentals

C# Edition

The Complete Handbook Volume 1

Anton Angelov
Automate The Planet

Table of Contents

Credits

First published: September 2023

Production reference: Published by Automate The Planet Ltd.
Address: https://www.automatetheplanet.com/

Book cover design and formatting by Martin Kolev
Proofread and edited by Daniel, aka. @mrproofreading
Technical Review by Automate The Planet Engineering

About the Author

Anton Angelov is CTO and Co-founder of Automate The Planet Ltd, inventor of BELLATRIX Test Automation Framework, and author of bestsellers "Design Patterns for High-Quality Automated Tests: Clean Code for Bulletproof Tests" in C# and Java. He has been nominated 5 times for "QA of the Year award", listed in the top 100 of most influential IT people in Bulgaria, and cited with the "Overall Contribution QA Community Award". Nowadays, he manages and directs teams of passionate engineers helping companies succeed with their test automation. Additionally, he consults companies, leads automated testing training series, writes books, and gives talks at the biggest QA conferences worldwide. You can find him on LinkedIn every day.

- 320+ Published Articles Automate The Planet
- 120+ Published Articles Code Project
- 60+ Published Articles DZone as Most Valuable Blogger
- 10+ Articles Published in Quality Magazines
- 50+ Given International Conference Talks and Keynotes
- 8 books published
- 7,000,000+ article views
- 1200 000+ amazing readers for 2022
- Read in 180+ countries

About the Reviewers

Above all, the author would like to extend his heartfelt gratitude to his comrades at Automate the Planet for their invaluable assistance with technical and editorial tasks, especially to Ivaylo Milanov, who contributed significantly. Given the expansive scope of the "Automated Testing Unleashed" series, including multiple perspectives in the editorial process was necessary rather than relying on a single individual to review all the content. Over the past three years, numerous interns have utilized the beta versions of the books as a cornerstone for their induction and skill enhancement programs. The regular and senior engineers at Automate the Planet, too, have found the series useful for refreshing knowledge on various topics and have, in turn, contributed invaluable insights.

The series underwent over 20 reviews, all conducted by engineers who are genuinely the best in their field, and together tackle some of the most demanding test automation projects. Without their collective wisdom and unwavering support, the quality of these books simply would not be what it is today!

Acknowledgements

This book encapsulates insights and wisdom from many talented IT professionals and engineers. Skillful programmers sometimes overlook that their knowledge is not solely a result of personal effort but a combination of various factors: luck, environment, and experiences. At this point in my life, I have gathered enough practical know-how to write these books. Yet, this would not have been possible without the influence and guidance of numerous people: my parents' hard work, lessons from my school and university teachers, and the knowledge I acquired from mentors and colleagues in previous companies. I have a natural thirst for learning, regularly immersing myself in new books and educational videos, significantly shaping my expertise.

In the past decade, I have contributed regularly to the Automate The Planet website, posting articles and conducting many live corporate training sessions. The "Automated Testing Unleashed" series is a rich blend of knowledge I have tried to share over the years. However, your support has been crucial to the website's success. So, a big "Thank You!" to all our fans and readers. I also appreciate the attendees of numerous international DEV and QA conferences where I have spoken.

I reached a significant milestone this year: I gave the main keynote at my 50th international conference. I'm grateful for your presence and your efforts to implement the ideas I discuss. I sincerely thank my colleagues at Automate The Planet for their invaluable assistance with technical and editorial tasks, particularly Ivaylo Milanov, for his significant contribution. My partner at Automate The Planet, Martin Kolev, deserves recognition for his work on visual enhancements, marketing, and the numerous detailed tasks around the project.
My friends, who have patiently listened to my geeky book talk, especially my wife, Stela, deserve special gratitude!

As an active member of society, I've organized various donation drives, contributed blood to hospitals, planted trees, and managed waste effectively. It is crucial to nurture a greener future for the next generations. I regularly organize book donation campaigns in Bulgaria, where the proceeds go toward tree planting. If you're elsewhere in the world, buying this book also contributes to the cause. We have already raised enough funds to plant over 10,000 trees. I encourage you to find and support similar initiatives in your countries. Let's work towards a better future for our children together.

Foreword

This book series is a comprehensive journey through the realms of software test automation, written to make the process understandable and accessible to both novices and experienced professionals. It offers a deep dive into various automation frameworks and methodologies alongside essential techniques and concepts crucial to mastering the art of automation testing. Every test automation engineer should have a broader knowledge of different technical topics and know how the applications work under the hood.

I wrote a single foreword for all books part of "Automated Testing Unleashed: The Complete Handbook".

Automated Testing Unleashed: Automated Testing Engineering Fundamentals Volume 1

Chapter 1. C# Programming Basics
Chapter 2. C# Object-oriented Programming
Chapter 3. C# Beyond Fundamentals
Chapter 4. Testing Fundamentals
Chapter 5. Test Automation Fundamentals
Chapter 6. Web Fundamentals
Chapter 7. Source Control Fundamentals
Chapter 8. HTML Crash Course
Chapter 9. CSS Crash Course
Chapter 10. JavaScript Crash Course
Chapter 11. Unit Testing Fundamentals
Appendix 1. High-quality Code

This volume offers an in-depth exploration of the vital technologies test engineers must grasp. It begins with a comprehensive study of C# programming, ranging from basic principles to advanced topics, laying a solid groundwork for programming and test automation.

As we advance, the book illuminates software testing fundamentals, underscoring its significance in our digital age. The segments on test automation essentials demystify common misconceptions, guiding you toward a clearer understanding of this vital area. We also delve into the web's foundational technologies - TCP/IP, HTML, CSS, and JavaScript - presenting invaluable context for crafting high-quality web automated tests.

Further, the book underscores the importance of source control in software development, focusing on GIT.

Toward the conclusion, we delve into unit testing fundamentals, a vital tool for creating complex UI tests. You'll encounter popular .NET ecosystem unit testing frameworks, gaining knowledge on leveraging them for comprehensive end-to-end testing.

In sum, this volume centers on understanding all crucial technologies we must know as software engineers in test, ranging from a deep comprehension of an OOP programming language to JavaScript and unit testing frameworks. This book is an all-encompassing guide for those eager to enhance their skills in automated testing.

Automated Testing Unleashed: Web Automated Testing Volume 2

Chapter 1. WebDriver Fundamentals
Chapter 2. WebDriver Beyond Fundamentals
Chapter 3. Chrome DevTools & BiDirectional APIs
Chapter 4. Selenium WebDriver-Based Tools
Chapter 5. Defining High-Quality Test Attributes
Chapter 6. Layout, Style, and Responsive Testing with Selenium

------

This comprehensive guide to Selenium WebDriver navigates from foundational to advanced aspects of web test automation. Readers will gain skills in executing JavaScript, managing cookies, leveraging the Actions API, and utilizing Selenium 4's revolutionary features, such as Chrome DevTools and BiDirectional API.

The book expands on an array of WebDriver-based tools that boost Selenium's potential, spotlighting cutting-edge automated testing types like layout, style, and responsive tests. Moreover, the book illuminates vital principles of high-quality test attributes and the SOLID principles, which are critical for every test engineer. It also clarifies often misunderstood terms in test automation, improving your comprehension and command of the technical language.

In essence, this book is a reliable companion for anyone keen on enhancing their skills in Selenium WebDriver and web test automation, delivering expert knowledge in an easy-to-understand manner.

Automated Testing Unleashed: API Automated Testing Volume 3

Chapter 1. API Testing with Postman Fundamentals
Chapter 2. API Testing with Postman Beyond Fundamentals

This comprehensive guide embarks on the journey by demystifying the fundamentals of API testing, employing Postman, one of the most celebrated tools in the industry. We examine Postman's robust capabilities and advanced features like creating collections, variables, and environments. As we traverse beyond the rudiments, the readers will be introduced to elements such as automated testing, scripting with JavaScript, and command-line interface (CLI) test running in Postman, establishing a solid foundation for the world of API testing. We also delve into the world of databases, explaining the ins and outs of SQL and highlighting the practical use of ORM frameworks for streamlined database operations. We further expand on the theme of automated testing, this time in the context of APIs using .NET libraries, exploring various libraries and their configurations.

With a forward-looking approach, we venture into innovative technologies like gRPC, OpenAPI, and various protocols such as OData, SOAP, and GraphQL. Each segment provides practical examples, enabling you to grasp the advanced concepts of these technologies and to implement them in automated testing.

In summary, this book takes you on an informative journey through the landscape of API testing, balancing fundamental concepts with advanced tools, libraries, and cutting-edge technologies.

Automated Testing Unleashed: Expert Level Automated Testing Volume 4

This volume opens by delving into Windows desktop application automation utilizing WinAppDriver, shedding light on automating UI interactions and employing design principles for robust tests. It then shifts gears to behavior-driven testing via SpecFlow, instructing on crafting detailed, business-readable specifications. Subsequently, it guides the reader through constructing utility classes to bolster testing capabilities. The journey continues as we submerge into mobile application automation with Appium, encapsulating Android and iOS platforms and revealing an assortment of critical commands to fortify your testing repertoire. The focus then swivels to web performance analysis and benchmarking employing Google Lighthouse and BenchmarkDotNet, providing the means to assess the effectiveness of your WebDriver code.

Further, the volume navigates advanced territories of modern web application testing, addressing sophisticated topics and automation tactics for cutting-edge web frameworks and complex web components. The book highlights the significance of adept test data management and environment setup, demonstrating strategies for data generation and the application of test data across diverse environments.

Finally, the handbook elaborates on continuous test execution and result analysis, explaining the subtleties of single-machine and distributed setups and showing cloud solutions for scalable test execution. A thorough analysis of CI/CD tools and test result analysis tools adds a hands-on aspect to the learning journey.

Automated Testing Unleashed: The Complete Handbook - Automated Testing Practice - Solving Real-World Challenges Volume 5

This book provides comprehensive solutions for most of the exercises featured in the first four books of the "Automated Testing Unleashed" series. In addition, it includes detailed explanations of crucial code segments to help enhance your understanding.

Ultimately, these books aim to be a reliable companion on your test automation journey, providing valuable insights and practical techniques.

Preface

Whether you are embarking on your trip or looking to refine your skills further, there is something here for everyone. Let's dive in!

What this book covers

Chapter 1. C# Programming Basics

In this chapter, you will completely understand C# programming language fundamentals. You will learn how to write code and understand how the language operates, which is often overlooked. The topics covered include data types, arrays, operators, and conditions, demonstrated through multiple examples and exercises. By the end of this chapter, you will have a solid understanding of the basics of C# programming, giving you a foundation for further learning in test automation QA and technical programming.

Chapter 2. C# Object-oriented Programming

This chapter will dive into object-oriented programming (OOP) fundamentals using C#. First, we'll explore how to reuse code blocks with methods and create user-defined classes with fields, functions, and properties. Next, we'll cover the core concepts of polymorphism and inheritance in OOP programming. Finally, we'll examine how interfaces, base classes, enumerations, and static methods work, giving you a complete understanding of the topic. By the end of this chapter, you'll have a firm grasp of the building blocks of C# OOP programming and be able to apply these concepts in practice.

Chapter 3. C# Beyond Fundamentals

This chapter will dive deeper into advanced C# programming concepts beyond the basics. We will start by discussing generic classes and methods, which can help us write more reusable code. Next, we will explore the various C# collections beyond arrays and lists and learn how to perform basic file and directory operations. Additionally, we will investigate delegates and extension methods, which are essential building blocks for software libraries. Lastly, I will briefly touch on the LINQ and Reflection APIs.

Chapter 4. Testing Fundamentals

This chapter will dive into software testing, starting with some key terminology. Then, we'll explore what testing is and look at different testing types and the fundamental test processes. We'll also touch upon some of the essential concepts at the ISTQB Foundation level. By the end of this chapter, you'll understand the basics of software testing, its importance, and how it fits into the software development life cycle.

Chapter 5. Test Automation Fundamentals

The upcoming chapter will cover the essential concepts beyond test automation. Before writing automated code, it's important to know what to automate and what not to automate. This chapter will discuss common misunderstandings about automated testing and help establish a solid test infrastructure. We will cover high-quality automated tests' attributes, benefits, and costs. We will also explore a system for selecting the appropriate solution for your project.

Chapter 6. Web Fundamentals

In this chapter, we will explore the workings of the web, an essential aspect of writing high-quality web automated tests. To do that, we will dive deep into the fundamental web technologies you need to know. We'll discuss the concepts of TCP/IP, HTML, CSS, and JavaScript and explain how they work together to create websites. Additionally, we will examine the structure, types, and headers of HTTP requests so that you can understand the mechanisms used in web communication.

Chapter 7. Source Control Fundamentals

This chapter imparts vital information that all software engineers ought to understand. We'll delve into the nature of source control, its indispensable role in software development, and its added advantages. We'll also examine one of the most popular tools in this field - GIT. This tool is integrated into larger platforms like GitHub, AzureDevOps, and Bitbucket, which we'll briefly explore. In addition, key operations such as code reviews, pull requests, merging code, and branches are on our radar for thorough understanding. We'll wrap up with a discussion on best practices related to creating automated test code and leveraging these systems.

Chapter 8. HTML Crash Course

In the upcoming chapter, we will dive into the basics of HTML web pages. We will start by analyzing a simple HTML web page and understanding its essential components. Then, we will explore all the necessary HTML elements and their attributes. Finally, you will see various examples, making it easier to understand how each element works and how to use them to build web pages.

Chapter 9. CSS Crash Course

In this chapter, we will explore how the styling of websites works with CSS. Understanding CSS is essential for writing high-quality automated tests for websites. We will thoroughly review all CSS selectors because we must use them in our automated tests. By the end of this chapter, you will understand how to use CSS to style your web pages and use it in your automated tests.

Chapter 10. JavaScript Crash Course

In this chapter, we will explore JavaScript, a core component of every web page that makes it interactive and dynamic. We will discuss how it is used in automated testing to solve complex problems where standard libraries lack the required utilities. You will find that many of the concepts covered in previous chapters for C# will also apply to JavaScript. We will learn the fundamentals of the programming language and discuss its features, including variables, data types, operators, loops, functions, and more. By the end of this chapter, you will have a solid foundation in JavaScript and be prepared to use it in automated testing.

Chapter 11. Unit Testing Fundamentals

In the upcoming chapter, we will delve into a crucial tool for writing complex UI tests - unit testing. Although I won't go into too much detail about component testing, mocking objects, etc., which is the responsibility of backend developers to unit test their code, we will discuss two popular unit testing frameworks in the .NET ecosystem and demonstrate how to leverage them for end-to-end testing.

Who Is This Book For?

"Automated Testing Unleashed" Book Series:
This quintessential series of five books is a comprehensive reservoir of foundational knowledge that will empower you to excel as a test automation engineer. With content that caters to both beginners stepping into the field and seasoned professionals, these books delve into an array of technical aspects related to our profession. I encourage you to consume them sequentially. Even if you're already familiar with most of the concepts, these books will likely expose you to new insights and provide a valuable opportunity to revisit and reinforce the ones you already know. Although I've crafted each chapter and book to stand independently, the ideal way to absorb and appreciate the full breadth and depth of the material is by progressing through them book by book, chapter by chapter.

Before You Get Started

Prior experience in OOP programming languages, such as C#, Java, etc., is not required, but having this knowledge will assist in grasping the concepts more quickly. The presented code in the book provides sufficient information to understand the concepts. If you purchase and read all five books, kindly contact me on LinkedIn, and I will add you to a private GitHub repository containing all exercise solutions and more. Please complete the exercises alone before checking the answers. This is my way of thanking you for purchasing the books instead of pirating them. You can also connect with me on LinkedIn if you have any questions about the book that still need to be addressed.

To build and execute the code, you will require a C# editors such as Visual Studio, Rider or Visual Studio Code, and you'll need to install .NET 6+.

Source Code & Excluse LinkedIn Group

You can grasp its central concepts by perusing the code snippets in the book. Yet, to get hands-on experience, it's advised to execute the solutions firsthand. To begin, clone the book's GitHub repository via this link: https://bit.ly/3YUCLuq

To gain access and confirm your book purchase, send me a screenshot of the book order or the Kindle via LinkedIn, along with your GitHub username.

As an added perk, I've initiated an exclusive LinkedIn group for the book's readers. There, I'll share supplementary resources and videos tailored for those who own any book series volume. This includes insights for career advancement, interview preparation, checklists, and in-depth videos on topics that couldn't fit within the book's pages. **To join, provide proof of purchase by sending a screenshot of your book order or the Kindle version via a LinkedIn message.** Exclusive group's link - https://bit.ly/3qPnBtP

At the end of every chapter, you'll encounter a set of exercises. Their solutions are housed in **"Automated Testing Unleashed: The Complete Handbook - Automated Testing Practice - Solving Real-World Challenges Volume 5."** This volume offers exhaustive solutions to most exercises from the initial four editions of the "Automated Testing Unleashed" collection. Furthermore, it elucidates vital code sections to deepen your comprehension. A dedicated GitHub repository accompanies it.

Conventions

In this book, you will find several styles of text that distinguish between different kinds of information. Here are examples of these styles and an explanation of their meaning.

Code words in the text are shown as follows: `CartPage`

A block of code is set as follows:

```
public void clickProceedToCheckout() {
    proceedToCheckout().click();
    _driver.waitUntilPageLoadsCompletely();
}
```

Important words or code snippets are shown in **bold**.

Remember that to make the example more concise and more comfortable to read, I haven't included the 'throws exception' part of the methods' signature.

NOTE

Definition description

Definition

Definition: Example

Definition description

Piracy

Only those who value the hard work and dedication that went into this endeavor and chose not to obtain the book unlawfully will enjoy the additional benefits, such as access to source code and the exclusive books club. Due to economic constraints, I recognize that affording books isn't feasible in certain parts of the world. This is precisely why I've set modest prices for all the books. The Kindle e-version, in particular, is priced lower than most comparable books, which typically have a much higher price tag.

Piracy of copyright material on the Internet is an ongoing problem across all media. Therefore, if you come across any illegal copies of the work, in any form, on the Internet, please provide me with the location address or website name immediately so I can pursue a remedy.
I appreciate your help in protecting the ability to bring you valuable content!

Reader Feedback & Questions

Feedback from the readers is always welcome. Let me know what you think about the book, and what you liked or disliked. Although I have taken every care to ensure the accuracy of the content, mistakes do happen. If you find a mistake in the book, whether in the text or code, I would be grateful if you would report it.

You can contact me on LinkedIn - https://bit.ly/2NjWJ19 if you have any problems with any aspect of the book, and I will do my best to address them.

Chapter 1. C# Programming Basics

This book is an essential resource for anyone looking to become a skilled QA Automation Engineer. While some programming knowledge is necessary to excel in this field, this book does not require an in-depth understanding of any programming language. Instead, it provides a comprehensive overview of the essential concepts and practices needed to succeed in automated testing.

While many books are available on specific programming languages, this book takes a broader approach, covering the fundamental principles and best practices of automated testing. It aims to provide you with a solid foundation in the key concepts and skills needed to excel in the field without overwhelming you with too much technical detail.

After covering the essential concepts and skills, the book will dive deeper into testing practices and tools that can help you automate the testing of various software pieces. By the end of the book, you will have the knowledge and skills to create and maintain efficient and effective automated testing solutions for various software applications.

Topics covered in this chapter:

- C# Programming Intro
- Your First C# Program
- Primitive Data Types and Variables
- Operators and Expressions
- Conditional Statements
- Loops
- Arrays

C# Programming Intro

C# (pronounced "See Sharp") is a modern and powerful programming language that is object-oriented and type-safe. It is designed to help you create secure and reliable applications running seamlessly in the .NET ecosystem.

C# has its roots in the C family of programming languages and is therefore highly familiar to C, C++, Java, and JavaScript programmers. In addition, its syntax is easy to understand and learn, making it a popular choice among developers in technical programming domains like test automation QA.

C# is an excellent choice for building various applications, from desktop and mobile apps to web-based applications and beyond. Whether you're just starting in your programming career or looking to expand your skills, C# is a powerful and versatile language that is well worth learning.

Introduction to .NET

C# programs run on the .NET platform, which includes the Common Language Runtime (CLR) and a set of class libraries. When C# code is compiled, it is transformed into an intermediate language (IL) stored in an assembly with the ".dll" extension. The CLR then loads the assembly into memory when the program is executed.

When the CLR encounters the IL code, it uses Just-In-Time (JIT) compilation to convert it into native machine instructions that the system can execute. This ensures that the code is optimized for the specific hardware and operating system it runs on. In addition, the CLR provides other services such as automatic garbage collection, exception handling, and resource management, making it easier for developers to create secure and reliable software.

One of the key advantages of .NET is its language interoperability, which allows IL code generated from C# to interact with code generated from other compliant languages like F#, Visual Basic, or C++. This means that developers can use the best tool for the job, regardless of the language or platform, and can easily combine different codebases to create more powerful and flexible software solutions.

.NET is a free, open-source development platform for building many kinds of apps, such as: web apps, web APIs, microservices, cloud native apps, mobile apps, desktop apps, games and many more. You can create .NET apps for many operating systems: Windows, macOS, Linux, Android, iOS and more.

> **NOTE**
>
> Microsoft released the .NET Framework in 2002, providing developers with a powerful platform for building Windows applications. Since then, the platform has evolved, and the current version is .NET Framework 4.8, which is still supported today.
>
> However, in 2014, Microsoft recognized the need for a more modern, cross-platform implementation of .NET and began working on a new, open-source successor to the .NET Framework. Initially called .NET Core, this new implementation went through several iterations and updates, with version 3.1 being the last version to use the Core suffix.
>
> The latest version of .NET, which succeeded .NET Core 3.1, is .NET 5.0. The name "Core" was dropped to emphasize that this is now the primary and official implementation of .NET. The decision to skip version 4 was made to avoid confusion with the existing .NET Framework 4.8.
>
> With its modern architecture, improved performance, and cross-platform support, .NET 7.0 is an excellent choice for developers in technical programming domains like test automation QA and software development, offering powerful tools and resources for building robust and scalable applications.

Integrated Development Environments IDEs

The integrated development environments for .NET include:

- **Visual Studio**
  It runs on Windows only. It has extensive built-in functionality designed to work with .NET. The Community edition is free for students, open-source contributors, and individuals.
- **Visual Studio Code**
  It runs on Windows, macOS, and Linux. It is free and open source. Extensions are available for working with .NET languages.
- **Visual Studio for Mac**
  It runs on macOS only. For developing .NET apps and games for iOS, Android, and web.
- **JetBrains Rider**
  Powerful cross-platform IDE that contains many smart code inspections. It is built by the company who created and maintains the most used IDE for Java - IntelliJ.

> **NOTE**
>
> For running all the examples and exercises in the book, I suggest using Visual Studio
> Community Edition. It is my preferred choice for IDE when developing apps or tests with C#
> and .NET. Moreover, the installer will install most of the SDKs and tools we need.
> Therefore, I suggest you download the latest version.

SDK and Runtimes

To develop and run .NET apps, you need the .NET runtime. If you pick Visual Studio for IDE, it
will install the runtime. When you install the SDK required for development, you will
automatically get the runtime. The .NET SDK includes:

- **.NET CLI** - command-line tools for local development and continuous integration
  scripts.
- **MSBuild build engine** - provides an XML schema for a project file that controls how
  the build platform processes and builds software.
- **.NET runtime** - provides a type system, assembly loading, a garbage collection, and
  other basic services.
- **Runtime libraries**

> **NOTE**
>
> In the context of Visual Studio, managed projects are loaded and built using **MSBuild**. The
> project files in Visual Studio have a `.csproj` extension and include MSBuild XML code
> executed when the project is built using the IDE. These project files import all the relevant
> settings and build processes required for typical development work.

The .NET Common Language Runtime (CLR) is a cross-platform runtime that operates on
Windows, macOS, and Linux. It is responsible for memory allocation and management in
applications. Additionally, the CLR functions as a virtual machine that can run applications
while generating and compiling code using a just-in-time (JIT) compiler.

NuGet is a package manager designed explicitly for .NET and is available as open-source
software. Each NuGet package is a compressed `.zip` file with the `.nupkg` extension containing
compiled code (DLLs) and other related files. These packages are distributed through a private

host or https://nuget.org. Developers can add a package, also known as a dependency, to their project if they want to utilize shared code and then call the package's API within their project's code.

Your First C# Program

To create your first C# program, download and install the latest version of Visual Studio Community Edition if you still need to do so. Once you have installed Visual Studio, create a new C# Console application by navigating to **File -> New -> Project**. Make sure to give your new project an appropriate name that reflects its purpose. Additionally, choose the preselected "current" version as the target framework to ensure that your project uses the most up-to-date framework available. With these simple steps, you'll be well on creating your very first C# program.

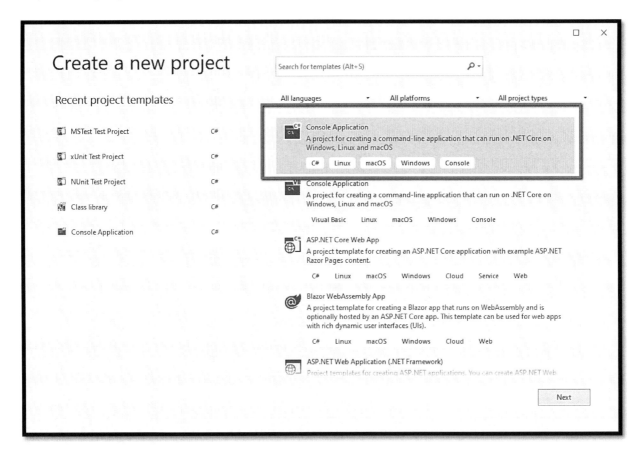

Your first C# application was generated automatically for you:

```
using System;

namespace MyFirstCSharpProject
{
    class Program
```

```
    {
        static void Main(string[] args)
        {
            Console.WriteLine("Hello World!");
        }
    }
}
```

To execute your application, press the green "**Play**" button or use the shortcut key CTRL + F5. Once executed, a new console window will open, displaying the message *"Hello World!"* to indicate that your application is running.

The provided C# program includes the standard namespace System via the using statement. It defines a class called Program, which contains the Main() method - the program entry point. Next, we print text to the console by calling the WriteLine() method, which is part of the Console class. It is essential to follow certain conventions when writing C# code, such as using PascalCase for class names and starting them with a capital letter. Additionally, the opening curly brace should be on a new line, and a TAB should indent the code block. Finally, the closing curly brace should be aligned with the corresponding opening curly brace. These rules are in place to ensure that the code is readable. However, it's worth noting that C# code can be formatted in various ways and still run correctly.

using

```
System
                                                   ;

    class          HelloCSharp                    {
         static
void        Main(              )   {   Console    .      WriteLine      ("Hello,
C#"     )  ;Console.
   WriteLine           (                "Hello again"
                      )                      ;}}
```

Before delving into further details on how to build your code, let's take a step back and
discuss how your code is organized into groups.

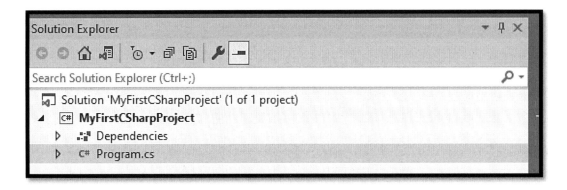

What Are Solutions and Projects in Visual Studio?

When you create an application or test in Visual Studio, it starts with a project. A project
contains all the files compiled into an executable, library, or website. These files can include
source code, icons, images, and more. Visual Studio leverages MSBuild to build each project in
a solution; each project consists of an MSBuild project file. Double-click on the project's icon
to view the contents of newer project files in Visual Studio. A project is part of a solution,
which is a container for one or more related projects, along with build information, Visual
Studio window settings, and miscellaneous files that are not associated with a specific project.
Visual Studio uses two file types to store settings for the solution:

- .sln - organizes projects, project items, and solution items in the solution.
- .suo - stores user-level settings and customizations, such as breakpoints.

A "solution folder" is a virtual folder that only exists in **Solution Explorer**, which allows you to
group projects within a solution. The solution also has a folder on the existing file system, and
each separate project has a folder inside the solution folder that bears its name.

How to Build Your Project?

Your program is built automatically when you click the "**Play**" button. During the build process, your C# source code is converted into IL code, which is stored inside .dll files. You can also manually build your project by opening the context menu (selecting the project and right-clicking) and clicking on the "**Build**" menu item.

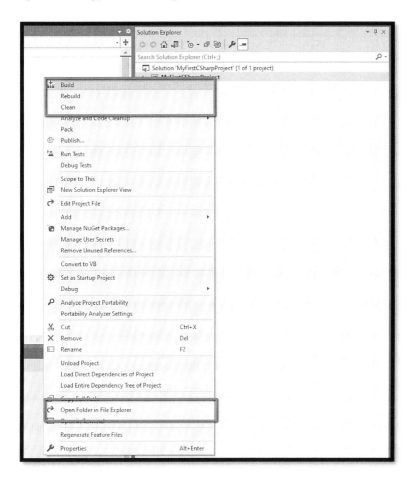

In addition, if you click "**Open Folder in File Explorer**", the actual folder on the file system will open. Once you've built the project, you can find the bin folder containing the outputs such as .dll, .exe, and other files.

NOTE

The "**Build**" command compiles code files (.dll and .exe) that have changed since the last build. On the other hand, the "**Rebuild**" command deletes all compiled files and recompiles them, regardless of whether the code has changed.

Exercises

1. Familiarize yourself with:
   a. Microsoft Visual Studio
   b. Microsoft Developer Network (MSDN) Library Documentation
2. Find information about `Console.WriteLine()` method.
3. Create, compile, and run a "Hello C#" console application.
4. Modify the application to print your name.
5. Write a program to print the numbers 2, 202 and 2002.
6. Create a console application that prints the current date and time.
7. Create a console application that calculates and prints the square of the number 32346.

NOTE

Please note that some exercises intentionally require more knowledge than the examples presented earlier. This widespread teaching methodology helps you learn how to search effectively in documentation and developer forums online. As a result, it's normal if you cannot complete some exercises. However, don't let this discourage you. Keep going and return to the exercises when you feel more comfortable and confident in your skills.

Primitive Data Types and Variables

The next section will cover data types and how to store and use data in C# programs using variables.

What Is a Data Type?

A data type is a set of values that share similar characteristics and determines the type of data stored in a variable in the computer memory. Examples of data types include positive integers (such as 1, 2, 3), alphabetical characters (like a, b, c), or days of the week (such as Monday and Tuesday). Each data type has a name, which is typically a C# keyword or .NET type, as well as a size and a default value.

Integer Types

Data Type	Values
sbyte	-128 to 127
byte	0 to 255
short	-32,768 to 32,767
ushort	0 to 65,535
int	-2,147,483,648 to 2,147,483,647
uint	0 to 4,294,967,295
long	-9,223,372,036,854,775,808 to 9,223,372,036,854,775,807
ulong	0 to 18,446,744,073,709,551,615

We may need to use different data types depending on the unit of measurement.

```
byte centuries = 25;
ushort years = 2009;
uint days = 840480;
ulong hours = 19536520;
```

Floating-point Types

float (±1.5 × 10−45 to ±3.4 × 1038), precision of 7 digits, 0.0F default value
double (±5.0 × 10−324 to ±1.7 × 10308), precision of 15-16 digits, 0.0D default value
decimal (±1.0 x 10^{-28} to ±7.9228 x 10^{28}), precision of 28-29 digits, 0.0M default value

Boolean Data Type

The `bool` keyword is used to declare a Boolean data type, which can have one of two possible values - `true` or `false`. This data type is commonly used in logical expressions, and the default value is `false`.

```
int a = 1;
int b = 2;
bool greaterAB = (a > b);
Console.WriteLine(greaterAB); // False
bool equalA1 = (a == 1);
Console.WriteLine(equalA1); // True
```

Character Data Type

A char data type represents symbolic information and is declared using the `char` keyword. Each symbol is assigned a corresponding integer code. The default value of this data type is `'\0'`.

```
char symbol = 'a';
Console.WriteLine($"The code of '{symbol}' is: {(int)symbol}");
```

String Data Type

To declare a sequence of characters in C# programming language, you can use the string data type, which is declared using the `string` keyword. By default, a string variable has a value of `null`, which means that no value has been assigned to it. To define a string, enclose it in quotation marks:

```
string s = "Automate The Planet";
```

Strings can be concatenated using the + operator:

```
string s = "Automate" + "The" + "Planet"; // results in "Automate The Planet"
```

Object Type

The `object` keyword is used to declare the base type for all other types and can hold values of any type:

```
object dataContainer = 5;
```

```
dataContainer = "Five";
```

What Is a Variable?

Variables are used in programming as placeholders to store and manipulate data that can be changed at runtime. Each variable has a name, data type, and value. The variable's name is used to refer to the data it holds, and the data type defines the type of data that can be stored in the variable. We can also change the value of the variable.

```
int number = 9;
```

In this example, we have declared a variable named `number` and assigned it a value of **9** using the **integer** (`int`) data type.

<data_type> <identifier> [= <initialization>];

Assigning Values

To set a value to a variable, we use the `=` operator. The name of the variable is placed on the left side, and the value of the corresponding data type is placed on the right side. For example:

```
int firstValue = 5;
int secondValue;
secondValue = firstValue;
```

In this example, the variable `firstValue` is assigned the value of **5** using the `int` data type. The variable `secondValue` is declared without an initial value, and later assigned the value of `firstValue` using the `=` operator.

Nullable Types

Nullable types can contain the values of the corresponding value type and a `null` value. They are declared using the `System.Nullable` struct and are wrappers over primitive types (such as `int?` and `double?`).

For example, the following code demonstrates declaring a nullable integer and assigning it a `null` value, then assigning it a value of 5:

```
int? nullInt = null;
Console.WriteLine("This is the integer with Null value -> {nullInt}");
nullInt = 5;
Console.WriteLine("This is the integer with value 5 -> {nullInt}");
```

The output of the code will be:

```
This is the integer with Null value ->
This is the integer with value 5 -> 5
```

Exercises

1. Declare five variables choosing the most appropriate type for each, either `byte`, `sbyte`, `short`, `ushort`, `int`, `uint`, `long`, or `ulong`, to represent the following values: 51240, -113, 4735941, 87, -20000.

2. Declare a `boolean` variable called `isFemale` and assign an appropriate value corresponding to your gender.

3. Declare two string variables and assign them "Hello" and "World". Next, declare an object variable and assign it with the concatenation of the first two variables (mind adding an interval). Finally, declare a third string variable and initialize it with the value of the object variable (you should perform type casting).

4. An IT company wants to keep a record of its employees. Each record would have the following characteristics - first name, family name, age, gender (m or f), ID number, and a unique employee number (38560000 to 38569999). Declare the variables needed to keep the information for a single employee using appropriate data types and descriptive names.

5. Declare two integer variables, assign them 5 and 10, and then exchange their values.

Operators in C#

In the upcoming section, we will explore the concept of operators, examine examples of various categories, and discuss when to use them effectively.

Category	Operators
Arithmetic	+ - * / % ++ --
Logical	&& || ^ !
Binary	&	^ ~ << >>
Comparison	== != < > <= >=
Assignment	= += -= *= /= %= &= |= ^= <<= >>=
String concatenation	+
Type conversion	is as typeof
Other	. [] () ?: new

Arithmetic Operators

In programming, arithmetic operators are used when performing mathematical operations. The plus (+), minus (-), and multiplication (*) operators are used the same way as in math. The division operator (/) is slightly different: if used on integers, it returns an integer (without rounding) or throws an exception. If used on real numbers, it returns a real number, infinity, or NaN (not a number). The remainder operator (%) returns the remainder from the division of integers. The special addition operator (++) increments a variable.

Example:

```
int squarePerimeter = 17;
double squareSide = squarePerimeter / 4.0;
double squareArea = squareSide * squareSide;
Console.WriteLine(squareSide); // 4.25
Console.WriteLine(squareArea); // 18.0625
int a = 5;
int b = 4;
Console.WriteLine(a + b); // 9
Console.WriteLine(11 / 3); // 3
```

```
Console.WriteLine(11 % 3); // 2
Console.WriteLine(12 / 3); // 4
```

Logical Operators

The logical operators are used to evaluate conditions and compare values. These operators take boolean operands and return a boolean result. The operator ! reverses the boolean value of an operand. The operators && (AND), || (OR), and ^ (XOR) perform logical operations on two operands.

Operation	||	||	||	||	&&	&&	&&	&&	^	^	^	^
Operand1	0	0	1	1	0	0	1	1	0	0	1	1
Operand2	0	1	0	1	0	1	0	1	0	1	0	1
Result	0	1	1	1	0	0	0	1	0	1	1	0

Example:

```
bool a = true;
bool b = false;
Console.WriteLine(a && b); // False
Console.WriteLine(a || b); // True
Console.WriteLine(a ^ b); // True
Console.WriteLine(!b); // True
Console.WriteLine(b || true); // True
Console.WriteLine(b && true); // False
Console.WriteLine(a || true); // True
Console.WriteLine(a && true); // True
Console.WriteLine(!a); // False
Console.WriteLine((5>7) ^ (a==b)); // False
```

Comparison Operators

In programming, we use comparison operators to compare variables. These operators include ==, <, >, >=, <=, and !=.

Here are some examples:

```
int a = 5;
int b = 4;
```

```
Console.WriteLine(a >= b); // True
Console.WriteLine(a != b); // True
Console.WriteLine(a == b); // False
Console.WriteLine(a == a); // True
Console.WriteLine(a != ++b); // False
Console.WriteLine(a > b); // False
```

In the code above, we declared two integer variables, a and b, and compared them using different comparison operators. Finally, the output of each comparison is written to the console.

Assignment Operators

The assignment operators allow you to assign a value to a variable using the =, +=, -=, /=, %=, *=, and ??= operators. For instance, x -= y equals x = x - y, with x evaluated once. The same rule applies to other operator combinations.

```
int x = 6;
int y = 4;
Console.WriteLine(y *= 2); // 8
int z = y = 3; // y=3 and z=3
Console.WriteLine(z); // 3
Console.WriteLine(x |= 1); // 7
Console.WriteLine(x += 3); // 10
Console.WriteLine(x /= 2); // 5
```

In C# 8.0 and later, the null-coalescing assignment operator ??= assigns the right-hand operand's value to the left-hand operand only if the latter evaluates to null.

Expressions

In programming, expressions are comprised of operators, literals, and variables that are evaluated to produce a value.

Here are some examples:

```
int a = 2 + 3; // a is assigned the value 5
int b = (a + 3) * (a - 4) + (2 * a + 7) / 4; // b is assigned the value 12
bool greater = (a > b) || ((a == 0) && (b == 0)); // greater is assigned the value true or
false based on the values of a and b
```

Note that parentheses can be used to group expressions and change the order of evaluation.

Exercises

1. Write an expression that checks if the given integer is odd or even.
2. Write an expression that calculates a rectangle's area by given width and height.
3. Write an expression that checks if the given positive integer number n (n ≤ 100) is prime. E.g., 37 is prime.
4. Write an expression that calculates trapezoid's area by given sides a and b and height h.

Conditional Statements

The upcoming section will discuss how C# allows us to perform different actions for different decisions using mathematical and logical conditions. We will explore the various available statements for this purpose.

Comparison Operators

Operator	Notation in C#
Equals	==
Not Equals	!=
Greater Than	>
Greater Than or Equals	>=
Less Than	<
Less Than or Equals	<=

The code snippet shows an example of using the less than or equals operator in C# to compare two integers and assign the resulting boolean value to a variable named `result`. In this case, the expression evaluates to `true`, and the value of the `result` variable is printed to the console:

```
bool result = 7 <= 8;
Console.WriteLine(result); // True
```

Logical Operators

Operator	Notation in C#

Logical NOT	!
Logical AND	&&
Logical OR	||
Logical Exclusive OR (XOR)	^

IF Statement

The `if` statement is the simplest conditional statement in C#, allowing you to test for a condition. The condition can be a boolean variable or expression or a comparison expression. If the condition is `true`, the code inside the `if` block is executed:

```
if (condition)
{
    statements;
}
```

IF-ELSE Statement

The `if-else` statement is a more complex and useful conditional statement. It executes one branch if the condition is `true` and another if `false`. The simplest form of an `if-else` statement is as follows:

```
if (expression)
{
    statement1;
}
else
{
    statement2;
}
```

Nested IF Statements

In C#, `if` and `if-else` statements can be nested, which means they can be used inside another `if` or `else` statement. Each `else` corresponds to its closest preceding `if` statement:

```
if (expression)
{
```

```
    if (expression)
    {
        statement;
    }
    else
    {
        statement;
    }
}
else
{
    statement;
}
```

Multiple IF-ELSE-IF-ELSE

When working with conditional statements, there may be cases where we need to use another `if` the construction in the `else` block. In such cases, the `else if` statement can be used.

For example:

```
int ch = 'Z';
if (ch == 'A' || ch == 'a')
{
    Console.WriteLine("Vowel [ei]");
}
else if (ch == 'E' || ch == 'e')
{
    Console.WriteLine("Vowel [i:]");
}
else if (/*other condition*/)
{
    // execute this block if the previous conditions are false and this condition is true
}
else
{
    // execute this block if all previous conditions are false
}
```

Switch-Case Statement

In this section, we will discuss the switch statement in C#, which selects a statement for execution from a list based on the value of the `switch` expression. The `break` operator exits the statement. The syntax for the `switch` statement is as follows:

```
switch (expression)
{
    case constant1: statement1;
```

```
        break;
    case constant2: statement2;
        break;
    case constantN: statementN;
        break;
    default: statement; break;
}
```

Here is how the `switch` statement works:

1. The expression is evaluated.
2. When one of the constants specified in a `case` label equals the expression, the statement corresponding to that `case` is executed.
3. If no `case` is equal to the expression, the `default` case is executed, or the control is transferred to the endpoint of the `switch` statement if there is no `default` case. Here is an example of a `switch` statement that displays the name of the day of the week:

```
switch (day)
{
        case 1: Console.WriteLine("Monday");
                break;
        case 2: Console.WriteLine("Tuesday");
                break;
        case 3: Console.WriteLine("Wednesday");
                break;
        case 4: Console.WriteLine("Thursday");
                break;
        case 5: Console.WriteLine("Friday");
                break;
        case 6: Console.WriteLine("Saturday");
                break;
        case 7: Console.WriteLine("Sunday");
                break;
        default: Console.WriteLine("Error!");
                break;
}
```

Exercises

1. Write an IF statement that examines two integer variables and exchanges their values if the first one is greater than the second one.
2. Write a program that shows the sign of the product of three real numbers without calculating it. Instead, use a sequence of if statements.

Loops

In the upcoming section, we will explore how to execute blocks of code multiple times using control statements called loops. We will discuss several types of loops, such as `while`, `do-while`, `for`, and `foreach`. Loops allow us to repeat the execution of a code block a fixed number of times or while a given condition is `true` for each collection member. It is important to note that loops that never end are called infinite loops.

While Loop

A `while` loop is a simple and commonly used loop. The loop continues to execute as long as the specified condition returns a `true` boolean value. Then, you can use the `break` operator to exit the loop:

```
while (condition)
{
    statements;
}
```

Do-While Loop

In this loop, the block of statements is executed first, and then the loop condition is evaluated. The loop is repeated if the condition is `true` and it is executed at least once:

```
do
{
    statements;
}
while (condition);
```

For Loops

The `for` loop is a commonly used loop consisting of an initialization statement, a boolean test expression, an update statement, and a block of statements that comprise the loop body.

Here is an example of a `for` loop:

```
for (initialization; test; update)
{
    statements;
}
```

The initialization expression executes once, just before the loop is entered. It is usually used to declare a counter variable:

```
for (int number = 0; ...; ...)
{
    // Can use the number here
}
// Cannot use the number here
```

The test expression evaluates before each iteration of the loop. If `true`, the loop body is executed; if `false`, the loop body is skipped:

```
for (int number = 0; number < 10; ...)
{
    // some code
}
```

After the loop's body is finished, the update expression executes at each iteration. It is usually used to update the counter:

```
for (int number = 0; number < 10; number++)
{
    // some code
}
```

The `continue` operator is used to end the iteration of the inner-most loop. For example, to sum all odd numbers in the range of [1, n] that are not divisors of 3, the following code can be used:

```
int n = int.Parse(Console.ReadLine());
int sum = 0;
for (int i = 1; i <= n; i += 2)
{
    if (i % 3 == 0)
    {
        continue;
    }
    sum += i;
}
Console.WriteLine($"sum = {sum}");
```

In the above code, the `continue` statement is used to skip adding the odd number to the sum if it is a multiple of 3. If this condition is met, the loop continues with the next iteration, allowing only the desired odd numbers to be summed.

Foreach Loops

The `foreach` loop in C# iterates over all collection elements. This loop is best suited when you want to iterate through all the elements of a collection without bothering about the index. In a `foreach` loop, the loop variable is the element in the collection, which takes on each collection value, one by one.

The basic syntax of a `foreach` loop in C# is as follows:

```
foreach (Type element in collection)
{
    statements;
}
```

Here, `Type` represents the data type of the elements in the collection, and `element` is the loop variable that takes on each collection value, one by one. The collection can be an array, a list, or any other group of elements of the same type.

For example, the following `foreach` loop iterates over all the days in an array and prints them to the console:

```
var days = new string[] { "Monday", "Tuesday", "Wednesday", "Thursday",
  "Friday", "Saturday", "Sunday" };
foreach (string day in days)
{
    Console.WriteLine(day);
}
```

Nested Loop

A composition of loops is called a nested loop - a loop inside another loop:

```
for (initialization; test; update)
{
    for (initialization; test; update)
    {
        statements;
    }
    \\...
}
```

In this example, the inner loop will execute its statements 5 times for each outer loop iteration. Once the inner loop completes its execution, the outer loop will continue with its next iteration.

Exercises

1. Write a program that prints all the numbers from 1 to 30.
2. Write a program that prints all the numbers from 1 to 30 that are not divisible by 3 and 7 simultaneously.

Arrays

In this section, we will discuss arrays in C#. An array is a sequence of elements of the same type, and the order of the elements is fixed. In addition, arrays have a fixed size, which can be accessed using the `Length` property. Finally, we use square brackets with the desired type of elements to declare an array. For example, to declare an array of integers and an array of strings:

```
int[] myIntArray;
string[] myStringArray;
```

To create an array, we use the `new` operator followed by the desired array size. For instance, to create an array of 5 integers:

```
int[] myIntArray = new int[5];
```

To access array elements, we use square brackets with the index of the desired element. The first array's element has an index of `0`, and the last has an index of `Length - 1`. For example, to retrieve and modify elements of an array of strings:

```
string[] array = {"one", "two", "three"};
for (int index = 0; index < array.Length; index++)
{
    Console.WriteLine(array[index]);
}
```

We process all array elements in the above code and print each item to the console. Here is a similar code where we print all cities in a `string[]` array using a `foreach` loop:

```
string[] capitals =
{
    "Sofia",
    "Moscow",
    "Berlin",
    "Paris"
};
foreach (string capital in capitals)
{
    Console.WriteLine(capital);
}
```

The `foreach` loop is a simpler way to iterate over array elements without indexing. We use the `foreach` loop when we only need to read and not modify the elements. The syntax of the `foreach` loop is:

```
foreach (type value in array)
```

Where `type` is the element type, `value` is the local name of the variable, and `array` is the array being processed.

Lists

Arrays have a fixed size that must be specified during creation, while lists can dynamically resize when elements are added or removed. Lists are implemented using the List<T> class in C#, where T is the type of elements the list will hold. You can use the Add() method to add an element to a list. To remove an element, you can use the Remove() method. In addition, the Count property can be used to get the list's current size.

This is equivalent to creating an integer array with a length of 5 and initializing its elements using a for loop:

```
List<int> intList = new List<int>();
for(int i=0; i<5; i++)
{
    intList.Add(i);
}
```

It is the same as:

```
int[] intArray = new int[5];
for(int i=0; i<5; i++)
{
    intArray[i] = i;
}
```

Exercises

1. Write a program that allocates array of 20 integers and initializes each element by its index multiplied by 5. Then, print the obtained array on the console.
2. Solve the same problem but use a list instead of the array.

Summary

In this chapter, we covered the necessary aspects of C# programming that are crucial to understanding the language. First, it's essential to have a high-level understanding of how things work under the hood. We then delved into creating a C# program and exploring the various data types and operators that C# provides. We also learned about the essential components of any program, such as code branches, storing data in arrays and lists, and iterating over them to perform various operations.

In the upcoming chapter, we will dive into object-oriented programming (OOP) fundamentals, which include methods, classes, interfaces, and more.

Chapter 2. C# Object-oriented Programming

In the next chapter, we'll cover the basics of object-oriented programming (OOP). Then, I'll show you how to reuse code blocks using methods and create user-defined classes that combine fields, functions, and properties. We'll also discuss important OOP concepts such as polymorphism and inheritance. Finally, we'll explore interfaces, base classes, enumerations, and static methods.

Topics covered in this chapter:

- Methods
- Classes and Objects
- Interfaces
- Base Classes
- Enumerations
- Static Classes and Methods
- Creating and Implementing a Class Hierarchy

Methods

Methods are a fundamental component of programming that serve as building blocks for solving small problems. They are pieces of code with a name that can be called from other parts of the code and can take parameters and return values. Using methods allows programmers to construct large programs from simple pieces, resulting in better organization and readability of code. Additionally, they help to avoid repeating code, making it easier to maintain and modify the code over time. With methods, code reusability can be significantly improved by using existing methods multiple times. Other terms for methods include functions, procedures, and subroutines.

Declaring and Creating Methods

Each method has a name that describes its purpose and is used to call the method. The methods declared as static can be called by any other method, static or not. The void methods do not return any results. Each method has a body containing the programming code, surrounded by {and}.

To declare a method, use the following syntax:

```
static void PrintCompanyInfo()
{
    Console.WriteLine("Automate The Planet");
    Console.WriteLine("automatetheplanet.com");
}
```

To call a method, use the method's name followed by parentheses and a semicolon. For example, to call the PrintCompanyInfo() method, we can write:

```
PrintCompanyInfo();
```

A method can be called from the Main() method, any other method, or itself (in a process known as recursion). If a method needs to receive information, you can use parameters (also known as arguments). Each parameter has a name and type. You can pass zero or several input values. For example, we can define a method called PrintMax() that takes two float parameters and prints the maximum of the two:

```
static void PrintMax(float num1, float num2)
{
    float max = num1;
    if (num2 > num1)
        max = num2;
    Console.WriteLine("Maximal number: {0}", max);
}
```

To call a method and pass values to its parameters, use the method's name followed by a list of expressions for each parameter:

```
PrintSign(-7);
PrintSign(balance);
PrintSign(5+4);
PrintMax(150, 209);
PrintMax(oldQuantity * 1.7, quantity * 3);
```

Methods can also return values of any type (int, string, array, etc.) by specifying the method's return type. To return a value from a method, use the return keyword followed by the value to be returned. For example, we can define a method Multiply() that takes two integers and returns their product:

```
static int Multiply(int firstNum, int secondNum)
{
    return firstNum * secondNum;
}
```

The return statement immediately terminates the method's execution and returns the specified expression to the caller. You can also use it to terminate void methods. The return keyword can be used several times in a method body, depending on the logic of the code.

Exercises

1. Write a method GetMax() with two parameters that returns the bigger of two integers. Write a program that passes two integers and prints the biggest of them using GetMax().

Classes and Objects

In object-oriented programming, objects represent real-world objects or abstract concepts. For example, objects can represent a bank, an account, a customer, a dog, a bicycle, a queue, and so on. These objects have states/data and behaviors. For instance, an account's data includes information about the account holder, balance, and type. Its behaviors include methods to withdraw, deposit, and suspend. We use variables/properties to represent the states/data and methods/functions to represent the behaviors. Therefore, we can define an object as a software bundle of variables and related methods.

What Is a Class?

> **Definition: Class**
>
> Classes serve as blueprints for creating objects at runtime. They define the characteristics and properties of an object, as well as the methods used to manipulate its behavior.

The classes define the structure of objects. They act as a template and define attributes represented by variables and properties that hold the object's state. Additionally, they contain a set of actions (behavior) realized by methods. Finally, a class defines the methods and types of data associated with the object.

Here's an example of a class in C# called `Car`:

```
class Car
{
    public Car(string color)
    {
        Color = color;
    }

    public string Color { get; set; }

    public string Describe()
    {
        return $"This car is {color}";
    }
}
```

This is how we use the class to create an instance of it:

```
static void Main(string[] args)
{
```

```
        Car redCar = new Car("Red");
        Console.WriteLine(redCar.Describe());

        Car greenCar = new Car("Green");
        Console.WriteLine(greenCar.Describe());
        Console.ReadLine();
}
```

We can use the class to create instances of objects that hold different sets of information. In this case, we created two instances. One is called `redCar` and another is named `greenCar`. Classes in C# can contain fields (member variables), properties, methods, constructors, and other parts discussed later in the book. Some examples of classes in C# include `System.Console`, `System.String`, `System.Int32`, `System.Array`, `System.Math`, and `System.Random`.

Fields

The fields are data members of a class. They can be variables and constants. By accessing a field, we don't invoke any actions of the object.

```
Car redCar = new Car("Red");
```

Properties

Properties are similar to fields. They both hold data and have a name and type. However, properties contain code that is executed when they are accessed. They are often used to control access to data fields, acting as wrappers around them, but they can also contain more complex logic.

Properties consist of one or more components called accessors, with at least one required. For example, the `get` accessor returns the property's value, while the `set` accessor sets the property's `value`.

NOTE

The `init` accessor is a new feature in C# 9 that initializes the value of a property but doesn't allow it to be changed later (similar to a read-only field).

Here is a code showing a property that has both `get` and `set` accessors:

```
private string _color;

public string Color
{
    get { return _color; }
    set { _color = value; }
```

```
}
```

In this example, `Color` is a property that wraps the private field `_color`. The `get` accessor returns the `value` of `_color`, while the `set` accessor sets its `value` to the provided argument.

In addition, C# 3.0 introduced auto-implemented properties, which allow the compiler to generate the `get` and `set` accessors automatically:

```
public string Color { get; set; }
```

In this case, the property `Color` is automatically implemented with both `get` and `set` accessors. Furthermore, the compiler generates a `private` backing field for the property, so you don't have to define one yourself.

NOTE

Please note that properties are not the same as fields, although they may use fields internally to store their values. The distinction between the two is important because properties allow you to add logic and control access to the underlying data.

Instance and Static Members

Fields, properties, and methods can be instance members (related to a specific object) or static members (related to the class itself). Instance members are unique to each object. For example, different dogs have different names. On the other hand, static members are common to all class instances—for example, `DateTime.MinValue` is shared between all instances of `DateTime`.

To access an instance member, we need to use the name of the instance followed by the member's name (field or property), separated by a dot ".":

```
<instance_name>.<member_name>
```

To access **static** members, we use the class name followed by the member's name:

```
<class_name>.<member_name>
```

Methods can manipulate the data of the object to which they belong or perform other tasks. Some examples of methods include `Console.WriteLine()`, `Console.ReadLine()`, `String.Substring(index, length)`, and `Array.GetLength(index)`.

Here is an example of calling static methods:

```
Console.WriteLine("Automate The Planet")
Console.ReadLine()
String.Substring(index, length)
Array.GetLength(index)
```

Here is a code for calling an instance method of a string:

```
String sampleLower = new String('a', 5);
String sampleUpper = sampleLower.ToUpper();
Console.WriteLine(sampleLower); // aaaaa
Console.WriteLine(sampleUpper); // AAAAA
```

The following statements call instance methods of the DateTime class:

```
DateTime now = DateTime.Now;
DateTime later = now.AddHours(9);
Console.WriteLine($"Now: {now}");
Console.WriteLine($"9 hours later: {later}");
```

This is an example of a static class with a static method:

```
public static class Rectangle
{
    public static int CalculateArea(int width, int height)
    {
        return width * height;
    }
}
```

To use a static method, you need to specify the class's name followed by the method's name, separated by a dot, and pass all required arguments:

```
Console.WriteLine("The area is: " + Rectangle.CalculateArea(5, 4));
```

Constructors

Constructors are special methods used to set initial values of the fields in an object. They are executed when an object of a given type is created and has the same name as the class that holds them. Constructors do not return a value and can have different sets of parameters. The constructor without parameters is called the default constructor.

To invoke a constructor, we use the new operator. For example, we can create an object to generate random numbers with the default seed by using the following constructor:

```
Random randomGenerator = new Random();
```

We can also use constructors to create objects with specific initial values. For example, we can create a string object with the value "Automate!" using the following constructor:

```
String s = new String("Automate!"); // s = "Automate!"
```

Similarly, we can create a `DateTime` object with the date and time of December 30, 2017, at 12:33:59 by using the following constructor:

```
DateTime dt = new DateTime(2017, 12, 30, 12, 33, 59);
```

We can also create an `Int32` object with the value of 2058 by using the following constructor:

```
Int32 value = new Int32(2058);
```

> **NOTE**
>
> Remember that one class can have multiple constructors, each with different parameters.

Enumerations

Enumerations, also known as enums, allow a variable to have a set of named values. Enumerations are declared using the `enum` keyword. For instance, to define an enumeration of colors, we can use the following code:

```
public enum Color
{
    Red,
    Green,
    Blue,
    Black
}
```

Here is an example of how we can use the `Color` enumeration:

```
Color color = Color.Red;
Console.WriteLine(color); // Red
```

We can also assign numerical values to the named values of an enumeration:

```
public enum Size
{
    Small = 1,
    Medium = 2,
    Large = 3
}
```

In this example, `Small` has the value of 1; `Medium` has the value of 2, and so on.

What Is a Namespace?

Namespaces are used to organize the source code more logically and manageably. The namespaces can be used via the using keyword. In addition, they allow us to use types in a namespace without specifying their full name.

For instance, instead of writing System.DateTime every time we use DateTime, we can add using System at the top of the file and write DateTime after that:

```
using <namespace_name>
using System;

DateTime date;
Random randomGenerator = new Random();
```

Exercises

1. Write a program that generates and prints to the console 10 random values in the range [100, 200].
2. Write a program that prints to the console today's day of the week. Use System.DateTime.

Creating and Implementing a Class Hierarchy

In the following section, we will discuss inheritance and how it can be achieved using base classes. Also, we will talk about polymorphism and C# interfaces.

Inheritance

Inheritance is the process of letting one class be derived from another class. It establishes an "is-a-kind-of" relationship between a base and a derived class. For example, we use inheritance to create subclasses that inherit attributes and methods from their base class. This helps in code reuse and allows for more efficient development of programs.

Interfaces

An interface is a type that contains only the signatures of methods and properties but not their implementation. Instead, it defines a set of related functionalities that can be implemented by any class or struct, which means it defines a contract that the class or struct must implement.

NOTE

The method signature is a unique identifier that defines a method or function. It is composed of the method's name and its parameter list. The method signature specifies the number of parameters, types, and orders. It does not include the return type of the method. The compiler uses the signature to ensure that methods are correctly declared and called. When two methods have the same signature, they are considered overloads of each other.

In this example, we define an interface named IExample that contains two members: a method GetResult() and a property Value:

```
public interface IExample
{
    string GetResult();
    int Value { get; set; }
}
```

We use a colon (:) to indicate that a class is implementing an interface:

```
public class ExampleImplementation : IExample
```

```
{
    public string GetResult() { return "result"; }
    public int Value { get; set; }
}
```

We create a class named `ExampleImplementation` that implements the `IExample` interface. It must provide an implementation for all the members defined in the interface.

> ## NOTE
>
> Interfaces can also inherit from other interfaces. However, a class inheriting from one of the derived interfaces must implement all signatures in the hierarchy. Also, keep in mind that you cannot instantiate an interface directly. You can instantiate only a concrete type that implements an interface.

Here is an example:

```
interface IAnimal
{
    void Move();
}

class Dog : IAnimal
{
    public void Move() {}
    public void Bark() {}
}

IAnimal animal = new Dog();
```

In this code snippet, we define an interface named `IAnimal` with the method `Move()`. Then we create a class `Dog` that implements the `IAnimal` interface and provides an implementation for the `Move()` method, as well as a method `Bark()`. Finally, we create an instance of the `Dog` class and assign it to a variable of type `IAnimal`.

Base Classes

The following statements show that the `Square` class derives from the `Rectangle` class, reusing its code, such as the constructor and the properties. In addition, the `override` keyword is used after the access modifier `public` to change the base implementation, allowing us to customize the behavior of child classes.

```
class Rectangle
{
    public Rectangle(int width, int height)
    {
        Width = width;
```

```csharp
            Height = height;
    }

    public int Height { get; set; }

    public int Width { get; set; }

    public int Area
    {
        get
        {
            return Height * Width;
        }
    }
}

class Square : Rectangle
{
    public override int Width
    {
        get
        {
            return base.Width;
        }
        set
        {
            base.Width = value;
            base.Height= value;
        }
    }

    public override int Height
    {
        get
        {
            return base.Height;
        }
        set
        {
            base.Height = value;
            base.Width = value;
        }
    }
}
```

In the example, the Square class derives from the Rectangle class, reusing its code - the constructor and the properties. We can use the keyword override after the access modifier public to change the base implementation, which helps us customize the behavior of the child classes. For instance, we specify that we want to call the property code declared in the base class instead of the current implementation using the base keyword. We can use this keyword instead if we use the same current property defined in the base class.

Access Modifiers

In C#, all types and type members have an accessibility level determining whether they can be accessed from other code in the same assembly or other assemblies. In addition, six accessibility modifiers can be used to control the level of accessibility for types and type members:

- **public** - a type or member with this modifier can be accessed anywhere in the current assembly or any other assembly that references it.
- **private** - only code defined in the same class can access the members with this modifier.
- **protected** - a type or member with this modifier can only be accessed by code within the same class or by code in a class derived from that class.
- **internal** - a type or member with this modifier can be accessed by any code within the same assembly but not from another assembly.
- **protected internal** - a type or member with this modifier can be accessed by any code within the assembly in which it's declared or by code in a derived class in another assembly.
- **private protected** - a type or member with this modifier can only be accessed within its declaring assembly, by code within the same class, or within a type derived from that class.

These accessibility modifiers are essential for creating secure and maintainable code by controlling how and where types and type members can be accessed.

Exercises

1. You are asked to model an application for storing data about people. You should be able to have a person and a child. The child is derived from the person. The only constraints are the following:
   - People should not be able to have negative age
   - Children should not be able to have age more than 15
   - Person - represents the base class by which all others are implemented
   - Define a constructor that accepts name and age
   - Override ToString() and display info about the class
   - Add a unique person ID and implement IEquatable<T> interface
   - Create two people and compare whether they are the same by comparing their IDs. Implement IComparable<T> for the age

2. You are working in a library. The task is simple - your program should have two classes - one for the ordinary books - Book, and another for the special ones - GoldenEditionBook.
   - Book - represents a book and holds title, author, and price. A book should offer information about itself in the format shown in the output below.
   - GoldenEditionBook - represents a special book with the same properties as any Book, but its price is always 30% higher.
   - If the author's second name starts with a digit- exception message is: "*Author not valid!*"
   - If the title's length is less than 3 symbols - exception message is: "*Title not valid!*"
   - If the price is zero or negative - exception message is: "*Price not valid!*"
   - Price must be formatted to one symbol after the decimal separator
   - Override ToString and use StringBuilder class to display the information about the class
   - Rewrite the ToString() to use $"" (string interpolation) instead of StringBuilder

3. Create a hierarchy of Animals. Your task is simple: there should be a base class which all others derive from. Your program should have 3 different animals - Dog, Frog, and Cat. Create deeper hierarchy and add two additional classes - Kitten and Tomcat. Kittens are female and Tomcats are male! Along with the animals, there should be also a class which classifies its derived classes as sound producible. You may guess that all animals

are sound producible. The only mandatory functionality of all sound producible objects is to ProduceSound(). For instance, the dog should bark.

Your task is to model the hierarchy and test its functionality. Create an animal of each kind and make them produce sound. On the console, for each animal you've instantiated, print its info on three lines.
On the first line, print: {Kind of animal}
On the second line print its {name} {age} {gender}
On the third line print the sound it produces: {ProduceSound()}

Each Animal should have name, age, and gender. All properties' values should not be blank (e.g., name, age, etc.). If you enter invalid input for one of the properties' values, throw an exception with the message: "*Invalid input!*". Each animal should have a functionality to ProduceSound()
Here is example of what each kind of animal should produce when, ProduceSound() is called
Dog: "Woof"
Cat: "Meow"
Kittens: "Meow Meow"
Frog: "Croak"

Summary

This chapter covered object-oriented programming (OOP) concepts, including code reuse methods and creating user-defined classes with fields, functions, and properties. We also discussed the core concepts of OOP programming, such as polymorphism and inheritance, and the workings of interfaces, base classes, enumerations, and static methods.

The next chapter will delve into more advanced topics beyond the basics of writing simple C# programs. For example, we will explore the use of generic classes and methods to write more reusable code, and explore the concepts of delegates and extension methods, which are essential building blocks for software libraries. Additionally, we will touch on the LINQ and Reflection APIs. Finally, we will learn about other C# collections beyond arrays/lists and how to perform basic operations with files and directories.

Chapter 3. C# Beyond Fundamentals

The upcoming chapter will explore more advanced topics related to writing C# programs. We'll begin by discussing generic classes and methods, which enable us to write more reusable and efficient code. Next, we'll delve into other C# collections beyond arrays and lists, and how to perform basic file and directory operations. Additionally, we'll investigate delegates and extension methods, often critical components of software libraries. Finally, we'll briefly touch on the LINQ and Reflection APIs.

Topics covered in this chapter:

- Generic Classes
- System Collections
- Generic Methods
- Delegates and Anonymous Functions
- Extension Methods
- Working with Files
- LINQ
- Reflection API

Generic Classes and Methods

Generics are a key feature of .NET, allowing for type parameters not specific to a particular data type. This provides greater code reuse, type safety, and performance. Generic interfaces, classes, methods, events, and delegates can all be created to encapsulate operations that are not specific to a particular data type. One of the most common uses for generic classes is with collections, such as lists, dictionaries, stacks, and queues. For example, the following code creates a list of integers using a generic `List<T>` class:

```
List<int> list = new List<int>();

for (int x = 0; x < 10; x++)
{
    list.Add(x);
}
```

Generic Classes

When defining a generic type, we specify a type parameter in angle brackets after the type name. So, for instance, we can define a `ValueStore` class that takes a type parameter `T`:

```
class ValueStore<T>
{
    public T Value { get; set; }
}
```

The type parameter can be used as the type of delegates, properties, fields, return types, and method parameters within the class. In this example, the `Value` property is generic because we use the type parameter `T` instead of a specific data type.

We can use any name for a type parameter, not just `T`. However, `T` is widely used as a name when only one type parameter exists. Therefore, using more descriptive names such as `TDriver`, `TKey`, `TValue`, and so on is recommended for better code readability.

We can also define multiple type parameters separated by a comma, like in the following example:

```
class DictionaryMap<TKey, TValue>
{
    public TKey Key { get; set; }
    public TValue Value { get; set; }
}
```

Here, we define a `DictionaryMap` class that takes two type parameters, `TKey` and `TValue`. The class has properties for a key of type `TKey` and a value of type `TValue`.

Instantiating Generic Classes

When creating an instance of a generic class, you need to specify the actual type in angle brackets `<T>`. So, for example, we can create an instance of the `ValueStore` class that is specific to strings as follows:

```
ValueStore<string> store = new ValueStore<string>();
```

In this case, the type parameter `T` is replaced with the `string` type, and the `Value` property of the class is of the type `string`. You can assign a `string` value to the `Value` property, but it will throw a compile-time error if you try to assign a value of a different type:

```
ValueStore<string> store = new ValueStore<string>();
store.Value = "Hello World!";
store.Value = 123; //compile-time error
```

System Collections

In the `System.Collections.Generics` namespace, you can find interfaces and classes that define generic collections. These collections cover most cases where you would need a collection in your code. Let's take a quick look at some of the most important ones:

- `Dictionary<TKey,TValue>`
- `KeyValuePair<TKey,TValue>`
- `List<T>`
- `Queue<T>`
- `Stack<T>`
- `SortedList<TKey,TValue>`
- `SortedDictionary<TKey,TValue>`
- `LinkedList<T>`

List<T>

`List<T>` is a generic version of `ArrayList` that allows you to access strongly typed objects by an index and sort and search them. Unlike `ArrayList`, there isn't any boxing or unboxing process involved. You can add items using `Add()` or `AddRange()`. Here is an example of how to use `List<T>`:

```csharp
var numbers = new List<int>();
numbers.Add(1);
numbers.Add(7);
Console.WriteLine(numbers[2]);
```

NOTE

In C#, we have an implicit type keyword called **var**. When you declare a variable using var, the compiler determines the type of the variable based on the value it is assigned. However, the variable is still strongly typed as if you had declared the type yourself. Using var can make your code more concise and easier to read, which is why I often use it in my code.

There are various ways to populate a list. One way is to use the `Add()` method, like so:

```csharp
var cities = new List<string>();
cities.Add("Sofia");
cities.Add("Berlin");
cities.Add("London");
cities.Add("Paris");
```

Alternatively, you can use the constructor to initialize a list:

```
var nonEuropeCities = new List<string>()
{
    "Rio",
    "Brasilia",
    "Miami",
    "LA"
};
```

To access elements in a list, you can use the index operator []:

```
var numbers = new List<int>() { 2, 3, 6, 13, 8, 10 };
Console.WriteLine(numbers[0]); // prints 2
Console.WriteLine(numbers[1]); // prints 3
Console.WriteLine(numbers[2]); // prints 6
Console.WriteLine(numbers[3]); // prints 13
```

You can also use the ForEach() method or a for loop to iterate over a list:

```
numbers.ForEach(num => Console.WriteLine($"{num}, ")); //prints 2, 3, 6, 13, 8, 10

for(int i = 0; i < numbers.Count; i++)
{
    Console.WriteLine(numbers[i]);
}
```

The List<T> class implements the IList<T> interface, which implements the IEnumerable interface. Therefore, you can use the LINQ query or method syntax to access elements in a list:

```
var cities = new List<City>() {
            new City { Id = 1, Name="Berlin"},
            new City { Id = 2, Name="London"},
            new City { Id = 3, Name="Lviv"},
            new City { Id = 4, Name="Paris"}
        };
// Get all cities with name starting with L.
var results = from c in cities
            where c.Name.StartsWith("L")
            select c;

foreach(var city in results)
{
    Console.WriteLine($"{city.Id}, {city.Name}");
}
```

NOTE

Don't worry. We will investigate in more detail what LINQ is and how to use it later in the chapter.

To remove an item from a list, you can use one of two methods. The `Remove(item)` method removes the first occurrence of the item, and the `RemoveAt(index)` method removes an element from the specified index:

```
var numbers = new List<int>(){ 10, 20, 30, 20, 10 };
numbers.Remove(20); // removes the first 20 from a list
numbers.RemoveAt(2); //removes the 3rd element
```

Finally, you can use the `Contains()` method to check whether or not an element is in a list:

```
var numbers = new List<int>(){ 11, 22, 33, 44 };
numbers.Contains(11); // returns true
numbers.Contains(15); // returns false
numbers.Contains(44); // returns true
```

SortedList<TKey, TValue>

`SortedList<TKey, TValue>` is an array of key-value pairs sorted by keys. The key must be unique and cannot be `null`. However, the value can be `null` or duplicate. It contains elements of type `KeyValuePair<TKey, TValue>`.

```
var numberNames = new SortedList<int, string>();
numberNames.Add(4, "Four");
numberNames.Add(1, "One");
numberNames.Add(5, "Five");
numberNames.Add(3, null);
numberNames.Add(10, "Ten");
```

`SortedList<T, V>` rearranges key-value pairs in the ascending order of keys when a key-value pair is added:

```
var numberNames = new SortedList<int,string>()
                        {
                            {2, "Two"},
                            {6, "Six"},
                            {0, "Zero"}
                        };

foreach(KeyValuePair<int, string> pair in numberNames)
{
    Console.WriteLine($"key: {pair.Key}, value: {pair.Value}");
}
```

Dictionary<TKey, TValue>

`Dictionary<TKey, TValue>` is a .NET generic collection that stores key-value pairs with no specific order. The keys must be unique and non-null, while the values can be `null` or duplicated. It consists of elements of the type `KeyValuePair<TKey, TValue>`.

Items can be added to the dictionary using the `Add()` method or the dictionary initializer syntax. You can access elements by their keys using the indexer `[]` or the `ElementAt()` method. You can also check if the dictionary contains a specific key using the `ContainsKey()` method.

Here's an example of creating and accessing dictionary elements:

```
var numberNames = new Dictionary<int, string>();
numberNames.Add(4, "Four");
numberNames.Add(1, "One");
numberNames.Add(5, "Five");
numberNames.Add(3, null);
numberNames.Add(10, "Ten");

Console.WriteLine(numberNames[4]); // prints "Four"
Console.WriteLine(numberNames[1]); // prints "One"
Console.WriteLine(numberNames[3]); // prints null

if (numberNames.ContainsKey(5))
{
    Console.WriteLine(numberNames[5]); // prints "Five"
}

for (int i = 0; i < numberNames.Count; i++)
{
    Console.WriteLine(
        $"Key: {numberNames.ElementAt(i).Key}, Value: {numberNames.ElementAt(i).Value}");
}
```

Stack<T>

In `Stack<T>`, elements are stored in a LIFO (Last In, First Out) order without boxing-unboxing. You can add elements using the `Push()` method and retrieve them using `Pop()` and `Peek()`. However, using an indexer `[]` is not supported. Here is a sample usage:

```
var numbers = new Stack<int>();
numbers.Push(1);
numbers.Push(2);
numbers.Push(3);
numbers.Push(4);

while (numbers.Count > 0)
{
    Console.Write(numbers.Pop() + ",");
}
```

In this example, we created a new stack of integers and added four numbers using the `Push()` method. We then retrieved each element from the stack using the `Pop()` method, which removes and returns the top element of the stack in LIFO order. The output of this code will be *"4,3,2,1,"*.

Queue<T>

Queue<T> is a generic collection that operates on a first-in-first-out (FIFO) basis without any boxing or unboxing. The elements can be added to the end of the queue using the Enqueue() method and retrieved from the beginning of the queue using the Dequeue() and Peek() methods. It does not support the use of the indexer [].

Here is an example of how to use the Queue<T> collection in C#:

```
var numbers = new Queue<int>();
numbers.Enqueue(1);
numbers.Enqueue(2);
numbers.Enqueue(3);
numbers.Enqueue(4);

while (numbers.Count > 0)
{
    Console.Write(numbers.Dequeue() + ",");
}
```

This will print *"1,2,3,4,"* to the console.

Tuple<T>

Tuple<T> is a generic class representing a data structure with a fixed number of elements, each of a specific type. The number of collection items is determined by the number of generic type parameters you specify when creating an instance of the Tuple<T> class.

Here's a code snippet of using a tuple to store a sequence of elements with different data types:

```
var city = Tuple.Create(1, "Bulgaria", "Sofia");
city.Item1; // returns 1
city.Item2; // returns "Bulgaria"
city.Item3; // returns "Sofia"

var numbers = Tuple.Create(1, 2, Tuple.Create(9, 4, 5, 6, 7, 8), 9, 10, 11, 12, 25);
numbers.Item3.Item1; // returns 9
numbers.Rest.Item1; // returns 25
```

As you can see, the Tuple.Create() method is used to create instances of the Tuple<T> class. The tuple elements are accessed using the ItemN properties, where N is the one-based index of the item in the tuple. Additionally, the Rest property provides access to a tuple containing the remaining elements of the tuple that are not explicitly named.

Exercises

1. Write a program that counts the number of occurences of each value in a given array of double values. Use `Dictionary<TKey,TValue>`.

Example: array = {3, 4, 4, -2.5, 3, 3, 4, 3, -2.5}
-2.5 -> 2 times
3 -> 4 times
4 -> 3 times

2. Implement the data structure "hash table" in a class `HashTable<K, T>`. Keep the data in an array of lists of key-value pair `<KeyValuePair<K, T>[]` with an initial capacity of 16. When the hash table load runs over 75%, resize to 2 times larger capacity. Implement the following methods and properties: `Add(key, value)`, `Find(key) ->` value, `Remove(key)`, `Count`, `Clear()`, `this[]`, `Keys`. Try to make the hash table support iterating over its elements with foreach.

Generic Methods

We declare generic methods with the type parameters for their return type or parameters:

```
public class DataRepo<T>
{
    private List<T> _repo = new List<T>;

    public void Add(T item)
    {
        _repo.Add(item);
    }

    public T Get(int index)
    {
        if(_repo.Count >= index)
        {
            return _repo[index];
        }
        else
        {
            return default(T);
        }
    }
}
```

Add() and Get() are generic methods in this example. The data type of the item parameter will be specified when instantiating the DataRepo<T> class.

We can also have generic methods in a non-generic class by adding the type parameter in angle brackets < > next to the method name:

```
public class ConsoleWriter
{
    public void WriteToConsole<TData>(TData data)
    {
        Console.WriteLine(data);
    }
}

var cwriter = new ConsoleWriter();
cwriter.WriteToConsole<int>(300);
cwriter.WriteToConsole(500);
cwriter.WriteToConsole<string>("Hi");
cwriter.WriteToConsole("Galaxy!");
```

In the previous example, we saw how generic methods could be declared with type parameters for their return type or parameters. Here's a sample snippet of how generic parameters can be used with multiple parameters, with or without non-generic parameters and return types:

```
public void Add(int index, T data) { }
public void Add(T data1, T data2) { }
public void Add<V>(T data1, V data2) { }
public void Add(T data) { }
```

The first method, `Add(int index, T data)`, takes an integer index and a generic data type T as parameters. The second method, `Add(T data1, T data2)`, takes two parameters of the same generic type T. The third method `Add<V>(T data1, V data2)` takes two parameters, one of generic type T and another of generic type V. Finally, the fourth method, `Add(T data)` takes a single parameter of the generic type T.

Generic Constraints

Constraints are a way to restrict the usage of certain types while instantiating generic classes. You can add one or more constraints on the generic type by using the `where` clause after the generic type name in the format `GenericClassName<T> where T : constraint1, constraint2`.

For instance, let's look at the following code:

```
class DataRepo<T> where T : class
{
    public T Data { get; set; }
}
```

In this case, we have restricted the `DataRepo<T>` class to accept only classes as data types. As a result, passing in value types will lead to a compile-time error. Here are some valid and invalid instantiations of `DataRepo<T>`:

```
DataRepo<string> repo = new DataRepo<string>(); // valid
DataRepo<Point> repo = new DataRepo<Point>(); // valid
DataRepo<IEnumerable> repo = new DataRepo<IEnumerable>(); // valid
DataRepo<ArrayList> repo = new DataRepo<ArrayList>(); // valid
DataRepo<int> repo = new DataRepo<int>(); // compile-time error
```

If you want to restrict the supplied type from having a constructor, you can use the `new()` constraint. A compile-time error will occur if the class doesn't have a constructor:

```
class DataRepo<T> where T : class, new()
{
    public T Data { get; set; }
}
```

```
DataRepo<Person> repo = new DataRepo<MyClass>(); // valid
DataRepo<ArrayList> repo = new DataRepo<ArrayList>(); // valid
DataRepo<string> repo = new DataRepo<string>(); // compile-time error
DataRepo<int> repo = new DataRepo<int>(); // compile-time error
DataRepo<IEnumerable> repo = new DataRepo<IEnumerable>(); // compile-time error
```

Constraints can also be used to limit the class to derive from a specific base class or implement a specific interface. A compile-time error is generated if the class doesn't derive from the specified base class:

```
class DataRepo<T> where T : IEnumerable
{
    public T Data { get; set; }
}

DataRepo<ArrayList> repo = new DataRepo<ArrayList>(); // valid
DataRepo<List> repo = new DataRepo<List>(); // valid
DataRepo<string> repo = new DataRepo<string>(); // compile-time error
DataRepo<int> repo = new DataRepo<int>(); // compile-time error
```

Here is a list of all constraints you can use:

Constraint	Description
class	The type argument must be any class or interface.
class?	The type argument must be a nullable/non-nullable class or interface.
struct	The type argument must be value types such as int, char, bool, float, etc.
new()	The type argument must be a reference type that has a public constructor.
base class name	The type argument must be, or derived from, the specified base class.
interface name	The type argument must be, or implement from, the specified interface.
notnull	The type argument can be non-nullable reference or value types.
unmanaged	The type argument must be non-nullable unmanaged types.

Delegates and Anonymous Functions

A delegate is a reference type that defines a method signature, allowing you to pass a method as a parameter. To declare a delegate, use the `delegate` keyword followed by a function signature. For example, you can create a delegate for a method that takes a string as a parameter:

```
public delegate void PrintDelegate(string msg);
```

To assign a method to a delegate, you can use the `new` keyword and specify the method name:

```
PrintDelegate pdel = new PrintDelegate(PrintMessage);

public void PrintMessage(string message)
{
    Console.WriteLine(message);
}
```

Alternatively, you can use the shorthand notation:

```
PrintDelegate pdel = PrintMessage;
```

You can also use a lambda expression to create a delegate:

```
PrintDelegate pdel = (string msg) => Console.WriteLine(msg);
```

To invoke a delegate, you can use the `Invoke()` method or call the delegate as if it were a method:

```
pdel.Invoke("Hello Galaxy!");
pdel("Hello Galaxy!");
```

Delegates can also be used as parameters for methods. For instance, you can create a method that takes a `PrintDelegate` parameter:

```
public static void InvokeDelegate(PrintDelegate pdel)
{
    pdel("Hello Galaxy");
}
```

You can then pass a delegate to this method to execute it:

```
PrintDelegate pdel = PrintMessage;
InvokeDelegate(pdel);
```

In this example, we create a delegate for the `PrintMessage()` method and then pass it to the `InvokeDelegate()` method. The `InvokeDelegate()` method executes the delegate and prints *"Hello Galaxy"* to the console.

Delegates are a powerful feature of C# that allows you to write more flexible and modular code.

Action and Func Delegates

The `Func` and `Action` types are built-in generic delegates. Therefore, they should be used for most common delegates instead of creating new custom ones.

```
public static void ConsolePrint(int num)
{
    Console.WriteLine(num);
}

public static void Main(string[] args)
{
    Action<int> printDel = ConsolePrint;
    printDel(10);
}
```

Action Delegate

The `Action` delegate can be initialized using the `new` keyword or directly assigning a method. An anonymous function can also be assigned to an `Action` delegate:

```
Action<int> printDel = ConsolePrint;
Action<int> printDel = new Action<int>(ConsolePrint);
Action<int> printDel = delegate(int i)
                       {
                           Console.WriteLine(i);
                       };
printDel(15);
```

You can also use a lambda expression with an `Action` delegate:

```
Action<int> printDel = num => Console.WriteLine(num);
printDel(15);
```

Func Delegate

`Func` is a type of delegate that takes zero or more input parameters and has a single return parameter, and is a generic delegate. The last parameter of the delegate type in angle brackets is considered the return type, while the other parameters are input parameter types. So, for instance, we can declare a `Func<int, int, int>` to represent a method that takes two int parameters and returns an int value.

To assign a method that matches the `Func` delegate, we can use the `new` keyword or directly assign a method. For example, we can assign a method, `Sum()`, that takes two int parameters and returns their sum to a `Func<int,int,int>` delegate:

```
public static int Sum(int a, int b)
{
   return a + b;
}

public static void Main(string[] args)
{
    Func<int,int,int> add = Sum;
    int result = add(20, 20);
    Console.WriteLine(result);
}
```

We can also assign an anonymous method to a `Func` delegate using the `delegate` keyword or a lambda expression. For example, we can use a `delegate` keyword to assign a method that returns the current date and time to a `Func<DateTime>` delegate:

```
Func<DateTime> getCurrentTime = delegate()
                                {
                                    return DateTime.Now;
                                };
```

We can also use a lambda expression to assign a method that takes two integer parameters and returns their sum to a `Func<int,int,int>` delegate:

```
Func<int> getCurrentDate = () => DateTime.Now;
Func<int, int, int> Sum = (a, b) => a + b;
```

Events

An `event` is a way for an object to notify other objects when an action occurs. The class responsible for raising the event is called the **Publisher**, while the class that receives the notification is referred to as the **Subscriber**. An event is an encapsulated delegate, and the object that raises the event doesn't know which object or method will receive the events it raises. For this reason, the event is usually defined as a member of the object that raises it.

Here's an illustration of how to define and raise an `event`:

```
public delegate void Notify();

public class ConsolePrinter
{
    public event Notify PrintCompleted;

    public void Print(string message)
```

```
    {
        Console.WriteLine(message);
        OnPrintCompleted();
    }

    protected virtual void OnPrintCompleted()
    {
        PrintCompleted?.Invoke();
    }
}
```

To raise the event, we use the `Invoke()` method. To react to an `event`, you define an event handler method in the receiver. This method must match the delegate's signature for the event you are handling. You then perform the needed actions in the event handler when the event is raised. Finally, to consume the event and subscribe to it, we use the `+=` operator:

```
public class Program
{
    public static void Main()
    {
        var cp = new ConsolePrinter();
        cp.PrintCompleted += cp_ProcessCompleted;
        bl.Print("Hello Galaxy!");
    }

    public static void cp_ProcessCompleted()
    {
        Console.WriteLine("Print Completed!");
    }
}
```

It is possible to pass data to an event through a data class. The base class for all the event argument classes is the `EventArgs` class. For example, use `EventHandler<TEventArgs>` to pass data to the handler:

```
public event EventHandler<bool> PrintCompleted;

protected virtual void OnPrintCompleted(bool isSuccessful)
{
    PrintCompleted?.Invoke(this, isSuccessful);
}
```

If you want to pass more than one value as event data, create a class deriving from the `EventArgs` base class:

```
public class PrintEventArgs : EventArgs
{
    public bool WasSuccessful { get; set; }
    public DateTime CompletionDate { get; set; }
}
```

Exercises

1. Using delegates, write a class `Timer` to execute specific methods at each t second.

Extension Methods

Extension methods allow adding methods to a class, struct, or interface without altering, deriving, or recompiling them. An extension method is a static method defined in a static class. The sole difference between an extension and a regular static method is that the first parameter, preceded by the `this` keyword, specifies the type that will be extended.

To illustrate, look at the following code:

```
namespace Bellatrix.Utilities;
public static class StringExtensions
{
    public static string RemoveSpaces(this string value)
    {
        return value.Replace(" ", string.Empty);
    }
}
```

To use this extension method, a `using` statement is required for the namespace where the static class containing the extension method is defined:

```
using Bellatrix.Utilities;
```

With the extension method in scope, it can be used on an instance of the extended type, like so:

```
public class Program
{
    public static void Main(string[] args)
    {
        string text = "Hello Galaxy!";

        string cleanedText = text.RemoveSpaces();

        Console.WriteLine(cleanedText);
    }
}
```

In this case, the `RemoveSpaces()` extension method is used to remove spaces from a string without needing to modify or derive from the string class.

Exercises

1. Implement an extension method `Substring(int index, int length)` for the class `StringBuilder` that returns a new `StringBuilder` and has the same functionality as `Substring` in the class `String`.

2. Implement a set of extension methods for `IEnumerable<T>` that implement the following group functions: `Sum()`, `Min()`, `Max()`, and `Average()`.

Working with Files

To write reliable automated tests, it's crucial to have a good understanding of working with files and directories. There are numerous situations where you need to read the contents of a file or verify if a directory exists. Therefore, in this section, we'll explore the `System.IO` namespace, which provides several useful classes and methods for handling these tasks.

System.IO.File Namespace

The static `File` class is a part of this namespace and allows you to perform I/O operations on the physical file system. It provides various utility methods such as `AppendAllText()`, `Copy()`, `Delete()`, `Exists()`, `Move()`, `Open()`, `ReadAllLines()`, `Replace()`, and `WriteAllText()`.

The `File.AppendAllLines()` method appends multiple text lines to a file, while `File.WriteAllText()` method writes text to a file. If the file does not exist, the method will create and open it. However, it will not append text but overwrite existing text.

The static `File` class can perform quick operations with physical files. For instance, you can check if a file exists using `File.Exists()`, copy and move files using `File.Copy()` and `File.Move()`, respectively. You can also create, open, and delete files using the methods provided by this class.

To illustrate, take a look at the following code:

```
string[] linesToBeAdded = {"line one", "line two", "line three"};
File.AppendAllLines(@"C:\testFile.txt", linesToBeAdded);
File.WriteAllText(@"C:\testFile.txt", "Come to my galaxy!");

bool isFileExists = File.Exists(@"C:\myFile.txt");
File.Copy(@"C:\myFile.txt", @"C:\NewMyFile.txt");
File.Move(@"C:\DummyFile.txt", @"D:\NewDummyFile.txt");
FileStream fs = File.Open(@"C:\myFile.txt", FileMode.OpenOrCreate);
StreamReader sr = File.OpenText(@"D:\myFile.txt");
File.Delete(@"C:\myFile.txt");
```

> **NOTE**
>
> To learn about all the methods available in the static `File` class, you can visit MSDN.

System.IO.FileInfo Namespace

The `FileInfo` class offers similar functionality to the static `File` class but with more control. You can create an instance of the `FileInfo` class and use it to open the file and read its content:

```
var fileInfo = new FileInfo(@"C:\myFile.txt");
using var fileStream = fileInfo.Open(FileMode.OpenOrCreate, FileAccess.ReadWrite,
FileShare.ReadWrite);
using var streamReader = new StreamReader(fileStream);
string fileContent = streamReader.ReadToEnd();
```

In this example, we create a new instance of the `FileInfo` class and pass the file path to its constructor. We then open the file using the `Open()` method of the `FileInfo` instance, which returns a `FileStream` object that we can use to read or write to the file. Finally, we create a `StreamReader` object to read the file's content and assign it to a string variable called `fileContent`.

NOTE

Files and streams are managed types that access unmanaged resources. These resources need to be properly closed and disposed of. The `using` statement provides a convenient syntax to ensure the correct use of `IDisposable` objects.

Here's an example of code without the `using` statement:

```
FileInfo fi = new FileInfo(@"C:\myFile.txt");
FileStream fs = fi.Open(FileMode.OpenOrCreate, FileAccess.ReadWrite, FileShare.ReadWrite);
StreamReader sr = new StreamReader(fs);
string fileContent = sr.ReadToEnd();
sr.Close();
fs.Close();
```

Here's the same code with the non-concise version of the `using` statement:

```
var fi = new FileInfo(@"C:\myFile.txt");
using(var fs = fi.Open(FileMode.OpenOrCreate, FileAccess.ReadWrite, FileShare.ReadWrite))
{
    using(var sr = new StreamReader(fs))
    {
        string fileContent = sr.ReadToEnd();
    }
}
```

The `using` statement guarantees that `Dispose()` is called even if an exception occurs within the `using` block. You can achieve the same result by putting the object inside a `try` block and then calling `Dispose()` in a `finally` block. This is how the compiler translates the `using` statement.

One thing to keep in mind is that you cannot perform read and write operations on the same `FileStream` object simultaneously. To write to a file, you can use the `StreamWriter` class, as shown in the following example:

```
var fi = new FileInfo(@"C:\myFile.txt");
using var fs = fi.Open(FileMode.OpenOrCreate, FileAccess.Write, FileShare.Read );
using var sw = new StreamWriter(fs);
sw.WriteLine("Another line from streamwriter");
```

The abstract class `System.IO.Stream` provides standard methods for transferring bytes and is used by various stream classes for different purposes, such as `FileStream`, `MemoryStream`, `BufferedStream`, `NetworkStream`, `PipeStream`, and `CryptoStream`.

System.IO.Directory Namespace

The `Directory` class provides static methods for manipulating directories and subdirectories. In addition, it includes various utility methods for working with physical files, such as `CreateDirectory()`, `Delete()`, `EnumerateDirectories()`, `EnumerateFiles()`, `Exists()`, `GetFiles()`, `Move()`, and `GetParent()`. For instance, to move all text files from a source directory to an archive directory, you can use the `EnumerateFiles()` method to retrieve a collection of text files, then loop through the collection and use the `Move()` method to move each file to the archive directory:

```
string sourceDirectory = @"C:\Source";
string archiveDirectory = @"C:\Archive";
var txtFiles = Directory.EnumerateFiles(sourceDirectory, "*.txt");

foreach (string currentFile in txtFiles)
{
    string fileName = currentFile.Substring(sourceDirectory.Length + 1);
    Directory.Move(currentFile, Path.Combine(archiveDirectory, fileName));
}
```

It's also possible to write more complex statements with the `Directory` class. For example, you can use LINQ to retrieve a collection of text files and then use that collection to query for all lines that contain a specific word or phrase:

```
string archiveDirectory = @"C:\Archive";

var files = from retrievedFile in Directory.EnumerateFiles(archiveDirectory, "*.txt",
SearchOption.AllDirectories)
            from line in File.ReadLines(retrievedFile)
            where line.Contains("Galaxy")
            select new
            {
               File = retrievedFile,
               Line = line
             };
```

```
foreach (var f in files)
{
    Console.WriteLine($"{f.File} contains {f.Line}");
}
```

System.IO.DirectoryInfo Namespace

The `DirectoryInfo` class provides more advanced functionality than the `Directory` class, similar to how `FileInfo` provides more advanced functionality than the `File` class. Here is a sample method that uses recursion to copy all the files and directories from a source directory to a target directory:

```
public static void CopyAll(DirectoryInfo source, DirectoryInfo target)
{
    if (Directory.Exists(target.FullName) == false)
    {
        Directory.CreateDirectory(target.FullName);
    }

    foreach (FileInfo fi in source.GetFiles())
    {
        fi.CopyTo(Path.Combine(target.ToString(), fi.Name), true);
    }

    foreach (DirectoryInfo diSourceSubDir in source.GetDirectories())
    {
        DirectoryInfo nextTargetSubDir = target.CreateSubdirectory(diSourceSubDir.Name);
        CopyAll(diSourceSubDir, nextTargetSubDir);
    }
}
```

System.IO.Path Namespace

The `Path` class provides static methods that work with string instances containing file or directory path information:

```
string path1 = @"c:\temp\myFile.txt";
string path2 = @"c:\temp\myDir";
string path3 = @"temp";

if (Path.HasExtension(path1))
{
    Console.WriteLine($"{path1} has an extension.");
}

Console.WriteLine($"The full path of {path3} is {Path.GetFullPath(path3)}.");
Console.WriteLine($"{Path.GetTempPath()} is the location for temporary files.");
Console.WriteLine($"{Path.GetTempFileName()} is a file available for use.");
```

The code checks if `path1` has an extension, gets the full path of `path3`, and retrieves the directory path for temporary files and a file name that can be used for temporary purposes.

System.IO.FileSystemWatcher Namespace

The `FileSystemWatcher` class allows you to listen for file system change notifications and raise events when a directory or file in the directory changes:

```
using var watcher = new FileSystemWatcher();
watcher.NotifyFilter = NotifyFilters.LastAccess | NotifyFilters.LastWrite;
watcher.Path = args[1];
watcher.Filter = "*.txt";
watcher.Changed += OnChanged;
watcher.Created += OnChanged;
watcher.Deleted += OnChanged;
watcher.Renamed += OnRenamed;
watcher.EnableRaisingEvents = true;

private static void OnChanged(object source, FileSystemEventArgs e)
{
        Console.WriteLine($"File: {e.FullPath} {e.ChangeType}");
}

private static void OnRenamed(object source, RenamedEventArgs e)
{
        Console.WriteLine($"File: {e.OldFullPath} renamed to {e.FullPath}");
}
```

This code sets up a `FileSystemWatcher` instance, specifies the path to monitor, and subscribes to events for file changes, creation, deletion, and renaming. When an event is raised, the corresponding event handler method is called, which can take further action as needed.

Exercises

1. Write a program that reads a text file and prints on the console its odd lines.
2. Write a program that concatenates two text files into another text file.
3. Write a program that reads a text file and inserts line numbers before each line. The result should be written to another text file.
4. Write a program that compares two text files line by line and prints the number of lines that are the same and the number of different lines. Assume the files have an equal number of lines.
5. Write a program that deletes from a text file all words that start with the prefix "test." The words should contain only the symbols 0...9, a...z, A...Z, _.
6. Write a program that removes from a text file all words listed in another text file. Handle all possible exceptions in your methods.
7. Write a program that reads a list of words from a file words.txt and finds how many times each word is contained in another file test.txt. The result should be written in the file result.txt, and the number of their occurrences should sort the words in descending order. Handle all possible exceptions in your methods.

Language Integrated Query LINQ

LINQ (Language Integrated Query) is a query syntax that provides a uniform way of retrieving data from various sources and returning results as objects. LINQ queries are written for classes implementing the `IEnumerable<T>` or `IQueryable<T>` interface. There are several advantages to using LINQ, such as not having to learn a new query language for each data source or format type, reducing the amount of code required compared to traditional approaches, improving code readability, and enabling the same syntax to query multiple data sources. In addition, LINQ provides type checking of objects at compile time and IntelliSense for generic collections. To use LINQ, you must include the `System.Linq` namespace with a `using` statement.

Lambda Expressions

The lambda expression concisely represents anonymous methods using a special syntax. It involves removing the delegate keyword and parameter type and adding a lambda operator `=>`. For example:

```
string[] cities = {"Berlin", "London", "Paris", "Kyiv" };
var citiesWithE = cities.Where(city => city.Contains('e'));

foreach(var name in citiesWithE)
{
    Console.Write(name + " ");
}
```

The `Where()` method filters the array based on a predicate that we pass through a lambda expression. We can even make the `foreach` statement shorter using lambda expression as shown below:

```
citiesWithE.ForEach(n => Console.Write(n + " "));
```

In the example, the `Where` method filters the array through a predicate that we pass through a lambda expression.

We can wrap the parameters in parentheses when passing more than one parameter to the lambda expression, like this:

```
string[] cities = {"Berlin", "London", "Paris", "Kiev" };
var citiesWithE = cities.Where((city, letter) => city.Contains(letter));
citiesWithE.ForEach(n => Console.Write(n + " "));
```

We can also have a lambda expression with no parameters by using empty brackets `()` together with the lambda operator `=>`, as follows:

```
() => Console.WriteLine("Parameterless lambda expression")
```

Furthermore, we can enclose expressions in curly braces if we want to have more than one statement in the lambda expression body:

```
(city, letter) =>
{
    Console.WriteLine("Lambda expression with multiple statements in the body");
    return city.Contains(letter);
}
```

Frequently Used LINQ Methods

To filter a collection based on a given criteria expression, we can use the Where() method, which will return a new collection:

```
var workers = new List<Worker>() {
        new Worker() { Id = 1, Name = "John", Age = 18 } ,
        new Worker() { Id= 2, Name = "Pesho",  Age = 15 } ,
        new Worker() { Id= 3, Name = "George",  Age = 25 } ,
        new Worker() { Id= 5, Name = "Ivan" , Age = 19 }
    };
var filteredResult = workers.Where(s => s.Age > 12 && s.Age < 20);

var filteredResult = workers.Where((s, i) => {
            if(i % 2 ==  0)
            {
              return true;
            }
            else
            {
              return false;
            }
        });
```

The First() and FirstOrDefault() methods return the first element that satisfies the specified condition:

```
Console.WriteLine($"1st element: {workers.First()}");
Console.WriteLine($"1st even element: {workers.FirstOrDefault(i => i % 2 == 0)}");
```

The Last() and LastOrDefault() methods return the last element that satisfies the specified condition:

```
Console.WriteLine($"Last element: {workers.Last()}",);
Console.WriteLine($"Last even element: {workers.LastOrDefault(i => i % 2 == 0)}");
```

The All() method evaluates each element in the given collection on a specified condition and returns true if all the items satisfy a condition. While Any() checks whether any element satisfies a given condition or not:

```
bool areAllWorkersOver30 = workers.All(w => w.Age > 30);
bool isAnyWorkerTeenAger = workers.Any(s => s.age > 14 && s.age < 20);
```

The `Contains()` method examines whether a specified element exists in the collection or not and returns a boolean:

```
var worker = new Worker() { Id = 3, Name = "George"};
bool result = workers.Contains(worker);
```

The `OrderBy()` method arranges the elements of a collection in either ascending or descending order:

```
var workersInAscOrder = workers.OrderBy(s => s.Name);
var workersInDescOrder = workers.OrderByDescending(s => s.Name);
```

The `Count()` method returns the number of elements in the collection or items that have satisfied the given condition:

```
int evenAgedWorkers = workers.Count(w => w.Age % 2 == 0);
```

Exercises

1. Write a LINQ query using the method syntax that finds the first name and last name of all workers between 18 and 24.
2. Using the extension methods `OrderBy()` and `ThenBy()` with lambda expressions, sort the workers by first and last names in descending order.
3. Rewrite the same with LINQ query syntax.
4. Write a program that prints from a given array of integers all numbers divisible by 7 and 3. Use the built-in extension methods and lambda expressions, use the LINQ method syntax. Then, rewrite the same with the LINQ query syntax.

Reflection API

Reflection is a feature that allows you to explore and alter the structure and behavior of a program during runtime. This can include obtaining information about types within assemblies, fields, properties, and methods. All the relevant classes for reflection are located in the System.Reflection namespace.

To obtain information about an assembly, you can use the Assembly class. For example, you can get the name and version of the currently executing assembly:

```
var assembly = Assembly.GetExecutingAssembly();
Console.WriteLine($"Assembly Name: {assembly.GetName().Name}");
Console.WriteLine($"Version: {assembly.GetName().Version}");
```

The Type class represents different types, including class types, interface types, array types, value types, enumeration types, type parameters, generic type definitions, and open or closed constructed generic types. You can get information about a type using typeof() or by obtaining the type from an object instance:

```
Type worker = typeof(Worker);
string name = worker.Name;
string workerTypeNamespace = worker.Namespace;
```

You can use the TypeInfo class to obtain more information about a type, such as the number of declared properties:

```
var assembly = Assembly.GetExecutingAssembly();
var types = assembly.GetTypes();
foreach(var type in types)
{
   var typeInfo = type.GetTypeInfo();
   Console.WriteLine($"{type.FullName} has {typeInfo.DeclaredProperties.Count()}
properties");
}
```

The MemberInfo class is used to obtain information about the attributes of a member, such as fields, properties, and methods:

```
Type workerType = typeof(Worker);
MemberInfo[] membersMetaData = workerType.GetMembers();
foreach (MemberInfo member in membersMetaData)
{
   Console.WriteLine($"{member.MemberType} {member.Name}");
}
```

The FieldInfo class is designed to help retrieve the attributes and metadata associated with a field:

```
Type workerType = typeof(Worker);
System.Reflection.FieldInfo[] fieldInfo = workerType.GetFields();
```

The `PropertyInfo` class is used to discover the attributes of a property and provides access to property metadata:

```
var type = typeof(Worker);
var propertyInfos = type.GetProperties();
foreach(PropertyInfo propertyInfo in propertyInfos)
{
    Console.Write(propertyInfo.Name);
    var accessors = propertyInfo.GetAccessors();
    foreach(var accessor in accessors)
    {
        Console.Write(accessor.Name);
    }
}
```

The `MethodInfo` class is used to discover the attributes of a method and provides access to method metadata:

```
MethodInfo[] methods = typeof(Worker).GetMethods(BindingFlags.Instance |
BindingFlags.Public);
foreach (MethodInfo info in methods)
{
    Console.Write(info.Name);
}
```

While you might only need to use Reflection API occasionally, it is an essential feature, especially if you plan on creating your frameworks, test runners, or another tooling.

Exercises

1. Get executing assembly. Get all types in the running assembly. In a loop, print all the type names where the namespace starts with "Work" - print one name per line.
   Hint: Watch out. The namespace can be null.
2. Create a new instance of `Worker`. Get instance type. Get the property `FullName` by name from the type. Set the property value to "Ivan Draganov" using Reflection. Find the `GetCharacteristics()` method by name in the `Worker` type. Invoke the `GetCharacteristics()` method using Reflection and pass a parameter `false`.

Summary

In the chapter, we explored advanced C# concepts beyond basic programming. We started by discussing generic classes and methods, which help us write more reusable code. We also covered various C# collections beyond arrays and lists and how to perform simple file and directory operations. Delegates and extension methods were also discussed as essential components of software libraries. Additionally, we briefly touched on LINQ and Reflection APIs.

In the next chapter, we will delve into the world of testing. We will cover key terminology related to testing, define what testing is, examine different testing types, and go over fundamental test processes.

Chapter 4. Testing Fundamentals

In the upcoming chapter, we'll gain an understanding of important terminology related to testing and explore what testing is all about. We'll also examine various types of testing and fundamental test processes. Our goal is to cover key concepts at the ISTQB Foundation level quickly.

Before we dive in, it's important to note that many extensive books are available that delve much deeper into these topics. If you're interested in learning more, you can find some of these resources in the bibliography section at the end of the book.

This chapter provides a foundation of terms we'll use later when writing automated tests. Understanding the different types of testing and techniques for designing test cases is crucial for successful automation. However, we'll only be touching the surface in this chapter. Feel free to skip ahead if you're already familiar with these concepts.

Topics covered in this chapter:

- What Is Testing?
- Testing Types
- Fundamental Test Process
- Bug Reporting
- Specification-based Test Design Techniques
- Types of Code Coverage

NOTE

ISTQB stands for the International Software Testing Qualifications Board, a globally recognized organization for software testing certifications. Established in Edinburgh in 2002, ISTQB is a non-profit association with legal registration in Belgium. They offer some of the most widely recognized quality assurance certificates worldwide.

NOTE

I attempted to rephrase the definitions and explanations in my own words, but it's clear that they're not original and need to be altered significantly. Many of these definitions come from the ISTQB Glossary, and some from the ISTQB syllabus. For a more in-depth understanding, I encourage you to visit their website. This is not meant to be an advertisement. I wanted to be transparent about the source of information. I didn't want to leave quotation marks out of every paragraph, so I included this information in one place. But, of course, it's impossible to cover everything in a single book, so I encourage you to research further any topics that interest you.

What Is Testing?

We'll begin by defining what testing is and discussing basic terms. The goal is to provide all team members with a shared understanding of the essential terminology of quality assurance and related processes. This will improve communication and enhance the quality of reviews. Furthermore, it will boost the testing capabilities of each team member.

Definition: Testing

Software quality definition found in IEEE Standard Glossary of Software Engineering Terminology:

The degree to which a system, component, or process meets specified requirements.

The degree to which a system, component, or process meets customer or user needs or expectations.

Testing is a comprehensive process, not a single task. It encompasses all life cycle stages, including static and dynamic testing, planning, preparation, and evaluation of software and associated work products. We'll delve into these activities in greater detail in the following sections.

The primary goals of testing are to detect defects in the software and prevent future bugs by improving the development process and standards. As quality assurance professionals, we help stakeholders build confidence in the system's quality and provide the information they need to make informed decisions. Depending on the context, we may also test the software to ensure it meets contractual or legal requirements or follows industry-specific standards. Early detection of problems can save significant time and money: fixing a problem at the requirements stage can cost as little as $1 while fixing it post-implementation can cost thousands. In some cases, software or system failures can even result in loss of life.

Too much testing can delay product release and increase the cost, while insufficient testing hides the risks of errors in the final product. Therefore, finding the right balance between testing effort and risk is essential to ensure the project is thoroughly tested while meeting timelines and budget constraints. We can adjust the testing effort based on the technical and business risk level in different areas.

> **Definition: Anomaly**
>
> Any condition deviates from expectations based on requirements specifications, design documents, user documents, standards, etc., or someone's perception or experience. As a result, anomalies may be found during, but not limited to, reviewing, testing, analysis, compilation, or use of software products or applicable documentation. [Sgt 18]
>
> **Definition: Bug/Defect/Fault/Problem**
>
> A flaw in a component or system that can cause the component or system to fail to perform its required function, e.g., an incorrect statement or data definition. A defect, if encountered during execution, may cause a component or system failure. [Sgt 18]
>
> **Definition: Failure**
>
> The actual deviation of the component or system from its expected delivery, service, or result. It is also called an 'external fault.' [Sgt 18]
>
> **Definition: Defect/Bug/Fault Masking**
>
> An occurrence in which one defect prevents the detection of another. [Sgt 18]

Seven Testing Principles

Before we investigate the different types of testing, let's review the seven essential principles that every quality assurance engineer should know:

1. Testing Indicates the Presence of Defects

Testing can reveal the presence of defects, but it cannot guarantee that there are no defects. However, it reduces the likelihood of undiscovered defects remaining in the software.

2. Exhaustive Testing is Infeasible

Testing some possible combinations of inputs and conditions is possible, except for very simple cases. Instead, we should use a risk analysis and prioritize our testing efforts.

3. Early Testing

Testing activities should begin as early as possible in the software development life cycle and be focused on specific goals. As we discussed earlier, fixing a bug earlier in the process is more cost-effective.

4. Defect Clustering

Testing efforts should be focused on the areas where defects are most likely to occur based on expected and observed defect density. A few modules often contain most issues found during pre-release testing or cause the most operational failures.

5. The Pesticide Paradox

Repeatedly using the same tests can reduce their effectiveness over time. As a result, previously undetected defects may go unnoticed. Therefore, it's important to regularly review and revise test cases and create new, varied tests.

6. Testing is Context-Dependent

Testing methods vary depending on the context. For example, safety-critical software is tested differently than an e-commerce website.

7. The Absence-of-Errors Fallacy

Finding and fixing defects is insufficient if the system is unusable and does not meet user needs and expectations. Therefore, ensuring that the software is functional and meets customer requirements is essential.

Testing Types

As a quality assurance engineer, it's crucial to have an understanding of different types of testing. So, let's review and define the various testing types. But first, let's explain some terms:

Definition: System Testing

The process of testing an integrated system to verify that it meets the requirements. [Sgt 18]

Definition: Component Testing

The testing of individual software components. [Sgt 18]

Definition: Component

A minimal software item that can be tested in isolation. [Sgt 18]

Definition: Integration Testing

This type of testing exposes defects in the interfaces and the interactions between integrated components or systems. [Sgt 18]

Definition: Functional Testing

It is based on an analysis of the specification of the functionality of a component or system. It answers the question: "What does the product do?". [Sgt 18]

Definition: Non-functional Testing

Tests the attributes of a component or system that do not relate to functionality, e.g., reliability, efficiency, usability, maintainability, and portability. It answers the question: "How well does the product behave?". [Sgt 18]

Definition: Acceptance Testing

Formal testing concerning user needs, requirements, and business processes is conducted to determine whether a system satisfies the acceptance criteria and to enable the user,

---

customers, or other authorized entities to determine whether to accept the software. [Sgt 18]

Definition: Acceptance Criteria

A component or system must satisfy the exit criteria to be accepted by a user, customer, or other authorized entity. [Sgt 18]

Re-testing vs. Regression Testing

Let's begin by defining the difference between two closely related terms: retesting and regression testing. Retesting involves testing again after a defect has been detected and fixed to verify that the problem has been resolved. This process is sometimes referred to as confirmation testing. On the other hand, regression testing involves retesting parts of previously tested modules after modifications have been made to the software. Regression testing aims to identify any new faults that may have been introduced due to the changes to the system. Regression testing can be performed at all levels of testing.

Functional Testing

As previously discussed, functional testing determines what the product does. To create test cases, we use specifications of the functional requirements. This type of testing is often called black-box testing or requirements-based testing. Later in the chapter, we'll review two common techniques for generating functional test cases. If we have use cases, they can serve as a useful starting point for creating test cases. Most of the automated tests we'll write will be functional, especially if they interact with the system only through its user interface (UI).

Non-functional Testing

Non-functional testing can be conducted at all levels of testing and is used to evaluate how well the system performs its functions. Non-functional testing helps answer the question of quality. Let's briefly review the core non-functional attributes that we need to test:

Definition: Reliability

The ability of the software product to perform its required functions under stated conditions for a specified period or a specified number of operations. [Sgt 18]

Definition: Usability

It is divided into the sub-characteristics of understandability, learnability, operability, attractiveness, and compliance. [Sgt 18]

Definition: Efficiency

The software's capability to provide appropriate performance relative to the number of resources used under stated conditions. [Sgt 18]

Definition: Maintainability

The ease with which a software product can be modified to correct defects, meet new requirements, make future maintenance easier, or adapted to a changed environment. [Sgt 18]

Definition: Portability

The ease with which the software can be transferred from one hardware or software environment to another. [Sgt 18]

Alpha vs. Beta Testing

Alpha testing occurs at the developer's site and involves a group of potential users and members of the developer's organization. During alpha testing, developers observe users as they use the software and take note of any issues. In contrast, beta testing involves sending the software to users who install and use it in real-world conditions. Users provide feedback by reporting any incidents they encounter while using the software to the development team.

Acceptance Testing

Acceptance testing focuses on the customer's perspective and evaluation. The customer is actively involved and tests in an environment that resembles the client's setup. The main objective is not to find defects but to assess the software from the customer's point of view. For example, when integrating a commercial off-the-shelf software product into a system, the client may only perform integration testing at the system level, followed by acceptance testing.

Maintenance Testing

Maintenance testing evaluates the effects of changes made to an operational system or the impact of changes to the environment on a working system. Any new or altered elements should be tested; regression testing is necessary. It's important to test even if only the environment has been changed and check the rest of the software for unintended side effects. The scope of maintenance testing is determined by the risk associated with the change, the size of the existing system, and the size of the change. Maintenance testing can be performed at any level and for any testing type, and it's crucial to conduct a careful impact analysis.

Definition: Impact Analysis

The change assessment to the layers of development documentation, test documentation, and components to implement a given change to specified requirements.

Maintenance testing may be triggered by planned modifications or enhancements to the system, such as adding new features or improving performance. It may also be necessary due to recent changes in the environment, such as an upgrade to the operating system or database, the retirement of a system, a migration to a different platform, or a migration of data.

Static vs. Dynamic Testing

Dynamic and static testing are complementary methods that effectively and efficiently find defects. Dynamic testing involves executing the software with input values and then examining and comparing the output to what is expected. This type of testing detects issues related to the non-functional attributes of the software code, such as memory leaks, performance problems, and storage issues.

In contrast, static testing helps detect defects early on before executing the tests. This is done by analyzing suspicious aspects of the code or design and calculating metrics, such as complexity measures. Static testing also helps identify defects that are not easily found through dynamic testing, improves the maintainability of the code and design, and helps prevent defects by learning from experiences during development.

Definition: Static Analysis

Analysis of software artifacts, e.g., requirements or code, carried out without execution of these software artifacts.

Fundamental Test Process

Test Planning

To conduct testing effectively, we need to follow a few steps. First, we must plan the testing to determine the scope, identify potential risks, and establish the testing objectives. Then, we choose the testing approach, which includes selecting the test case design techniques, identifying the test items, determining coverage, and working with the teams involved in testing. We also need to specify the necessary testware. Finally, we need to determine the exit criteria.

Definition: Test Basis

All documents from which the requirements of a component or system can be understood. The documents on which we base the test cases. [Sgt 18]

Definition: Test Condition

An item or event of a component or system that could be verified by one or more test cases, e.g., a function, transaction, feature, quality attribute, or structural element. [Sgt 18]

Definition: Test Design

The process of transforming general testing objectives into tangible test conditions and test cases. [Sgt 18]

Definition: Test Suite

A set of several test cases or automated tests for a component or system under test SUT.

Definition: Test Log

A chronological record of relevant details about the execution of tests. [Sgt 18]

Definition: Testware

Artifacts produced during the test process that are required to plan, design, and execute

---

tests, such as documentation, scripts, inputs, expected results, set-up and clear-up procedures, files, databases, environment, and any additional software or utilities used in testing. [Sgt 18]

Test Analysis and Design

During the testing phase, we review and analyze the basis for testing. We identify any gaps or ambiguities in the specifications to prevent defects from appearing in the code. As we mentioned earlier, it's much more cost-effective to catch bugs at this stage instead of during the later stages of development. Quality assurance engineers assess the testability of the test basis and test objects and communicate any necessary changes to support the testing process. Afterward, we prioritize the test conditions based on the analysis of the test specification, business importance, and system impact.

Test design involves identifying the necessary test data to support the test cases, including the initial conditions, actions, and expected results. We also design the test environment setup and identify any required infrastructure and tools.

Test Implementation and Execution

The next step is to execute the test suites and individual test cases, either manually or by using execution tools. We log the testing results and compare the actual and expected results. Any discrepancies are reported as incidents and analyzed to determine their cause. The following section will discuss the bug-reporting process in more detail.

Definition: Debugging

The process of finding, analyzing, and removing the causes of failures in the software. [Sgt 18]

Definition: Exit Criteria

The set of conditions was agreed upon with the stakeholders to permit a process to be officially completed. The purpose of exit criteria is to prevent a task from being considered completed when outstanding parts of the task have not been finished. In addition, exit criteria are used to report against and to plan when to stop testing.

Bug Reporting

Logging bugs properly is a critical task for every quality assurance engineer. Unfortunately, many people need clarification on what information to include in a bug report. This section will discuss the crucial elements of an issue report and examine the various statuses and transitions. The bug reporting process can be complex, but I will explain why I added additional statuses. The statuses and transitions between them can vary from project to project, so it's essential to research and create a bug workflow that suits your needs.

Bug Statuses

For Triage - the bug is reviewed by senior QA and development team members to determine whether it is a bug. If it is deemed a bug, the team decides on the next steps: immediate analysis, archiving, or deferring for later consideration.

Analysis - the developer thoroughly reads the issue description and starts debugging to locate the problem. During this phase, various issue fields are populated with information, such as the root cause analysis and bug taxonomy grouping, which will later be used for reporting measurements. If the problem is located, the bug can be moved to
the **Fixing** or **Deferred** status, depending on the time required to fix it. If the issue cannot be reproduced, it is transferred to the **Cannot Reproduce** status and then monitored for further observations (moving it to **Monitoring** status).

Deferred - deferred bugs are not considered high priority and will be considered for fixing later. For example, if a new development is planned for a particular feature, all deferred bugs related to that feature can be reviewed, and a decision can be made on whether to fix some.

Archived - we have determined that the issue is a valid bug, but we won't categorize it as Deferred because we believe it won't be a high priority to fix in the future. Nevertheless, we maintain a record of all these bugs to help reduce the number of duplicates. In addition, keeping track of them is important for logging purposes.

Communicate - there are times when logged problems are challenging to determine whether they are actual issues. Often, there needs to be more information regarding these problems in the documentation or requirements. If we decide the problem is worth investigating, we must first consult the product owner to get their input and understand how the feature is intended to behave.

Cannot Reproduce - sometimes, it can be challenging to recreate more complicated issues, even if they have been described in detail in the bug report. In these cases, we set the bug status to **Cannot Reproduce** for record-keeping purposes. Before doing this, we generally monitor the issue for a certain period to see if it can be recreated. If the issue cannot be recreated, it is considered **Cannot Reproduce**.

Monitoring - if a bug cannot be found during the analysis process, we will take some time to monitor it. This way, we can see if the bug will reappear. If, after two weeks, the bug hasn't resurfaced, we will change its status to **Cannot Reproduce**.

Reopened - before reporting a bug, we should always check if it has been logged. Sometimes, we may find that the bug already exists but has been marked as **Done**. So, instead of creating a new report, we'll move the bug to the **Reopened** status. This not only saves time on data entry but also provides essential information for measuring the quality of our work.

Fixing - we mark a problem as **Fixing** once we have determined the root cause and have agreed that there is sufficient time to resolve it.

Code Review - once a developer has fixed a bug, they will test it locally. Then, they will create a pull request and ask a colleague to review their code.

Integration Testing - after the bug has been approved through code review, it is deployed to the DEV environment for retesting and regression testing. The bug reporter, usually a QA, will perform these tests.

Failed Testing - during retesting, it may become apparent that the bug still needs to be fixed. Therefore, the bug is set to **Failed Testing** instead of immediately returning to the **Fixing** status, which allows us to collect additional quality metrics.

Integration Testing - the bug is retested on the TEST environment with other stories currently under development.

For Deployment - once we have confirmed that the bug has been fixed, we can safely roll it out to the production environment.

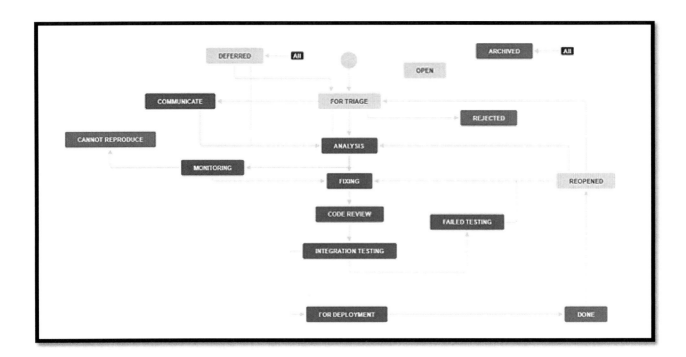

Main Fields

The following details are essential when logging a bug:

Title - a brief, meaningful explanation of the problem.
Description - a detailed explanation of the problem.
Actual Results - the observed results of the test.
Expected Results - the expected behavior of the tested functionality.
Steps to Reproduce - a step-by-step list of how to recreate the issue.
Environment - the environment where the problem was observed and any relevant setup details.
Assignee - the person responsible for analyzing and fixing the issue.
Reporter - the person who reported and logged the bug.
Attachments - relevant screenshots, videos, dumps, or other files to help explain the issue.
Priority - the level of importance assigned to the bug, indicating its urgency to be fixed."
Severity - the level of impact the bug has on the system or user experience. This can range from minor to critical.

Priority Levels

In order of decreasing importance, the available priorities are:

1. **Critical** - blocks development and/or testing work, production cannot run, causes crashes, loss of data, or a significant memory leak. Any issue that prevents the project from being built is automatically assigned a priority of 1 and requires immediate attention.
2. **High** - a major or important loss of function that requires urgent action.
3. **Medium** - a lower priority loss of function that does not require immediate attention.
4. **Low** - a small problem with no impact on functionality.

Definition: Severity

The degree of impact that a defect has on the development or operation of a component or system. [Sgt 18]

Severity Levels

BLOCKING	
Why should the QA assign the status?	QA cannot do manual testing/Smoke automation tests are failing.
Example	Functional/configuration issues leading to yellow screen, missing module, etc.
What should be done by QA?	Log a bug or send an email and verbal notification.
What should be done by DEV?	Resolve as soon as possible.
CRITICAL	
Why should the QA assign the status?	The main part of the feature is not working as expected.
Example	Core functional/unusable UI issues that lead to a form not submitting, the buy button not working, a form is not syncing data, etc.
What should be done by QA?	Log a bug and notification.
What should be done by DEV?	Give attention.

HIGH	
Why should the QA assign the status?	It is not recommended to release without fixing this.
Example	Functional/broken UI - UI differences from design, validations, etc.
What should be done by QA?	Log a bug.
What should be done by DEV?	Fix this after all Blocking and Critical bugs.
MEDIUM	
Why should the QA assign the status?	Good to fix if we have time.
Example	Minor functional/UI issues - off-the-happy path scenario, some responsive problems for specific resolutions/browsers, etc.
What should be done by QA?	Log a bug.
What should be done by DEV?	Do this if the story's estimated time is not reached.
LOW	
Why should the QA assign the status?	Documentation purposes.
Example	URL with the issue.
What should be done by QA?	Log a bug.
What should be done by DEV?	Check this out.

Specification-based Test Design Techniques

Many developers aim to reach 100% code coverage through their unit tests. In this section on test design, I'll show you how to use specification-based techniques to cover more requirements in your tests. Unfortunately, I've encountered many automated tests, most of which don't cover the requirements. So, think about how you write your tests. Are you taking test inputs from the application's specifications? If not, you should be! By the end of this chapter, you'll know how to design test cases based on specifications using two key techniques: **Equivalence Partitioning** and **Boundary Value Analysis**.

NOTE

Chapter 10. Unit Testing Fundamentals will delve into the intricacies of writing effective unit tests. This section will provide a comprehensive overview of the topic, covering everything from test design techniques to the ins and outs of code coverage.

The following is a simple class that calculates the monthly subscription price for Sofia's transportation lines:

```
public static class TransportSubscriptionCardPriceCalculator
{
    public static decimal CalculateSubscriptionPrice(string ageInput)
    {
        decimal subscriptionPrice = default;
        int age = default;
        bool isInteger = int.TryParse(ageInput, out age);

        if (!isInteger)
        {
            throw new ArgumentException("The age input should be an integer value between 0
- 122.");
        }

        if (age <= 0)
        {
            throw new ArgumentException("The age should be greater than zero.");
        }
        else if (age > 0 && age <= 5)
        {
            subscriptionPrice = 0;
        }
        else if (age > 5 && age <= 18)
        {
```

```
            subscriptionPrice = 20;
        }
        else if (age > 18 && age < 65)
        {
            subscriptionPrice = 40;
        }
        else if (age >= 65 && age <= 122)
        {
            subscriptionPrice = 5;
        }
        else
        {
            throw new ArgumentException("The age should be smaller than 123.");
        }

        return subscriptionPrice;
    }
}
```

This class is a static utility that takes a client's age as input and returns the monthly subscription price based on the following age ranges:

- For ages 0 < Age <= 5, the price is 0 lv
- For ages 5 < Age <= 18, the price is 20 lv
- For ages 18 < Age < 65, the price is 40 lv
- For ages 65 <= Age <= 122, the price is 5 lv.

Most developers approach test writing by reading the code and then the specifications. Their primary goal is to achieve 100% code coverage through the tests they write. However, this approach could lead to missed requirements, and the tests may fail if the code contains bugs. To ensure the code meets the specifications, it's important to design tests based on the requirements, not the code. **Equivalence Partitioning** and **Boundary Value Analysis** can help achieve this goal. In this article, I'll show you how to use these techniques to design tests that genuinely cover the requirements. I'll be using NUnit for demonstration, as it offers convenient attributes for test writing.

```
[TestFixture]
public class TransportSubscriptionCardPriceCalculatorTests
{
    private const string GreaterThanZeroExpectionMessage = "The age should be greater than
zero.";
    private const string SmallerThan123ExpectionMessage = "The age should be smaller than
123.";
    private const string ShouldBeIntegerExpectionMessage = "The age input should be an
integer value between 0 - 122.";

    [Test]
    public void ValidateCalculateSubscriptionPrice_Free([Random(min: 1, max: 5, count: 1)]
                                                        int ageInput)
```

```
        {
            decimal actualPrice =
TransportSubscriptionCardPriceCalculator.CalculateSubscriptionPrice(ageInput.ToString());

            Assert.AreEqual(0, actualPrice);
        }

        [Test]
        public void ValidateCalculateSubscriptionPrice_20lv([Random(min: 6, max: 18, count: 1)]
                                                             int ageInput)
        {
            decimal actualPrice =
TransportSubscriptionCardPriceCalculator.CalculateSubscriptionPrice(ageInput.ToString());

            Assert.AreEqual(20, actualPrice);
        }

        [Test]
        public void ValidateCalculateSubscriptionPrice_40lv([Random(min: 19, max: 64, count: 1)]
                                                             int ageInput)
        {
            decimal actualPrice =
TransportSubscriptionCardPriceCalculator.CalculateSubscriptionPrice(ageInput.ToString());

            Assert.AreEqual(40, actualPrice);
        }

        [Test]
        public void ValidateCalculateSubscriptionPrice_5lv([Random(min: 65, max: 122, count: 1)]
                                                            int ageInput)
        {
            decimal actualPrice =
TransportSubscriptionCardPriceCalculator.CalculateSubscriptionPrice(ageInput.ToString());

            Assert.AreEqual(5, actualPrice);
        }

        [Test]
        [ExpectedException(typeof(ArgumentException), ExpectedMessage =
ShouldBeIntegerExpectionMessage)]
        public void ValidateCalculateSubscriptionPrice_NotInteger()
        {
            decimal actualPrice =
TransportSubscriptionCardPriceCalculator.CalculateSubscriptionPrice("invalid");

            Assert.AreEqual(5, actualPrice);
        }

        [Test]
        [ExpectedException(typeof(ArgumentException), ExpectedMessage =
GreaterThanZeroExpectionMessage)]
        public void ValidateCalculateSubscriptionPrice_InvalidZero()
        {
```

```
        decimal actualPrice =
TransportSubscriptionCardPriceCalculator.CalculateSubscriptionPrice("0");

        Assert.AreEqual(5, actualPrice);
    }

    [Test]
    [ExpectedException(typeof(ArgumentException), ExpectedMessage =
SmallerThan123ExpectionMessage)]
    public void ValidateCalculateSubscriptionPrice_InvalidGreater122()
    {
        decimal actualPrice =
TransportSubscriptionCardPriceCalculator.CalculateSubscriptionPrice("1000");

        Assert.AreEqual(5, actualPrice);
    }
}
```

Using random data in tests is not a recommended approach. Some test automation engineers still use this technique, but it can lead to inconsistent and unreliable test results. For example, tests using random data may pass with some generated values but fail with others.

NOTE

In **Chapter 11. Unit Testing Fundamentals**, we will delve deeply into NUnit, one of the major unit test frameworks in the .NET world. We use NUnit to write unit, integration, and automated tests. In addition, it provides many useful tools, such as integration with Visual Studio for writing, debugging, executing tests, and viewing results, as well as a CLI test runner. For example, to mark a class as a test fixture, we use the [TestFixture] attribute; to mark a method as a test, we use the [Test] attribute.

In our examples, we will utilize two additional NUnit attributes, [Random] and [ExpectedException]. The [Random] attribute allows us to execute tests a specified number of times, generating parameter values within set boundaries. The [ExpectedException] attribute verifies that the tested code throws the specified exception and the appropriate error message.

For now, don't worry about writing NUnit tests. Instead, focus on the test scenario generation process. We use the same approaches for writing manual test cases.

To achieve 100% code coverage, just 7 tests are needed. Let's examine them:

[Random(min: 1, max: 5, count: 1)] then **Price = 0**, covers the first else if:

```
else if (age > 0 && age <= 5)
{
    subscriptionPrice = 0;
}
```

[Random(min: 6, max: 18, count: 1)] then **Price= 20**, covers second else if:

```
else if (age > 5 && age <= 18)
{
    subscriptionPrice = 20;
}
```

[Random(min: 19, max: 64, count: 1)] then **Price= 40**, covers the third else if:

```
else if (age > 18 && age < 65)
{
    subscriptionPrice = 40;
}
```

[Random(min: 65, max: 122, count: 1)] then **Price= 5**, covers the senior price:

```
else if (age >= 65 && age <= 122)
{
    subscriptionPrice = 5;
}
```

AgeInput= "invalid", validates the first exception scenario when the user passes a non-integer value:

```
if (!isInteger)
{
    throw new ArgumentException("The age input should be an integer value between 0 -
122.");
}
```

AgeInput= 0, covers the second defensive check:

```
if (age <= 0)
{
    throw new ArgumentException("The age should be greater than zero.");
}
```

AgeInput= 1000, causes the test to go through the last validation check about the maximum age:

```
else
{
    throw new ArgumentException("The age should be smaller than 123.");
}
```

With just seven tests, we've reached 100% code coverage, but, likely, these tests won't detect regression bugs if a conditional operator such as "<", ">", ">=", or "<=" is changed. This approach to writing tests also doesn't guarantee the code is correct. If the tests are based on flawed code, they won't help us deliver better, bug-free software. That's where specification-based test design techniques come in to help.

Specification-Based Tests: Based on Equivalence Partitioning

To start with, let me explain what is meant by specification-based testing.

Definition: Specification-based Testing

Specification-based testing is a testing approach that involves designing test cases based on test objectives and conditions derived from requirements. For example, this approach creates tests that exercise specific functions or investigate non-functional attributes like reliability or usability.

Equivalence Partitioning is a testing approach that seeks comprehensive test coverage while minimizing the required test cases. This method involves dividing a set of test conditions or values into equivalence partitions or classes, with only one value being selected for testing within each partition. The idea behind this technique is that if one condition or value in a partition passes, all other conditions or values in the same partition will also pass, and if one fails, all others will also fail. While Equivalence Partitioning is particularly useful for testing small input ranges, it becomes more challenging to apply for larger ranges, such as 2-10000.

Equivalence Partitioning adheres to one of the seven testing principles: **exhaustive testing is impossible**. Therefore, instead of testing every possible combination of inputs and preconditions, we can use risks and priorities to focus our testing efforts. For instance, if we have 15 input fields on a single screen, each with five possible values, it would require over 30 billion tests to cover all the valid combinations. Such a large number of tests is not reasonable given project timescales. Therefore, risk assessment and management are essential activities in any testing project.

Although writing 1 to 10 tests for smaller input ranges may be possible, writing hundreds of thousands or even millions of tests for larger sets is often impractical. Therefore, we can use specification-based test design techniques to reduce the required test cases to the minimum necessary. If we were to write code for production and test it, we would likely use Test-Driven Development and design test scenarios based on the specification requirements.

Let's see an example:

```
private const string GreaterThanZeroExceptionMessage = "The age should be greater than
zero.";
private const string SmallerThan123ExceptionMessage = "The age should be smaller than 123.";
private const string ShouldBeIntegerExceptionMessage = "The age input should be an integer
value between 0 - 122.";

[TestCase("0", 0, ExpectedException = typeof(ArgumentException), ExpectedMessage =
GreaterThanZeroExceptionMessage)]
[TestCase("5", 0)]
[TestCase("15", 20)]
[TestCase("25", 40)]
[TestCase("80", 5)]
[TestCase("1000", 0, ExpectedException = typeof(ArgumentException), ExpectedMessage =
SmallerThan123ExceptionMessage)]
[TestCase("invalid", 0, ExpectedException = typeof(ArgumentException), ExpectedMessage =
ShouldBeIntegerExceptionMessage)]
public void ValidateCalculateSubscriptionPrice(string ageInput, decimal expectedPrice)
{
    decimal actualPrice =
TransportSubscriptionCardPriceCalculator.CalculateSubscriptionPrice(ageInput);

    Assert.AreEqual(expectedPrice, actualPrice);
}
```

To validate the TransportSubscriptionCardPriceCalculator, we have defined three exception messages for invalid age inputs. These messages are stored in constant strings. The following test cases are used to validate the TransportSubscriptionCardPriceCalculator:

- When ageInput is "0", the expected output is 0, and an ArgumentException with GreaterThanZeroExceptionMessage is expected.
- When ageInput is "5", the expected output is 0.
- When ageInput is "15", the expected output is 20.
- When ageInput is "25", the expected output is 40.
- When ageInput is "80", the expected output is 5.
- When ageInput is "1000", the expected output is 0, and an ArgumentException with SmallerThan123ExceptionMessage is expected.
- When ageInput is "invalid", the expected output is 0, and an ArgumentException with ShouldBeIntegerExceptionMessage is expected.

We call the TransportSubscriptionCardPriceCalculator.CalculateSubscriptionPrice method with the ageInput parameter and assign the result to the actualPrice variable. Finally, we use the Assert.AreEqual() method to compare the expectedPrice and actualPrice variables.

The tests in the code example use the NUnit `[TestCase]` attribute, which allows the same test method to be executed with different parameters specified in the attribute constructor. In this case, seven tests are performed, with the first parameter representing the age input and the second representing the expected price. These test cases are derived using equivalence partitions, and while the number of tests is not increased, the tests are based on the specification requirements rather than the code itself. Additionally, these tests were written before the code, following a Test-Driven Development approach.

	1	2	3	4	5	6	7
Age	... 0	1 ... 5	6 ... 18	19 ... 64	65 ... 122	123 ...	NaN
Price	invalid	0 lv	20 lv	40 lv	5 lv	invalid	Invalid
Tests	0	5	15	25	85	1000	"invalid"

Based on the table, it can be observed that there are a total of seven equivalence partitions, which consist of four valid partitions and three invalid ones. All of these partitions are covered with the values from the last row of the table. While this technique is relatively simple, people make common mistakes when applying it. First, the different subsets cannot have too many members in common. If a value is present in two partitions, it may be impossible to define how it should behave in the different cases. Moreover, none of the subsets can be empty. It is useless for testing if you cannot select a test value from a set.

Specification-Based Tests: Based on Boundary Value Analysis

So, what is the Boundary Value Analysis?

Definition: Boundary Value Analysis

It is a black-box test design technique in which test cases are designed based on boundary values. But then, what are boundary values? Boundary values are input or output values on the edge of an equivalence partition or at the smallest incremental distance on either side of a border, such as, for example, the minimum or maximum value of a range.

Boundary Value Analysis is a technique that builds upon Equivalence Partitioning by selecting test cases at the edges of equivalence classes. Its coverage criterion requires that every valid and invalid boundary value be included in at least one test. The key difference is that at least two boundary values are selected from each equivalence class, resulting in roughly twice as many tests. However, not all equivalence classes have boundary values, and Boundary Value Analysis is only applicable when the members of an equivalence class are ordered.

How Many Boundary Values Are There?

Two schools of thought exist on how many boundary values to use. Some believe only two values should be derived from each edge of the equivalence partition. For example, in the condition 0 < Age > 6, the boundary values for the first edge will be 0, 1, and for the second edge, 5, 6. Boris Beizer, in his book Software System Testing and Quality Assurance, explains the other option: three values per boundary, where each edge is considered one of the test values, in addition to each of its neighbors. For the previous condition, 0 < Age > 6, the test values for 0 will be -1, 0, and 1. The test values for 6 will be 6, 5, and 7. I have experimented with both approaches during my career and believe that using Boris Beizer's technique, despite the increase in test case count, has helped me find more bugs. Therefore, I encourage you to use Boris Beizer's technique.

To achieve 100% boundary value analysis coverage, only the first 16 tests are needed. Still, I have included four additional tests to cover scenarios where test values belong to a common equivalence partition but may produce different results. The tests have been designed to validate age inputs ranging from -1 to 123:

0 < Age <= 5, Left Edge: -1, 0, 1, Right Edge: 4, 5, 6

5 < Age <= 18, Left Edge: 4, 5, 6, Right Edge: 17, 18, 19

18 < Age < 65, Left Edge: 17, 18, 19, Right Edge: 64, 65, 66

65 <= Age <= 122, Left Edge: 64, 65, 66, Right Edge: 121, 122, 123

Although this technique is relatively straightforward, there are common errors to avoid when applying it. For example, the subsets cannot have many members in common, and none may be empty. It is also worth noting that Boundary Value Analysis only applies when the members of an equivalence class are ordered.

Here is the code for the 20 tests I created using Boundary Value Analysis:

```csharp
private const string GreaterThanZeroExpectionMessage = "The age should be greater than
zero.";
private const string SmallerThan123ExpectionMessage = "The age should be smaller than 123.";
private const string ShouldBeIntegerExpectionMessage = "The age input should be an integer
value between 0 - 122.";

[TestCase("-1", 0, ExpectedException = typeof(ArgumentException), ExpectedMessage =
GreaterThanZeroExpectionMessage)]
[TestCase("0", 0, ExpectedException = typeof(ArgumentException), ExpectedMessage =
GreaterThanZeroExpectionMessage)]
[TestCase("1", 0)]
[TestCase("4", 0)]
[TestCase("5", 0)]
[TestCase("6", 20)]
[TestCase("17", 20)]
[TestCase("18", 20)]
[TestCase("19", 40)]
[TestCase("64", 40)]
[TestCase("65", 5)]
[TestCase("66", 5)]
[TestCase("121", 5)]
[TestCase("122", 5)]
[TestCase("123", 0, ExpectedException = typeof(ArgumentException), ExpectedMessage =
SmallerThan123ExpectionMessage)]
[TestCase("a", 0, ExpectedException = typeof(ArgumentException), ExpectedMessage =
ShouldBeIntegerExpectionMessage)]
[TestCase("", 0, ExpectedException = typeof(ArgumentException), ExpectedMessage =
ShouldBeIntegerExpectionMessage)]
[TestCase(null, 0, ExpectedException = typeof(ArgumentException), ExpectedMessage =
ShouldBeIntegerExpectionMessage)]
[TestCase("2147483648", 0, ExpectedException = typeof(ArgumentException), ExpectedMessage =
ShouldBeIntegerExpectionMessage)]
[TestCase("-2147483649", 0, ExpectedException = typeof(ArgumentException), ExpectedMessage =
ShouldBeIntegerExpectionMessage)]
public void ValidateCalculateSubscriptionPrice1(string ageInput, decimal expectedPrice)
{
    decimal actualPrice =
TransportSubscriptionCardPriceCalculator.CalculateSubscriptionPrice(ageInput);

    Assert.AreEqual(expectedPrice, actualPrice);
}
```

In conclusion, Boundary Value Analysis is a useful technique that helps ensure test cases are designed to cover the boundary values of input or output values. By carefully selecting the number of boundary values for each equivalence partition, we can reduce the required tests while achieving comprehensive test coverage.

Where Would You Find Boundary Values?

When determining the boundary values for an equivalence class, we can typically rely on the specification requirements to guide us. These requirements outline how the system should behave in various use cases and can inform our choice of boundary values. However, there may be instances where the specification does not provide clear guidance on appropriate boundary values. We may use test oracles to help identify suitable values in such cases.

Definition: Test Oracle

A source to determine expected results compared with the actual results of the software under test. An oracle may be the existing system (for a benchmark), a user manual, or an individual's specialized knowledge, but it should not be the code.

An example scenario is when you are developing a calculator application without full specifications on how it should behave in certain cases. In such cases, you can use the Windows built-in calculator as a test oracle to validate the behavior of your application. Using specification-based testing design strategies like Equivalence Partitioning and Boundary Value Analysis can help you write the minimum number of unit tests required to cover all the requirements. These techniques can prevent the practice of designing tests based on potentially faulty code, which can produce passing but incorrect tests. While there is no perfect test design technique, using your system knowledge, intelligence, and intuition to try different test values is crucial. In the next chapter, we will review the different types of code coverage.

Types of Code Coverage

Code coverage analysis is a technique to assess software testing quality, often done using dynamic execution flow analysis. There are various types of code coverage analysis, ranging from simple to complex, and some require advanced tool support. Many people mistakenly believe they have achieved comprehensive testing when Visual Studio code coverage reports 100%. However, this is not always the case. Let me provide a few examples of the different types of code coverage.

Statement Code Coverage

The simplest form of code coverage is called Statement Code Coverage. This type of coverage is commonly used in Integrated Development Environments (IDEs), such as Visual Studio. The main objective of statement coverage is to execute all statements in the code with the fewest possible tests. For example, consider the following code:

```
private void PeformAction(int x, int y)
{
        DoSomething();
        if (x > 3 && y < 6)
        {
                DoSomethingElse();
        }

        DoSomething();
}
```

To achieve statement coverage, you only need to execute one test with values x = 4 and y = 5. Therefore, testing all possible combinations of conditions within the IF statement is not necessary.

Statement Coverage = (Number of executed statements)/(Total Number of Statements)* 100%

Branch Code Coverage (Decision Coverage)

The next type of code coverage is called Decision Code Coverage. It ensures that every decision in the code is executed with both possible outcomes, **TRUE** and **FALSE**:

```
private void PeformAction(int x, int y)
{
    DoSomething();
    if (x > 3 && y < 6)
    {
        DoSomethingElse();
```

```
    }
    else
    {
        Console.WriteLine(x + y);
    }

    DoSomething();
}
```

In the example, we have an IF statement with two conditions, x > 3 and y < 6. To achieve Decision Code Coverage, we need two tests:

- x = 4 and y = 5 => IF Executed
- x = 2 and y = 5 => ELSE Executed

This type of coverage ensures that all possible paths, including the less used ones, are executed.

Branch Coverage = (Number of Branches)/(Total Number of Branches)* 100%

The calculation counts every executed branch only once.

```
private void PeformAction(int x, int y, bool shouldExecute)
{
    if (shouldExecute)
    {
        DoSomething();
        if (x > 3 && y < 6)
        {
            DoSomethingElse();
        }
        else
        {
            Console.WriteLine(x + y);
        }

        DoSomething();
    }
}
```

The branch of the `shouldExecute` will be executed twice in our tests, but it should be counted only once in the formula.

NOTE

100% Branch Coverage guarantees 100% statement coverage. Also, it requires more tests.

Branch Condition Coverage

Code often contains complex conditional expressions that depend on multiple smaller conditions called atomic parts. An atomic part is a condition that does not include logical operations such as AND, OR, or NOT but may consist of symbols such as "<", ">", or "=". A single condition can be made up of multiple atomic parts.

For example, consider the following code:

```
private void PeformAction(int x, int y, int z)
{
    DoSomething();
    if ((x > 3 && y < 6) || z == 20)
    {
        DoSomethingElse();
    }
    else
    {
        Console.WriteLine(x + y);
    }

    DoSomething();
}
```

To achieve 100% Branch Condition Coverage, we must test every atomic part with TRUE and FALSE values. The above example has 3 atomic parts: x > 3, y < 6, and z == 20. Therefore, we need to perform two tests:

- x = 2, y = 4, z = 21 ((F && T) || F) => F
- x = 4, y = 7, z = 20 ((T && F) || T) => T

Testing all atomic parts with TRUE and FALSE values ensures that every possible branch condition has been executed at least once.

NOTE

The Branch Condition Coverage is weaker than Statement Coverage and Branch Coverage because it is not required to execute every statement.

```
private void PeformAction(int x, int y)
{
    DoSomething();
    if (x > 3 && y < 6)
    {
        DoSomethingElse();
    }
```

```
    else
    {
        Console.WriteLine(x + y);
    }

    DoSomething();
}
```

Here you can accomplish 100% Branch Condition Coverage with again 2 tests:

- x = 2, y = 3 (F && T) => F
- x = 4, y = 7 (T && F) => F

But you don't have 100% Statement Coverage. So, the code in the IF won't be executed.

Branch Condition Combination Code Coverage

All combinations of the atomic parts should be applied:

- x = 2, y = 3 (F && T) => F
- x = 4, y = 7 (T && F) => F
- x = 4, y = 3 (T && T) => T
- x = 2, y = 7 (F && F) => F

It is a more comprehensive code coverage than statement and branch coverage. However, the number of tests required can grow exponentially, as it requires testing all combinations of atomic parts in a condition that can be 2^n with n atomic parts. This makes it a costly technique to implement. Additionally, not all combinations of atomic parts may be possible, further complicating the process.

```
private void PeformAction(int x, int y)
{
    DoSomething();
    if (3 <= x && x < 5)
    {
        DoSomethingElse();
    }
    else
    {
        Console.WriteLine(x + y);
    }

    DoSomething();
}
```

3 <= x (F) && x < 5 (F) - the combination is not possible because the value x shall be smaller than 3 and greater or equal to 5 at the same time.

Condition Determination Coverage

The Condition Determination Coverage overcomes the issues discussed earlier. Unlike the previous method, it doesn't require testing all possible combinations of atomic parts. Only those combinations that can affect the overall logical value of the condition need to be tested.

```
private void PeformAction(int x, int y)
{
    DoSomething();
    if (4 <= x || y < 6)
    {
        DoSomethingElse();
    }
    else
    {
        Console.WriteLine(x + y);
    }

    DoSomething();
}
```

If we want to achieve 100% Branch Condition Combination Coverage, we need four tests:

- x = 2, y = 3 (F || T) => T
- x = 4, y = 7 (T || F) =>T
- x = 4, y = 3 (T || T) => T
- x = 2, y = 7 (F || F) => F

However, we can exclude the third and fourth tests to achieve 100% Condition Determination Coverage. This is because even if we change the first or second atomic part from False to True, or vice versa, the outcome won't change.

Summary

This chapter covered vital testing concepts, including terminology, types, and fundamental test processes. We have explored ISTQB Foundation-level concepts and delved into how to use specification-based test design techniques, such as Equivalence Partitioning and Boundary Value Analysis, to design automated test cases. Additionally, we have reviewed the various types of code coverage.

The next chapter will focus on core test automation concepts, including its benefits and costs, what to automate, and what not to automate. Finally, we will discuss the issues that test automation solves and introduce an assessment system to help you choose the appropriate test automation solution.

Chapter 5. Test Automation Fundamentals

In the following chapter, we will learn concepts beyond test automation. Before you are ready to write automated code for the web or any other platform, you must understand what to or not to automate. It is best if we discuss the people's automated testing misunderstandings. Knowing the high-quality automated test attributes and the benefits that test automation can bring you will help establish a solid test infrastructure. However, we will also investigate its costs and a system for picking the right solution.

Topics covered in this chapter:

- What Should We Automate?
- Automated Testing Benefits
- Myths about Automated Testing
- Why not Automate?
- Test Automation Costs
- How Not to Automate
- Attributes of High-Quality Automated Tests
- Defining the Primary Problems that Test Automation Solve
- Assessment System for Evaluating Test Automation Solutions

What Should We Automate?

We should strive to automate tasks that are tedious such as regression testing. Or others that are hard to do manually, such as performance testing. Test automation can also automate other parts of the test process. Unfortunately, 10% code change still requires testing 100% of the features. Often, when the time before release is short, so is the time for testing, and ironically, managers decide to sacrifice regression testing in favor of testing new features. The irony is that the most significant risk to the user is in the existing features, not the new ones!

It would be best to write automated tests only when there's a strong business case. These tests will help decrease the test execution period and reduce overall effort. Test automation will help cover additional quality risks and reduce the cost of failure. As we discussed earlier, the issue has been detected and fixed. It is cheaper for the company. This will allow us to increase coverage so that errors are revealed before they can do real damage in production.

For some companies, the main goal is "faster time to market." But, sometimes, time is worth more than money, especially if it means releasing a new product or service that generates revenue. Automation can help reduce time to market by allowing test execution to happen 24X7. Let's review some other benefits you can get from automated testing.

Definition: Automated Testing

Automated testing uses software tools to execute predefined tests, validate expected outcomes, and compare them against actual results. It involves creating and running test cases, using automation frameworks, scripts, or tools. Automated testing aims to enhance testing efficiency, reduce manual effort, and provide prompt feedback on software quality.

Definition: Test Automation

Test automation encompasses a broader scope, encompassing the automation of various testing activities. This includes automating test environment setup, test data generation, result reporting, and other related tasks. As a result, test automation aims to streamline the overall testing process, boost productivity, and enable continuous testing in agile and DevOps environments.

Definition: Quality Engineering

Quality Engineering is an approach to software development that prioritizes ensuring and

---

enhancing the quality of software products and processes throughout the entire software development lifecycle. It is a discipline that combines engineering principles, best practices, and methodologies to deliver high-quality software solutions. Quality Engineering focuses on incorporating quality considerations and practices from the initial stages of software development, enabling teams to provide robust and reliable software that meets customer expectations.

Quality Engineering involves:

Test Planning and Strategy - developing a comprehensive plan and strategy for testing, defining objectives, scope, and test environments.

Test Design and Execution - creating and executing test cases, scripts, and scenarios to validate software functionality, performance, security, and usability.

Test Automation - implementing automated testing frameworks and tools to improve efficiency, speed, and repeatability.

CI/CD Integration - integrating quality practices into CI/CD pipelines for early issue detection and faster releases.

Defect Management - tracking and resolving software defects throughout the development process.

Performance and Scalability Testing - assessing software performance and scalability under different conditions.

Security Testing - identifying and addressing security vulnerabilities in software applications.

Usability and UX Testing - evaluating software usability and user experience.

Metrics and Reporting - collecting and analyzing quality-related metrics to assess effectiveness.

Process Improvement - continuously improving development and testing processes.

Quality Engineering aims to incorporate quality throughout the software development lifecycle, emphasizing collaboration, automation, and best practices to deliver high-quality software that meets customer requirements and provides an excellent user experience.

Automated Testing Benefits

We save effort and time, and we reduce risks through better coverage. Test automation allows more test cases to be run and reduces repetitive work. Easier and faster testing allows for running more tests, achieving better test coverage, and pushing up overall coverage reduces risks. Ultimately, it increases confidence upon release.
Another significant benefit is consistency and repeatability. Test tools improve testing consistency and repeatability. For example, tests can be executed in the same order and frequency.

Myths about Automated Testing

- Automated testing can replace manual testing and humans.
- Testing can be fully automated.
- One test tool is suitable for all tasks.
- Automation is entirely suitable for new functionality.
- Automated tests will find more bugs.
- Every test case can be automated.
- Testing can be fully automated.

Why not Automate?

There are many cases where you should not automate. Let's discuss some of them.

Certain applications are inherently unstable by design. The cornerstone of test automation is the premise that the expected application behavior is known. When this is not the case, it is usually better not to automate. Automation will be almost impossible if you can't control the application test environment and data.

Suppose you have inexperienced QAs who are new to the team. If the person/people writing the tests are not sufficiently experienced- their tests will have doubtful value. Remember, an automated test is only as good as the person who created it. If you don't have enough time or resources to manually complete your testing in the short term, don't expect test automation to help you.
Look at automation for the longer term. Remember that automation is a strategic solution, not a short-term fix.

Test Automation Costs

There are two types of costs to be considered - **initial** and **recurring**.

Initial expenses include evaluating and selecting the right test automation solution. At the end of the chapter, we will review an assessment system to help you pick the right tool because shortcutting this may come expensive. Depending on whether it is free or paid, you may need to purchase a license for it. Even if you don't need to buy the solution, adapting an open-source one or developing your own may cost even more.

The **initial costs** also include knowledge building. All engineers will have to invest time learning the tool and how to use it properly. Even if you are not paying for an outside provider to lead training, the company is still paying for the time the engineers need to spend researching and learning the tool. This time sometimes includes also intra-organizational knowledge transfer between different teams. You must consider the time necessary to design and document the test automation architecture and integrate the tool with your existing test process, other test tools, and your team.

Some **recurring costs** include maintaining the test automation solution and the test scripts. How long does an automated test last before it must be updated? You must consider the time required for tool upgrades and new staff onboarding. Other recurring expenses are ongoing license fees, support fees for the solution, and ongoing training costs.

Even if an **open-source tool costs** nothing to buy, it will cost time and effort to learn, use, and maintain. Therefore, evaluate open-source tools as you would commercial tools - rigorously and against your systems, not by running a canned demo.

How Not to Automate?

Unrealistic Expectations

Test tools are not silver bullets. Unfortunately, unrealistic expectations are widespread in organizations with limited experience with test automation. So, make sure people have proper expectations. In addition, the time savings come only when automated tests can be executed more than once.

Underestimating the Cost of Introducing

Underestimating the time, cost, and effort required to introduce the tool. You must be prepared to build test frameworks, integrate with other tools, set standards and guidelines for the automation solution, and train those who will use the tool. Sometimes this involves outside training or external consulting.

Underestimating Maintenance

You should be aware of the effort required to maintain the tests. Often, organizations fail to budget realistically for test maintenance, which leads to running tests that result in many false positives and negatives when engineers don't have sufficient time to develop the tests correctly and create brittle hard-to-maintain testware.

Doing the Wrong Things Faster

You should be careful which test cases you automate. There might be existing manual tests that are incomplete or incorrect. Using them as a basis for your automated tests might be wrong. Before automating, double-check manual test cases, data, and scripts. It's more expensive to fix them later.

Automation is More Than Capture/Replay

Usage of capture-replay tools often produces brittle, hard-to-maintain test scripts and test data, resulting in a frequent need for updates when the software under test changes. This leads to escalating costs of test maintenance.

Automation Is More Than Test Execution

As we will discuss thoroughly during the book, you need a complete process where you document, manage, and maintain the tests, tools for executing them, reporting the results, and managing the test environment.

Duplication of Effort

Certainly, each tester will automate the tests in their own distinct and personalized way, which often results in significant duplication of effort and may lead to conflicts when the tests are combined, as required.

Consider consultants as your personal trainers, who are there to guide you through your exercises rather than perform them for you! For instance, paying someone else to do your sit-ups won't help you flatten your stomach.

Attributes of High-Quality Automated Tests

Optimization

Creating a single test for each requirement is advisable to ensure a better testing experience. However, tests that are too long can become unstable and prone to errors. Ideally, every test should focus on a specific business requirement or a known defect. This approach enables selective execution of tests, like verifying whether a bug has been fixed.

In contrast, tests linked with multiple requirements may be overly complicated and should be divided into smaller, separate tests that address individual requirements. This makes the testing process more manageable and efficient.

Proper Naming

To improve the accuracy of error diagnosis, it is essential to provide precise information about what each test case covers in case it fails. For instance, a comprehensive test case that covers multiple features or functions could fail for various reasons, making it challenging to identify the root cause of the error. Therefore, the diagnostics required to understand the error can be minimized by specifying the exact areas that each test case covers. This approach enhances the effectiveness of the testing process and facilitates prompt resolution of any identified issues.

Independence

It's crucial to avoid any dependence between test cases. For instance, consider whether one test case's outcome relies on another. If the previous test case fails to run or is not executed correctly, the following test case will also fail as the required item for deletion won't be available. Additionally, if one test case is intended to begin at a specific location but requires a previous test case to navigate through the application to that point, it should be avoided at all costs. This approach enhances the reliability and effectiveness of the testing process and enables prompt identification and resolution of issues.

Modularity

It's vital to organize test cases in a way that aligns with the structure of the application being tested. By doing so, any changes made to the application can be quickly localized and tested to ensure they function correctly. In addition, to avoid redundancy and improve the efficiency of test automation, it's recommended not to duplicate common methods required by all tests within each automated test. Instead, they should be shared as part of the overall test solution. This helps streamline the testing process and makes managing and maintaining the overall test suite easier.

Maintainability

On average, 25% of an application is rewritten each year. If the tests associated with the modified portions cannot be changed with reasonable effort, they will be obsolete. Without maintainability, you cannot accumulate passing tests. Instead of gradually increasing code coverage, you will be discarding, ignoring, and deleting tests and will have to write them from scratch. Therefore, we will learn how to design automated tests to be easy to update and minimize the regression in our test suites.

Idempotency

Tests can be executed repeatedly and with the same results. So, they should be deterministic. They should always pass, and when it fails, ensure that there is a real bug in the code or environment. The mystery tests accumulate if you don't know what a test does or why you will be reticent to delete it, which leads to large amounts of tests that aren't used but require maintenance.

Defining the Primary Problems that Test Automation Solve

To list the various benefits of test automation frameworks, I must say that they naturally derive and extend the multiple benefits of test automation. Of course, before discussing their advantages we must define the problems they try to solve. Like most things in business and software development- there is a constant battle for resources- money and time. People often ignore these costs because they are not the ones paying the bills and receive their checks every month, no matter what. To define what is needed to deliver high-quality software, we must understand what the problems are in the first place.

Sub Problem 1 - Repetition and People Boredom, Less Reliable

It is okay if you must manually execute the same test case once per month. But if you must do it 3 times daily, we as humans tend to get bored quickly. Another natural thing that happens is that we begin to ignore the little details, which is exactly where thugs like to hide and lay eggs. Even the most conscientious tester will make mistakes during monotonous manual testing.

Automation Solution Hypothesis
ASH-1: Execute Same Tests Over and Over Again

When you have a way to execute all tests the same way repeatedly, you have more time to concentrate on writing new tests. Also, you can have more time to learn new tools, programming languages, and test techniques.

Subsequent Problems
SP-1: Automated Tests Are Not Stable

Many teams face this issue. Their tests are not correctly written, and because of that, they fail randomly. Or even worse- providing **false-positive** or **false-negative** results.

NOTE

False-positive - a test result in which a defect is reported, although no such defect exists in the test object. False-negative - a test result that fails to identify the presence of a defect that is present in the test object.

SP-2: Initial Investment Developing These Tests

The process of creating stable automated tests that verify the right things is an expensive undertaking. You need to invest in tools, frameworks, staff training, test data preparation, creation of test environments, test execution integration in CI/CD, and test result visualization.

Sub-Problem 2 - Engineers Are Not So Good with Numbers, Accuracy

If you have to test a user interface, it is a relatively doable job. Comparing labels and messages, clicking buttons, filling up forms, and eventually checking if something is populated in the DB. However, with time the systems got much more complicated. How do you compare huge XML/JSON messages or files without tools? It is hard to manually check if 100000 orders are upgraded successfully with all calculations. In many cases, automated scripts can do a much better job than us.

Automation Solution Hypothesis
ASH-2: Reuse Automatic Coded Checks

Once you write the logic for verifying that a single order is well migrated, you can create data-driven tests and execute the tests an unlimited number of times. The test result for run 15670 will be with the same precision and accuracy as the 1400 one.

Subsequent Problems
SP-3: Initial Investment Creating Shared Test Libraries

Sometimes, creating a solution that can be generalized for testing many scenarios and many test cases takes lots of effort. Sometimes you may not have the right people to create the library since significant coding and design skills may be required. Or even if you have these engineers, they may need to work on something else. It may be a significant time and money investment to code it right.

SP-4: Are Automated Tests Trustworthy? Test the Tests?

Even if you have the time to create these libraries. How do you make sure that they work correctly? It is code, so it may contain bugs. Do you spare time to develop tests for the tests or accept the risk of the checks not working correctly? Do you go to the next test once your assertion has passed? Did you check that it can fail?

SP-5: Library Modification

Creating the initial version of the library may be easy. But it is a different thing whether it is designed in a way to support future modifications. Changes in the requirements and applications are natural; our tests should evolve with them. Unfortunately, many IT professionals forgot that. In many cases, it is easier for them to rewrite the tests instead of making a little tuning because the code may not support that.

SP-6: Library Customization- Another Team's Context?

The whole point of creating a shared library is to be used by multiple teams across the company. However, the different teams work in different contexts. For example, they may have to test something a little bit different. So, the library code may not work out of the box for them. How easy will it be for them to extend or customize it? Is it even possible to do it? Will they need to invest time to create the same test feature again with the required modifications?

SP-7: Knowledge Transfer

Shared libraries are great, but do the engineers across all teams know whether they have a particular feature of your framework? For example, do they know you have already created automated checks?

If they don't know something exists, they will create it again. This is especially true for new team members. If you were a part of the team building the test features, you know most of them. However, when you have just joined the team someone must teach you if you don't have a way to find this information. Otherwise, you will face the problems we mentioned.

SP-8: Test API Usability

Is it easy for the users to understand how to use the library? Even if people know that something is there but don't know how to use or make it work, this will result in creating the same thing again.

If the API is not concise and is confusing, then you will need to invest time to teach the new team members one by one how to utilize it.

Sub-Problem 3 - Time for Feedback- Release

You don't want to release the new version untested when you need to release a security hotfix immediately. However, if you have 5000 test cases and your 10 QAs need 5 days to execute them by hand- this is slower, right?

Automation Solution Hypothesis
ASH-1: Execute the Same Tests Over and Over Again
ASH-3: Utilize the Speed of Automated Tests

Let's face it- computers are much faster than us. Even if you drink 5 coffees and click fast, you will be much slower than a well-written automated test. Even if you can match its speed, you will eventually get tired or miss some crucial details. Instead of waiting 1 week for all 5000 test cases to be executed by 5 QAs, you can run all your automated tests distributed on multiple machines for a couple of hours.

Subsequent Problems
SP-9: Test Speed

As mentioned, the automated tests are fast. However, this is not always the case. If the tests are not written properly, they can get quite slow. Some engineers use big pauses in their automation to handle various challenges in automating web or mobile apps. Another possible scenario where tests can get quite slow is when you put retry logic for various failing statements until the test succeeds. Or just retry all failing tests multiple times.

Sub-Problem 4 - Regression Issues Prevention

Regression Testing: "Testing of a previously tested program following modification to ensure that defects have not been introduced or uncovered in unchanged areas of the software as a result of the changes made."

Because of time pressure, "less important" tests are often not executed manually. This happens because of tight deadlines and when some of your people are unavailable- holidays, sickness, or your team is short-staffed.

Automation Solution Hypothesis
ASH-4: Execute All Tests before Deploying the App

You can execute all your tests before deploying. The app is deployed only if all tests pass. Since the automated tests are quite fast, you can deploy the tested version after 30-60 minutes.

Also, since the setup of tests is quite easy, the developers can execute some of the most important tests on their machines and fix the regression problems even before submitting the new code.

Subsequent Problems
SP-9: Test Speed
SP-10: CI and CD Readiness

Some older automation solutions are tough to execute from the command line interface- meaning it is hard to integrate them into your continuous integration or deployment tools.

Whatever tool or framework you use, it should allow being integrated relatively easily into CI systems. The same is valid for produced test results by the tool or framework. Usually, after CI execution, you want to publish them somewhere.

Sub-Problem 5 - Skipping Part of the Scope

After you test something, show your managers what you have tested. This can be hard if you don't have a test case management system. Some people cannot be trusted. They can lie that they executed something or just forgot to do it. This is not the case with automated solutions.

Automation Solution Hypothesis
ASH-4: Execute All Tests before Deploying App

Subsequent Problems
SP-9: Test Speed
SP-10: CI and CD Readiness

Sub-Problem 6 - Ping-pong

With a dedicated QA team, there was the so-called ping-pong game of throwing bugs. How does this happen?

1. The developer produces a new app version and deploys it without testing.

2. The QA starts testing when he gets free (this may not happen immediately). Testing begins 4 hours after the new version.

3. The QA logs a bug 2 hours later. After that, however, the developer may head home.

4. The developer fixes the bug early in the morning and deploys a new version without testing it. This takes 1 hour.

5. The QA starts testing 3 hours later and finds that the first bug got fixed, but another regression appeared.

6. The QA logs the regression bug 30 minutes later.

7. The developer is still there but started to work on a new feature, so they promise to fix the new bug tomorrow.

Automation Solution Hypothesis
ASH-4: Execute All Tests before Deploying App
ASH-5: Developers Execute Automated Tests Locally

So, for a single feature to be tested and released, you needed 2-3 days. If you have automated tests, the developer could execute them on their machine or at least the most important ones. Even if this is not possible, nowadays, the most critical tests are performed right after the code is deployed, even if we are talking about UI/System tests. If any regression bugs appear, you will catch them within 1 hour after the code's submission.

Subsequent Problems
SP-9: Test Speed
SP-10: CI and CD Readiness
SP-11: Easiness of Local Test Solution Setup

How easily can a new colleague set up everything needed to run the automated tests locally? Do you have instructions? How much time will they need? Unfortunately, in some cases, they need half a day to install and configure everything required. This is a bummer since we programmers tend to be lazy most of the time or have many other things to code. So, many people will prefer to skip the process and just not follow it because there are too many steps.

SP-12: Easiness of Local Test Execution

If you have lots of tests, the developer probably won't be able to execute them before their code check-in.

How easy is it to locate which tests they need to execute?

When the tests are executed, can I continue working, or should I go for a coffee? Some automation frameworks make it impossible to work during the test run. For example, browsers appear on top of all other programs; tests get the mouse focus, move your mouse, or do real typing with your keyboard.

Is it possible for the tests to be executed locally but in an isolated environment like Docker?

Can the tests be executed smoothly against the developer's local environment instead of against the shared test environment?

Sub-Problem 7 - Money, Time, and Effort for Maintaining Test Artifacts

What are the test artifacts? For example, these are all manual test cases you have. When a specific part of the application changes, you need to analyze and update your test cases. Otherwise, you have to rewrite them each time, even using a more sophisticated test case management system. This may be a task. This is why some more "agile" companies decide that the QAs won't use detailed test cases, leading to untested or not-well-tested areas of the app. This is especially true if you have to test part of the application developed and tested by people who are not part of the company anymore.

Automation Solution Hypothesis
ASH-6: Easier Tests Refactoring and Modification

Automated tests are testing artifacts too. But if you have a proper test automation framework and test structure, a single change can update multiple test cases simultaneously instead of editing each one by itself. In addition, most modern IDEs provide tons of refactoring support features.

In most cases, once a manual test case is automated, you don't need it anymore, so you can archive it.

Subsequent Problems
SP-5: Library Modifications

Sub-Problem 8 - Various App Configurations

To test a modern website, you must ensure it works on Edge, Firefox, Chrome, Opera, Internet Explorer, and Safari. In addition, if your software is related to banking or a similar service- you need to check if the app works the same way on the latest 5-10 versions of these browsers. But wait, you must check the website's responsiveness on various screen sizes and mobile resolutions. Making all these tests manually is doable, but they require lots of effort and sometimes money to buy and configure all these devices. Moreover, layout testing is hard for humans. Verifying "pixel-perfect" designs without tools or code is a considerable challenge.

Automation Solution Hypothesis
AHS-7: Reuse Tests for Different Platform Setups

You can easily reuse the same tests for different browsers or mobile devices with various resolutions through code. Also, the code can enable you to perform pixel perfect layout testing if needed.

Subsequent Problems
SP-13: Cross-technology and Cross-platform Readiness

Is it possible to execute the tests with no code modifications on various browsers? Are the tests behaving the same way in different browsers? For example, if you use a pure WebDriver code, it will be almost impossible. How much code do you have to write to change the size of the browser or change the mobile device on which the tests will be executed? In most cases, it is better to skip the large configuration boilerplate code.

SP-14: Cloud Readiness

Some companies have their own farms of devices and computers with various browser configurations. However, nowadays the cloud providers such as LambdaTest, SauceLabs, BrowserStack or CrossBrowserTesting are a reasonable solution to the problem. Can your tests be executed there? How much code is needed to switch from cloud to local tests execution?

SP-15: Docker Support

Another alternative of the cloud providers is to run your tests in Docker containers. However, the setup can be hard. Can your automation solution be integrated easily with Docker (Selenoid, Selenium Docker)? Does it provide pre-created configured images with all browser versions or mobile emulators?

SP-16: Complex Code Configuration

It is one thing your tool or framework to support various browsers, devices, cloud or Docker integrations. But it is entirely another how much code you need to write to make it happen. It is not only about the initial creation but also if the requirements change, how easy is it to reconfigure the tests to use another configuration?

Sub-Problem 9 - Low QA Team Morale

When you manually execute the same tests over and over again, testers get bored as mentioned. Most of us want to have fun and do something new occasionally. So, we usually get demotivated doing the same things and not improving ourselves. This is one of the primary reasons why people want to change their teams or quit their jobs.

Automation Solution Hypothesis
ASH-8: Test Automation Novelty

Thinking how to automate a particular app's functionality, prepare the test data or integrate your tests in CI is an exciting and challenging job. Most testers feel challenged working on test automation and have to continuously learn new things, which motivates them even more.

Subsequent Problems
SP-1: Automated Tests Are Not Stable
SP-4: Are Automated Tests Trustworthy? Test the Tests?
SP-17: Test Speed Creation

Time spent on maintaining the existing tests is essential. It can take significant time from the capacity of the QA team. However, for people to be motivated, it should be relatively easy to create new tests. For sure, QA engineers will be frustrated if for the whole sprint they can produce only a few tests. It shouldn't be rocket science to create a simple test. Or even if the scenario is more complicated, it should be easy to understand what needs to be done to automate it.

SP-18: Troubleshooting, Debuggability, Fixing Failing Tests Easiness

As we mentioned, a big part of maintainability is troubleshooting existing tests. Most in-house solutions or open-source ones don't provide lots of features to make your life easier. This can be one of the most time-consuming tasks. Having 100 failing tests and finding out whether there is a problem with the test or a bug in the application. If you use plugins or complicated design patterns, the debugging of the tests will be much harder, requiring lots of resources and expertise. Even if you spot the problem, how easy is it to fix it? Do you fix the code only in one place to fix multiple tests? In case the library didn't reuse most of the logic but for example copy-paste it, then the fixing will take much more time. If you use a 3rd party framework (open-source or commercial one), is its support fast and helpful?

Sub-Problem 10 - Questioned Professionalism

Every QA wants to be a professional and be recognized for the job done well. However, as mentioned if you have tight deadlines, management pressure to test and release the app as soon as possible, you cut out of the scope of your testing by executing only the most important test cases. Anyhow, most of the time when a new bug is found on Production, QAs feel responsible that they didn't catch it. In some cases, developers are not aware that this is not our fault and we had to cut out of the scope. So, they start to question how good we are. Even in some edge cases people get fired or don't get bonuses.

Automation Solution Hypothesis
ASH-4: Execute All Tests before Deploying App
ASH-5: Developers Execute Automated Tests Locally
ASH-8: Test Automation Novelty
ASH-9: More Time Writing New Tests- Exploratory Testing

With time you will have more and more automated tests, checking for regression bugs. This will reduce the time for performing the same tests over and over again. Also, the locating-fixing bug cycle will be drastically shortened, since the developers will be able to execute the tests locally or all tests will run before deploying the app. The QA team will be more motivated since it will execute more exciting tasks- thinking how to automate more complicated and challenging scenarios. Moreover, we will be able to spend more time experimenting- using manual testing techniques such as exploratory testing to locate new bugs.

Subsequent Problems

SP-1: Automated Tests Are Not Stable
SP-4: Are Automated Tests Trustworthy? Test the Tests?
SP-17: Test Speed Creation
SP-19: Upgradability

Fixing unstable tests is not the only time-consuming task of having an in-house automation framework. Every two weeks new browser versions are released. With each of them, a new version of the low-level automation libraries is released- WebDriver, Appium, WinAppDriver. However, since these libraries and tools are open-source, nobody can guarantee that they will be bug-free or backward compatible with everything you have. From my own experience, this task takes at least 3-4 hours per week if no significant problems appear. If a problem occurs, it can take much more time. This is especially true if you need to support all browsers and a couple of their versions (not only the last one). The same is even more valid for mobile automation low-level libraries since there is an unlimited number of devices and configurations.

Because of these problems, many teams upgrade less often to spare some time. However, not testing on the latest versions of the browsers hide many risks of not locating regression bugs.

Sub-Problem 11 - Provide Evidence What You Did

When you manually test something, it is hard to prove what you did. Sometimes it may go by unnoticed by developers and other colleagues because it is something "invisible". Of course, in more mature test processes you have detailed manual test cases, test reports, etc. but in general- why not be honest? When you write code, it is much more noticeable and measurable what you did. Because of this issue, I have heard many IT professionals complaining that they cannot get a promotion or a bonus. For me, this is one of the reasons why QAs should want better reporting tools- to show developers and management what they did. (Software won't improve because you have a fancy dashboard showing how many test cases you have executed.)

Automation Solution Hypothesis
ASH-10: More Visible Results

Since most of the test cases will be translated into coded tests- it will be more visible what the tests are. The code is something that can be measured and seen. The test results can be displayed in beautiful dashboards or sent via emails if needed.

Subsequent Problems
SP-20: Test Code Readability

Sometimes, your developer fellows or managers may want to check what you did. If you name your tests and methods correctly, using page objects and other design patterns, it will be much easier for other engineers to understand what your tests do. If this is true, it will be questionable whether you need more detailed reports.

SP-21: Test Results, Reports, Logs, Portal Integrations

If you use an in-house framework, does it produce well-looking test result files? Are these files compatible with the most popular extensions for CI tools? How much effort is required to visualize them with these tools? Is it even possible? There are at least 2 popular open-source solutions for visualizing test results (ReportPortal, Allure), is it possible to integrate your test results with these tools?

Sub-Problem 12 - Holidays and Sickness, 24 Hours

If you have 1 QA per app area and they go on holiday or gets sick. How do you release your application? Do developers start testing or what? Most people can work up to 8 hours. Of course, there are situations where your managers tell you that you need to come on Saturday to test the new version because you need to release it on Monday. But you won't often hear-"Let's stay up 2 nights in a row to finish everything". Engineers need to sleep and rest. (automated tests don't care whether it is 3 in the morning, Sunday or New Year's Eve)

There is another aspect of this problem. When someone decides to leave your team or the company, all of their knowledge is lost. Regularly automating new functionalities leaves valuable knowledge within the team.

Automation Solution Hypothesis
ASH-1: Execute Same Tests Over and Over Again
ASH-4: Execute All Tests before Deploying App
ASH-5: Developers Execute Automated Tests Locally
ASH-11: Tests as Documentation

If the automated tests are readable enough and the test scenario is visible through reading the code, even if you are missing, your colleagues will know what the test does. If they can quickly orient themselves what is automated and what is not, they will know what they need to check manually till your return.

Subsequent Problems
SP-7: Knowledge Transfer
SP-8: Test API Usability
SP-20: Test Code Readability

SP-21: Test Results, Report, Logs

Sub-Problem 13 - Some Things Cannot be Tested Manually

How do you perform a load or performance test manually? I can say the same about testing "pixel perfect" designs. Probably you can use some non-automated way using tools, but it is hard.

Automation Solution Hypothesis
ASH-12: Reuse Automated Tests for Complex Test Scenarios

You can reuse and reconfigure some of your existing automated tests to perform performance and load tests. Also, you can use different APIs from the framework to test pixel- perfect layout testing.

Subsequent Problems
SP-5: Library Modifications
SP-17: Test Speed Creation
SP-18: Troubleshooting, Debuggability, Easiness Fixing Failing Tests
SP-22: Learning Curve

Is it easy to figure out how to create these complex performance or load tests? Do you need to read huge documentations (if they even exist) or can you figure out everything from the demo example or the public API comments while typing in the IDE? How much time does a new team member need to learn to write and maintain these tests?

Do you need to spend countless hours passing your knowledge to them, or the authors of the framework give you better alternatives?

Sub-Problem 14 - Consistency

If there is no documentation on how to write automated tests, different people might write them differently. For example, one may use page object models. Another may use vanilla WebDriver directly, and so on. The same is valid for naming methods, elements, and tests. These inconsistencies lead to hard-to-understand/read/maintain test code.

Automation Solution Hypothesis
ASH-13: Unified Coding Standards

A significant part of the test automation frameworks is that they give everyone involved unified ways of writing tests. Unified team standards make the tests look identical and much easier to write. In addition, the shared libraries part of the framework provides an API that makes it clear to the user which scenario will be executed if the particular method is called.

Subsequent Problems
SP-7: Knowledge Transfer
SP-8: Test API Usability
SP-20: Test Code Readability
SP-22: Learning Curve
SP-23: Unified Coding Standards

Coding standards are good. However, you need an automated way to enforce them. Does the framework you use give you a default set of coding standards? Does it give you an automated way to apply and follow them? Is it easy for people to see what they did wrong? Is it easy to customise the default set of rules? (Some popular solutions for Java are EditorConfig and CheckStyle-IDEA)

Sub-Problem 15 - Faster Scale-up and Scale-down

Let's say that you many things to test for the new release. You have 2 QAs in the team, but the manager must bring in one more to finish on time. These transitions don't happen for a day. With longer release cycles, this is doable and may be the right decision, but when you release each week and need more workforce, this approach cannot scale. Imagine that you scale up for the next release after two months, and now you have 4 QAs, but after that, the summer comes. The releases will stop for a while (in an imaginary scenario where all developers go on vacation). Two QAs will be enough to test all new features. What happens with the 2 additional QAs you brought to the project? Do you move them again? It is not only a problem with how you scale up but also how you scale down.

Automation Solution Hypothesis
ASH-14: Cloud Test Agents and Docker

Living in the era of public clouds, you can have additional test agent machines for a few minutes. The same is valid if you use Docker to execute your automated tests. If you use the appropriate runner, the tests can be distributed across remote machines and executed in parallel.

Subsequent Problems
SP-14: Cloud Readiness
SP-15: Docker Support
SP-24: Parallel and Distributed Test Execution

Does your framework support your automated tests to be executed in parallel? For example, is there a runner for your tests to run them in parallel or distribute them across multiple machines?

Assessment System for Evaluating Test Automation Solutions

What is the primary task of many software engineers in test nowadays? It is to develop or find the right test automation solution for achieving fast, reliable, easy to understand and maintain tests that can be integrated into CI/CD pipelines. I will share some approaches they regularly use with clients during consulting to achieve these goals and discuss common mistakes. One of the many errors is that the engineers are not doing proper research and setting the right requirements upfront, which leads to losing time developing their solutions and maintaining lots of problematic tests later. In this last section of the chapter, you will learn some fundamental assessment criteria for automation testing designs, why they are essential and how to apply them in practice. We will discuss acquiring the proper requirements for the searched solution and how to conduct the research the right way. Afterwards, the presented assessment framework can help you to find the right test automation solution.

Many companies, at some point, decide to start automating their QA activities if they have some. Or for some new projects, want to establish test automation from the start. So, they must pick the right tool/solution for doing that. This article will be about approaching the problem, selecting the tools to evaluate, comparing them, and deciding which is best.

What Is the Usual Approach?

From my professional experience as a consultant, many companies make poor decisions at this particular step, one of the most important ones. Many of them have only manual QAs. The usual approach is to assign this process to the most senior, who may have only basic programming experience or almost zero experience with test automation. Or another usual practice is the transfer one junior/regular developer to help with the effort.

The problem is that none of these roles has the expertise to decide the best solution, nor do they have the experience to predict and estimate the cost of creating your solution or customizing an existing one. Usually, there is a massive conflict of interests because these roles prefer to create their own thing, not considering the actual cost because they want to learn and improve during this time. Usually, it is hard for managers to see this conflict because they don't have experience with such solutions and testing.

Assessment Framework

Phase 1: Gather Requirements

First, you must create a list of requirements you want to achieve. For example, automate the login, create accounts, submit tickets, run tests nightly, etc. You can do that by team brainstorming, asking senior division members, hiring a consultant, or conducting stakeholder interviews. Remember that stakeholders such as business owners often don't have the technical expertise or understanding of the testing process.

Phase 2: Research Existing Solutions

Pick the so-called HARD requirements and ignore, for now, the nice-to-have stuff. Then, based on your HARD requirements, the solution should have - after filtering the frameworks/tools and picking a few - 3 to 5 most serious candidates. We will further use these solutions for creating a PoC (proof-of-concept) and assessment.

"HARD" Requirements Examples:

- Automate Web
- Open source
- No License Costs
- Community Support
- Basic Documentation/Tutorials
- Frequent Updates.

Phase 3: Define Assessment Criteria

The next phase is to define the criteria you will use to compare the solutions. Since all of them are more or less subjective, we provide a rating from 1 to 5 for each of them. In a minute, I will show you an example. But let's first discuss them. By the way, this is just an example. You can put whatever you believe is important for you. For me, it is usually the solution is programmatic - not to use UI tools.

Here there are the following:

- Automate Web
- Automate Mobile
- Automate React
- Good Documentation
- Parallel Execution
- Easy Tests Creation
- Tests Stability

- Tests Readability
- Failures Troubleshooting
- Source Control Support
- Easy CI Execution
- Reporting Tools Support
- Paid Support/Consulting
- Customization Time Required
- Framework Extend Support
- Fast Learning

And a few bonus ones:

- Code Conventions
- Test Environment Configurations
- Responsive Testing
- Secrets Management
- Specific Tools Integrations
- Use SUT Technology Stack (Microsoft Technologies/JAVA)
- Use a Non-programming Solution

Phase 4: Implement Proof of Concept

Form a working group of technical experts. Implement 2-3 tests for each solution. It is better if all participants do it.

Phase 5: Rate Each Assess Criteria

Each team member will create a table for each solution. For each solution, we will have a separate column. For all criteria, we will have rows. So, once you have the PoC for all the solutions, each participant will put a rating for each measure for each solution. Then, at the bottom, we calculate an average for all criteria, the final score for the solution. You can further extend the rating phase by prioritizing the different criteria and providing a "WEIGHT" index for them. For example, put a rating between 1 and 5. 5 is the highest score. If there is a WEIGHT index, you must multiple by it. For example, 1.5 for good documentation.

Criterion	Solution 1	Solution 2	Solution 3	Solution N
Good Documentation (1.5w)	4 (6)	3 (4.5)	3 (4.5)	...
Easy Tests Creation (1.2w)	4 (4.8)	5 (6)	3 (3.6)	...
Troubleshooting	3	5	5	...
Parallel Execution	5	2	2	...
Tests Readability	5	5	5	...
....	...	...	...	...
AVG	4.76	4.5	4.02	...

Phase 6: Working Group Total Rating

Phase 6: Working Group Total Rating After we have the ratings of all participants, we create a final rating table. Each working group person should provide ratings based on the PoC. Then, you can also put the WEIGHT index again based on the participants' seniority/authority/role. In the example, Participant 1 is the QA Lead in the first row, so we multiply all scores by 4.

Criterion	Solution 1	Solution 2	Solution 3	Solution N
Participant 1 (4w)	5 (20)	3 (12)	2 (8)	...
Participant 2 (2w)	3 (6)	4 (8)	3 (6)	...
Participant 3	3	5	5	...
Participant 4 (0.5w)	4 (2)	5 (2.5)	5 (2.5)	...
Participant 5 (0.5w)	4 (2)	5 (2.5)	5 (2.5)	...
....	...	...	...	...
AVG	6.6	6	4.8	...

Phase 7: High-level Test Automation Strategy

1. Create Abstract Test Cases Suite
2. Set Priorities and Categories
3. Put Test Cases in 3 Phases
4. Create a Test Automation Requirements
5. Provide Estimates for Phase 1 Test Cases
6. Provide Estimates for Requirements

What will you need as a test environment, and test data preparation for working on phase 1 tests?

- Mock server and web page fixture generator
- Test Data Web Service with 3 endpoints - creating test users, test purchases, validating completed orders
- Custom framework components for working with test data tables?
- Custom logic for validating PDF information
- Logic for generating session cookies by username
- Bypass captchas on the test environment

Phase 8: Final Decision

You need to answer a few essential questions if you should use an existing solution.

Are you going to use the existing solution?
How much time will you need to implement it?
How much will it cost to maintain and support it?
Do you have an easy way to learn it? Are there any pieces of training?

Or these if you want more to develop your solution.

How much will it cost?
Do you have the expertise to do it?
How much will it cost to support it over time?

Summary

In the chapter, we learned the test automation core concepts. Then, we discussed people's automated testing misunderstandings, high-quality automated tests' attributes, and the benefits that test automation can bring to help establish a solid test infrastructure. We also investigated its costs and a system for picking the right solution.

In the next chapter, before learning how to automate web apps in-depth, we will investigate how the websites work. First, we will discuss the HTTP protocol, and what happens when you type the website URL into the browser tab. It is essential to understand how the web works; otherwise, you won't be capable to design the proper manual and automated tests.

Chapter 6. Web Fundamentals

In the following chapter, we will learn how the web works. To write high-quality web automated tests, it is essential to understand how the websites work. We will investigate what happens when you load a website. We will answer questions such as *"What are TCP/IP, HTML, CSS, and JavaScript?"*. You will find information about HTTP requests, their structure, types, headers, etc.

To tackle unexpected deviations, good knowledge of the surrounding context is required. Thus, knowing and understanding how the WWW operates, in general, might be the context a QA engineer or software developer needs. Therefore, we will explore some fundamental concepts and technologies that every QA professional needs to master if they truly desire to understand "what is going on under the hood."

Topics covered in this chapter:

- What Happens When You Load a Website?
- What Is HTTP?
- What Is TCP?
- Extensibility - Header Metadata
- Action, Verb, or Method
- The Sweetness of the Cookie
- Where is HTTP Headed?

What Happens When You Load a Website?

On the one hand, we have the client - the browser. On the other hand, the server is responsible for returning the website's content. They communicate through TCP/IP.

What happens, exactly?

1. The browser connects to the DNS server and finds the actual IP address of the website URL you typed.
2. The browser sends an HTTP request message to the server, asking it to send a website copy. The data sent between the client and the server is sent across the internet using TCP/IP.
3. If the server approves the client's request, it sends the client a "200 OK" message and then starts sending the website's files to the browser as a series of small chunks called data packets.
4. The browser parses the response and checks the data and metadata enclosed. Based on that, it decides what to do.
5. The browser assembles the small chunks from various parallel requests into a complete web page and displays it to you.

Definition: DNS

DNS stands for domain name server. Domain Name Servers are like an address book for websites or a C# dictionary. When you type a website URL in your browser, the browser retrieves the server's IP address by asking the DNS server. This way, the client and server can communicate with each other.

In the case of websites, the response would contain a specific piece of metadata that tells the browser that the response data is of type text/html. This allows the browser to parse the data attached to the response as HTML code. However, HTML does not include any instructions regarding what the site should look like and only defines the structure instructing the browser, which content is a heading, which is an image, which is a paragraph, etc. To describe a web page's appearance/presentation, we use CSS. To define the functionality/behavior, we use JavaScript.

Definition: HTML

"HTML (Hypertext Markup Language) is the most fundamental building block of the web. It defines the meaning and structure of web content.", - Mozilla MDN Web Docs

Definition: Assets

A collective name for all the other stuff that makes up a website, such as images, music, video, Word documents, and PDFs.

Definition: CSS Cascading Style Sheets

"Cascading Style Sheets (CSS) is a stylesheet language used to describe the presentation of a document written in HTML or XML. CSS describes how elements should be rendered on screen, paper, speech, or other media. CSS is among the core languages of the open web and is standardized across Web browsers according to W3C specifications.", - Mozilla MDN Web Docs

Definition: JavaScript

An object-oriented computer programming language. It is commonly used to create interactive effects within web browsers.

NOTE

Do not confuse JavaScript with the Java programming language. The two programming languages have very different syntax, semantics, and uses.

Now let's dive deep into defining HTTP.

What Is HTTP?

What is HTTP, how does it work, and where did it all start? According to the official HTTP documentation, supported by the W3C (World Wide Web Consortium), the Hypertext Transfer Protocol is a stateless and extensible application-level request/response protocol that operates by exchanging messages across a reliable transport- or session-layer "connection". So now, what does all that mean?

In the early days of the WWW, when the web was envisioned and implemented by Tim Berners-Lee and his team at CERN, HTTP was one of the fundamental pillars that would transform our lives forever. The initial draft of the protocol had no version; it was later identified as HTTP/0.9 to differentiate it from the upcoming versions. Sometimes referred to as a one-line protocol, HTTP/0.9 is simple enough to transport text documents (HTML). Any text document could have been returned to the requesting party with only one GET method.

The next phase of this fascinating evolution was HTTP/1.0., when extensibility was conceived. The notion of headers was introduced for the requests and responses. By providing metadata about the transmitted content, HTTP becomes flexible and extensible.

Implementation of the protocol's features resulted from a try-and-see approach over the first half of the 90s. As a result, there is no actual standard for its implementation, even though a real definition with the described common practices of the 1.0 version emerges from the stormy early WWW years up until HTTP/1.1.

The most notable improvements in 1997's HTTP/1.1 version are:

- A connection can be reused, saving time to reopen it numerous times to display the resources embedded into the single original document retrieved.
- Pipelining has been added, allowing it to send a second request before the answer for the first one is fully transmitted, lowering the communication latency.
- Chunked responses are now also supported.
- Additional cache control mechanisms have been introduced.
- Content negotiation, including language, encoding, or type, has been introduced and allows a client and a server to agree on acceptable content to exchange.
- Thanks to the Host header, the ability to host different domains at the same IP address now allows server colocation.

Although Google would later remove the support for SPDY, this research project for creating a new application-layer protocol will pave the way for HTTP/2. SPDY's initial focus was to reduce latency. The basic changes made to HTTP/1.1 to create SPDY included: "true request pipelining without FIFO (First in First Out) restrictions, message framing mechanism to simplify client and server development, mandatory compression (including headers), priority scheduling, and even bi-directional communication." In the end, here is a summary of this version's main differences from its predecessor. The HTTP/2 protocol has several prime differences from the HTTP/1.1 version:

- It is a binary protocol rather than text. Therefore, it can no longer be read and created manually. Despite this difficulty, improved optimization techniques can now be implemented.
- It is a multiplexed protocol. Therefore, parallel requests can be handled over the same connection, removing the order, and blocking constraints of the HTTP/1.x protocol.
- It compresses headers. These are often similar among requests, which removes duplication and overhead of data transmitted.
- It allows a server to populate data in a client cache in advance of it being required through a server push mechanism.

ISO, OSI - Fun Game of Acronyms

Let us start with the stateless part from the former definition.
The most straightforward explanation is that the recipient can understand each request message in isolation from other messages. This simplifies the server design because there is no need to allocate storage to deal with conversations in progress dynamically.
As part of the Open Systems Interconnection model (OSI Model), HTTP is an application-layer protocol type. In a broader sense, the application layer is responsible for processing an application's end-users. The following graph shows that the HTTP protocol is part of the 7th, last layer. The OSI model could be defined as a concept-based model that defines and sets standards in computing or telecommunication systems. If you read aloud the previous sentence again, it might just remind you of the ISO standards used in all kinds of industries. You cannot be closer to the truth. The body responsible for OSI coming to life is the International Organization for Standardization (ISO).

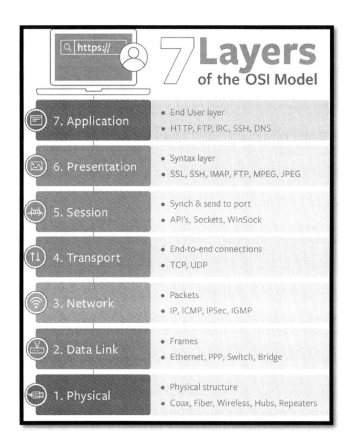

Next on the line is HTTP's operational concept.

What Is TCP?

Transmission Control Protocol (TCP) provides communication between an application program and the Internet Protocol (frequently written as TCP/IP.) An application does not need to require packet fragmentation on the transmission medium or other mechanisms for sending data via TCP. While IP handles the actual delivery of the data, TCP keeps track of 'segments' - the individual units of data transmission that a message is divided into for efficient routing through the network.

Due to unpredictable network behavior, IP packets can be lost or delivered out of order; TCP detects and minimizes these issues by reordering packet data or requesting redelivery. However, this accuracy comes with a trade-off in speed. TCP is known more for reliability than UDP, for instance, but this accuracy comes from trading speed, sometimes coming with a delay of several seconds.

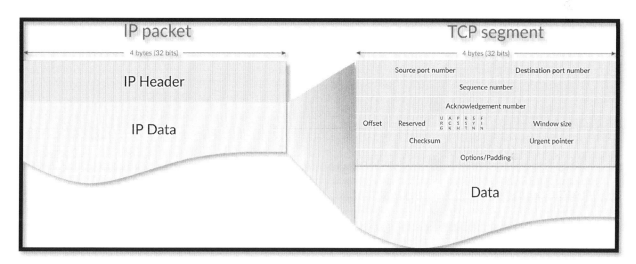

The figure above graphically depicts where the IP packet stands to TCP.

The data portion of each IP packet is formatted as a TCP segment. Each segment is divided into a header and data. The header part itself consists of many fields. These are all the blue-colored sectors of the header. Without getting too much into it, we should check out the three characters' long acronyms, **Checksum**, **Acknowledgment**, and **Sequence** numbers.

Step 1: Establish a connection

When two computers want to send data to each other over TCP, they first need to establish a connection using a three-way handshake (TWH). In terms of simplicity, imagine that those two computers meet on the street of a small town.

Machine A: *"Hey there, can you tell a joke?"*

Machine B: *"If you are asking me if I am able to tell jokes, I am proud to confirm that I can and I will."*

Machine A: *"Great, I am ready to hear it."*

Step 2: Send packets of data

When a packet of data is sent over TCP, the recipient must always acknowledge what they received. **Sequence** and **Acknowledgment** number fields are responsible for keeping track of whether data was successfully received, lost, or accidentally sent twice.

Step 3: Close the connection

Either computer can close the connection when they no longer want to send or receive data. To initiate closing a connection, the requesting machine should set the FIN bit to 1. After that, the process is the same as the three-hand shake in step 1.

When dealing with this type of data transportation, losing packages and the wrong order of receiving them are the most common issues. UDP, an alternative to the TCP protocol, can identify when data is corrupted. However, it can't handle those issues. In this regard, UDP's faster speed of data transaction is less preferable to TCP, which can take package loss or unintentional package reordering at a speed cost.

Extensibility - Header Metadata

Headers are metadata used in both requests and responses. There are multiple headers part of the HTTP standard. First introduced in HTTP/1.0, they make the protocol easy to extend. New functionality can even be introduced with a simple agreement between the client and server about the new header's semantics. Simply put, for application-specific logic, HTTP headers can be added. However, this also means that both the server and client need to know about those newly added headers. Otherwise, a server will not recognize the header when receiving a request or vice versa in terms of a client receiving the response. Headers are to be separated into four groups:

- **General header**: Headers applying to both requests and responses but with no relation to the data eventually transmitted in the body.
- **Request header**: Headers containing more information about the resource to be fetched or about the client itself.
- **Response header**: Headers with additional information about the response, like its location or about the server itself (name and version, etc.).
- **Entity header**: Headers containing more information about the entity's body, like its content length or its MIME-type.

Also, if you check the official registry of all HTTP headers, you will notice some of them starting with the "X-" prefix. This is a deprecated convention for custom headers implemented outside the existing protocol specifications. However, this convention is no longer applicable.

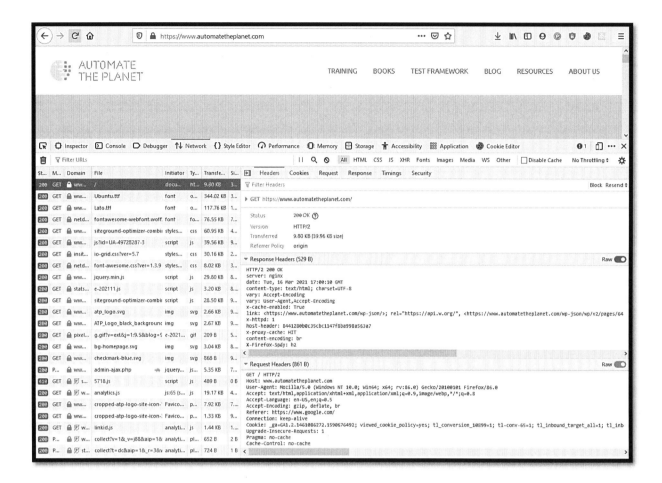

The figure above shows how headers fit in a request/response pair.

Action, Verb, or Method

The HTTP protocol defines 8 methods, sometimes referred to as verbs, although nowhere in the protocol's specification verb is used to notify the server what action should be performed on the identified resource. The first version of HTTP defined only one method - GET. Following the next version. HTTP/1.0 added new methods - HEAD and POST. The third method list expansion happened in the third version - 1.1. where OPTIONS, PUT, DELETE, TRACE, and CONNECT were implemented. If you haven't noticed yet, they are case-sensitive and always uppercased. The most staggering question that one might ask themselves is the possibility of adding new methods. The answer is an absolute yes. An example of that is Web-based Distributed Authoring and Versioning (WebDAV). It is a set of extensions to the HTTP protocol. The idea behind it is to edit and manage files on remote web servers collaboratively.

The following list compromises every standard HTTP method's name and a short description of its use case:

- **GET** - the GET method is used to retrieve information from the given server using a given URI. Requests using GET should only retrieve data and should have no other effect on the data.
- **HEAD** - same as GET, but only transfers the status line and header section.
- **POST** - a POST request is used to send data to the server, for example, customer information, file upload, etc. using HTML forms.
- **PUT** - replaces all current representations of the target resource with the uploaded content
- **CONNECT** - establishes a tunnel to the server identified by a given URI.
- **DELETE** - removes all current representations of the target resource given by a URI.
- **OPTIONS** - describes the communication options for the target resource.
- **TRACE** - performs a message loop-back test along the path to the target resource

Some of these methods are also known as safer than others. The basic principle of what determines the HTTP method as safe is its results. If the method does not alter the server's state, i.e., performs a read-only operation, then this method is safe. GET, HEAD, and OPTIONS are safe. On the other hand, PUT or POST is not safe since they create or alter existing resources.

The Sweetness of the Cookie

Before entering the realm of cookies, let us review two concepts. If you recall the protocol's definition, you might remember its stateless property. That means the client always needs to open a new connection for a new request. **What is a session?**

1. The client establishes a TCP connection (or other types of transport layer).
2. The client sends its request and waits for the answer.
3. The server processes the request, sends back its answer, provides a status code and appropriate data.

Although, as of HTTP/1.1, the connection is no longer closed after completing the third phase, which means the second and third phases can be performed any number of times, data is still not shared across requests during this session.

On the other hand, sometimes, we need to keep data from a request across more than one request. This is where Cookies come into play. A cookie is a name/value pair sent to the client browser from the server-side application.

Back to Fig.4, where the request's metadata is, there is a Cookie field. Again, notice that semicolons separate many key/value pairs. The most fundamental use cases of cookies are:

Session management
Manages if the user is logged in or in an e-commerce world, where keeping data for items in a shopping cart could be a hideous implementation if it were not cookies coming to the rescue. Those use-cases are part of session management.

Personalization
User preferences, themes, and any other settings for a particular website.

Tracking
Recording and analyzing user behavior - almost all digital advertising relies on those cookies. After receiving an HTTP request, a server can send one or more Set-Cookie headers with the response. The browser usually stores the cookie, and then the cookie is sent with requests made to the same server inside a Cookie HTTP header. An expiration date or duration can be specified, after which the cookie is no longer sent. Additional restrictions to a specific domain and path can be set, limiting where the cookie is sent.

Where is HTTP Headed?

HTTP/3.0 is the next iteration in this protocol's evolution. There are significant advancements and changes to the underlying method of utilization. First of all, HTTP/2 itself is not the issue that potentially will be fixed - instead, it is implemented by vendors. Because this protocol is often "baked in" to routers, firewalls, and another network, any deviation from HTTP/2 is often seen as invalid, or worse, an attack. These devices are configured only to accept TCP or UDP between contacted servers and their users within a rigorous, narrow definition of what expected traffic should look like - any deviation, such as when a protocol has been updated or new functionality has been introduced, is almost instantly rejected.

This issue is known as protocol ossification and is a considerable problem in resolving the underlying issues of HTTP/2. In terms of clarity, ossification happens when new Protocol features or changes in behavior are introduced, eventually being considered bad or illegal by systems or devices. New TCP options are either severely limited or outright blocked, so fixing HTTP/2 becomes less an issue of "what do to fix" and more an issue of "how to implement the fix."

The second most crucial fundamental problem addressed by the Internet Engineering Task Force (IETF), the body responsible for HTTP development and standardization, is TCP's relatively significant latency. Compared to UDP, TCP data safety features prevent transporting data packages fast enough. This is the most relevant difference from UDP. In a sense, HTTP as a protocol is synchronous. You send a request. You wait for a response. But, of course, HTTP provides parallelism by ensuring that any number of requests can be sent independently over separate connections. In this hostile world for protocol innovation, a superhero, a rescuer, is planned to play a big part in getting things right. Say hello to QUIC. This is not an acronym - it is pronounced as a plain old English word - "quick".

UDP is a transport layer network protocol initially designed at Google, implemented, and deployed in 2012. The initial QUIC handshake combines the typical three-way handshake you get with TCP with the TLS 1.3 handshake, which provides authentication of the endpoints and negotiation of cryptographic parameters. For those familiar with the TLS protocol, QUIC replaces the TLS record layer with its framing format while keeping the same TLS handshake messages.

Not only does this ensure that the connection is always authenticated and encrypted, but it also makes the initial connection establishment faster as a result: the typical QUIC handshake only takes a single round-trip between client and server to complete, compared to the two roundtrips required for the TCP and TLS 1.3 handshakes combined.

In the case of transporting data over TCP, a loss of a segment results in blocking all subsequent segments until a retransmission arrives with no respect to the application streams encapsulated in the following segments. Beyond its faster handshake process, QUIC ensures that lost packets carrying data for an individual stream only impact that specific stream. Data received on other streams can continue to be reassembled and delivered to the application.

Summary

To summarize, HTTP is one of the pillars that keep WWW up and running. Several improvements jump kept this protocol relevant to the ever-changing tech landscape. From HTTP/0.9 to HTTP/3.0, it has witnessed the introduction of various new properties, functionalities, and extensibility utilization. We covered the fundamental mechanisms and some of the most important attributes such as Headers, HTTP Methods, and TCP's principal role. In the end, the new QUIC protocol was introduced, which is poised to define HTTP/3.0 in the near future.

In the upcoming chapter, we delve into the essence of source control systems, a vital tool for any software engineer. We will explore its role in effective team collaboration and development, focusing on the widely used GIT. You'll gain insights into larger platforms it integrates with, like GitHub, AzureDevOps, and Bitbucket, along with crucial operations such as code reviews, pull requests, and merges.

Chapter 7. Source Control Fundamentals

This chapter imparts vital information that all software engineers ought to understand. For effective teamwork in our engineering group, a method for exchanging and integrating our code is crucial. Source control systems facilitate this process. Therefore, in this section, we'll delve into the nature of source control, its indispensable role in software development, and its added advantages. We'll also examine one of the most popular tools in this field - GIT. This tool is integrated into larger platforms, like GitHub, AzureDevOps, and Bitbucket, which we'll briefly explore. In addition, key operations, such as code reviews, pull requests, merging code, and branches, are on our radar for thorough understanding. We'll wrap up this section with a discussion on best practices related to creating automated test code and leveraging these systems.

These topics will be covered in this chapter:

- What is Source Control?
- What Is GIT?
- GIT Key Concepts
- GIT CLI Commands
- GIT Tools
- Automated Tests Development Source Control Best Practices

What is Source Control?

Source control, or version control, is a system that meticulously records our modifications. This tool provides a framework for collaboration, enabling us to work on the same codebase simultaneously. If needed, we can examine the modification history to see who made specific changes and when those changes were made. One of its significant features is that it allows us to undo any modifications, taking us back to a previous version if necessary.

In addition to these key features, source control provides a project safety net. In case of system failure or data loss, we can recover our work from the repository, reducing the risk of losing significant progress. It also simplifies handling multiple versions of a product, whether they're different builds for testing, production, or unique client needs. Furthermore, source control systems often integrate with other software tools, offering a seamless workflow. For instance, they can link with issue tracking systems to keep a log of why specific changes were made, improving traceability. Facilitating concurrent work also minimizes the risk of overwriting code and helps resolve conflicts when different team members edit the same parts of the code.

In essence, source control is not merely a tool but a critical component of modern software development methodology, enhancing teamwork, traceability, and risk management.

Types of Version Control Systems

Version control systems are fundamental tools in software development, assisting teams in managing and tracking changes to their code. They fall into two main categories: Centralized Version Control Systems (CVCS) and Distributed Version Control Systems (DVCS).

1. **Centralized Version Control Systems (CVCS)** - There's a single, central repository of the code in this type. Developers get the latest code copy from this central repository onto their machines and then upload the changes back to the repository. These systems are easy to understand and use. However, the central repository may become a single point of failure if it crashes. Examples of CVCS include Subversion (SVN) and Team Foundation Server (TFS):
   a. **Subversion (SVN)** is an open-source CVCS. It maintains a centralized repository of the code and keeps track of all its changes, allowing developers to revert to any previous version if necessary.
   b. **Team Foundation Server (TFS)**- Developed by Microsoft, TFS is a CVCS that combines version control, issue tracking, and application lifecycle management. It's a

comprehensive suite for project management, especially favored in the .NET environment.

2. **Distributed Version Control Systems (DVCS)** - Unlike CVCS, DVCS allows multiple repositories. Each engineer has a full copy of the project on their local system. This model enables flexible workflows and is more resilient to system failures, since each copy is a full backup. Examples of DVCS include Git and Mercurial:

   a. **Git** is a free and open-source DVCS. It allows for efficient branching and merging, making it ideal for agile development. Git is famous for its speed, flexibility, and support for non-linear development workflows.

   b. **Mercurial** is another open-source DVCS. It emphasizes simplicity and ease of use, with a design that handles large projects and ensures every operation is safe and intuitive.

There's also the **Concurrent Versions System (CVS)**, a predecessor to SVN. However, it's mainly out of favor today due to its many limitations.

One tool worth mentioning is **TortoiseSVN**, which isn't a version control system but an SVN client. It provides a user-friendly interface, integrating into the Windows shell to make using SVN easier. Similar tools exist for Git, like TortoiseGit.

All these tools have their strengths and cater to different needs, so the choice depends on the project's specific requirements.

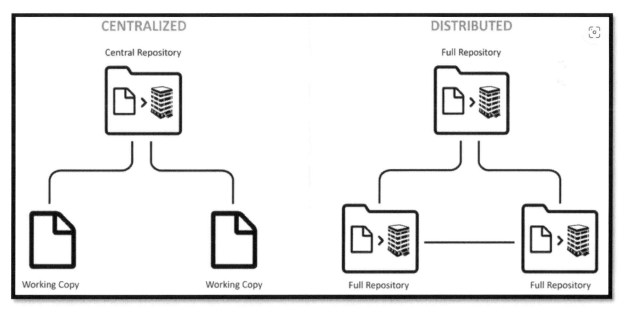

Image credit: This image is taken from the research article "A Comprehensive Study of Version Control Systems: Git and Mercurial" on ResearchGate, available at https://www.researchgate.net/figure/Centralized-Version-Control-vs-Distributed-Version-Control_fig2_316553817. I appreciate the authors for their work and ResearchGate for providing a platform for sharing academic resources.

What Is GIT?

In today's world, Git has solidified its position as the go-to standard for version control. Therefore, the rest of this chapter will primarily dive into the associated concepts and best practices of Git.

As discussed, Git is a distributed version control system. This design allows users to have the entire codebase and its complete history on their local machines, empowering them to make offline changes. However, this functionality doesn't include pushing and pulling changes from the remote server, which we will clarify shortly.

Git originated in 2005, spearheaded by Linus Torvalds, to support the development of the Linux kernel. Since then, its robust features and performance have proven Git's value in many projects.

Additional important aspects of Git are its versatility and adaptability. Git's branching system is notably efficient, allowing developers to create, switch, and merge branches rapidly. Furthermore, Git's 'Stash' and 'Rebase' features offer more flexibility during development. 'Stash' lets you save changes that aren't ready for a commit, while 'Rebase' provides a way to integrate changes from one branch into another. Finally, one of Git's most appreciated strengths is its broad ecosystem of tools and integrations. Platforms like GitHub, Bitbucket, and GitLab leverage Git to provide code hosting, issue tracking, continuous integration, and other services, augmenting the benefits of using Git in your software development process.

GIT Key Concepts

Let's start exploring the key GIT terms and concepts:

1. **Commit** is a captured state of your project at a specific moment. It contains a record of code changes and a unique identifier (an SHA-1 hash). Each commit includes metadata, like the author, timestamp, and a commit message describing the changes.
2. **Branch** is a pointer to a particular commit. It represents an independent line of development. You can change a branch without affecting the **main codebase**, also known as the **main (master)** branch. Once the changes on a branch are stable, they can be merged back into the **main** branch or another branch.
3. **Pull** retrieves modifications from a remote repository and integrates them into your active branch. This action is commonly employed to incorporate updates from collaborators in a shared project.
4. **Push** is a command in Git sends your commits to a remote repository. After making changes and committing them on your local machine, you 'push' them so others can access them.
5. **Rebase** essentially transports or merges a series of commits to a different base commit. It's a way to integrate changes from one branch into another. Instead of creating a merge commit, it rewrites the commit history, making the project history more linear and easier to understand.
6. **Stash** temporarily saves changes you don't want to commit immediately, allowing you to switch branches without committing your current changes. When you're ready, you can retrieve and apply the stashed modifications.
7. **Merge** is a command that combines the changes made in different branches. If two people have changed the same part of a file in different branches, Git will try to blend the changes. If it can't, it will indicate a **merge conflict** that needs to be manually resolved.
8. **Fork** represents a duplicate of a repository. By forking a repository, you create a personal space where you can make alterations freely without impacting the source project.
9. **Clone** is essentially a local copy of a repository that resides on your own computer rather than on a remote server. This cloned version carries all elements of the original repository, including files, historical records, and branches.
10. **Pull Request** serves as a mechanism to propose contributions to an open development project. This process begins when a developer creates a clone of a repository, implements modifications, and then formally requests these alterations to be reviewed and potentially incorporated into the main repository. Pull requests are specific to collaborative

platforms, like GitHub, Bitbucket, and GitLab. They allow code review and discussion about the proposed changes before integrating them into the project. This way, the project maintainers can review the changes and suggest modifications, making pull requests a critical part of collaborative development.

11. **Remote** refers to a version of your project hosted on a server on the internet or network, apart from your local version. You can have several remotes to work with where you push your local changes or fetch updates.

12. **Checkout** allows you to navigate between branches created in your repository. It is a way to switch to different workspaces.

13. **Tag** is a pointer to a particular commit, typically used to capture a point in history that is version related, such as v1.0, v1.1, and so on. This is particularly useful for software releases.

14. **Fetch** retrieves updates from a remote repository without merging them into your current branch. This lets you review the changes before integrating them into your local branches.

15. **Diff** displays differences between commits, branches, or your working directory and your commits.

GIT CLI Commands

Git provides a command-line interface for interaction. To utilize it, you first need to install Git. Visit https://git-scm.com/downloads and choose the appropriate version for your operating system. Once installed, you can open your command-line interface and use Git's CLI to perform all our discussed actions.

```
usage: git [-v | --version] [-h | --help] [-C <path>] [-c <name>=<value>]
           [--exec-path[=<path>]] [--html-path] [--man-path] [--info-path]
           [-p | --paginate | -P | --no-pager] [--no-replace-objects] [--bare]
           [--git-dir=<path>] [--work-tree=<path>] [--namespace=<name>]
           [--config-env=<name>=<envvar>] <command> [<args>]

These are common Git commands used in various situations:

start a working area (see also: git help tutorial)
    clone      Clone a repository into a new directory
    init       Create an empty Git repository or reinitialize an existing one

work on the current change (see also: git help everyday)
    add        Add file contents to the index
    mv         Move or rename a file, a directory, or a symlink
    restore    Restore working tree files
    rm         Remove files from the working tree and from the index

examine the history and state (see also: git help revisions)
    bisect     Use binary search to find the commit that introduced a bug
    diff       Show changes between commits, commit and working tree, etc
    grep       Print lines matching a pattern
    log        Show commit logs
    show       Show various types of objects
    status     Show the working tree status

grow, mark and tweak your common history
    branch     List, create, or delete branches
    commit     Record changes to the repository
    merge      Join two or more development histories together
    rebase     Reapply commits on top of another base tip
    reset      Reset current HEAD to the specified state
    switch     Switch branches
    tag        Create, list, delete or verify a tag object signed with GPG

collaborate (see also: git help workflows)
    fetch      Download objects and refs from another repository
    pull       Fetch from and integrate with another repository or a local branch
    push       Update remote refs along with associated objects

'git help -a' and 'git help -g' list available subcommands and some
concept guides. See 'git help <command>' or 'git help <concept>'
to read about a specific subcommand or concept.
See 'git help git' for an overview of the system.
```

Let's review the most used:

Initialize a Git repository

```
git init
```

Clone a remote repository

```
git clone [url]
```

Add files to the staging area

```
git add [file-name] or git add . (to add all files)
```

Commit changes

```
git commit -m "commit message"
```

Check the status of your files (whether they're staged, unmodified, or modified)

```
git status
```

Pull changes from a remote repository

```
git pull [remote] [branch]
```

Push changes to a remote repository

```
git push [remote] [branch]
```

Create a new branch

```
git branch [branch-name]
```

Switch to another branch

```
git checkout [branch-name]
```

Merge another branch into your current branch

```
git merge [branch-name]
```

View the commit history

```
git log
```

Stash changes (stash changes in a dirty working directory away)

```
git stash
```

Apply stashed changes back

```
git stash apply
```

Fetch changes from a remote repository without merging them

```
git fetch [remote]
```

View differences between commits, branches, etc

```
git diff [source branch] [target branch]
```

Tag a specific commit

```
git tag [tag name] [commit ID]
```

Rebase your branch

```
git rebase [base branch name]
```

Examples

I think you will get the concepts even better if we use some of the beforementioned commands to work with the book's Git repository https://github.com/AutomateThePlanet/Automated-Testing-Unleashed-Volume-3.

- **Clone the repository**

Start by cloning the repository on your local machine. Launch your command line interface and move to the directory where you wish to place the cloned repository. Next, execute the following command:

```
git clone https://github.com/AutomateThePlanet/Automated-Testing-Unleashed-Volume-3.git
```

This will create a copy of the repository in your chosen directory.

- **Check the status of your files**

To verify the status of the files (whether they are modified, staged, or unmodified), run the command:

```
git status
```

This will provide an overview of all the files that have been modified, staged, or untracked.

- **Create a new branch**

If you plan to make changes, creating a new branch is good practice. This helps keep the 'master' branch clean and stable. Run the command:

```
git branch my_automated_testing_getting_started
```

This creates a new branch named `my_automated_testing_getting_started`.

4. Switch to the new branch

To start working on your new branch, you need to switch to it using the command:

```
git checkout my_automated_testing_getting_started
```

5. Add and commit changes

Once you've made some changes to the code, you need to add these changes to the staging area before committing them. For example, if you've updated a file called `FirstUITests.cs`, you'd use the command:

```
git add FirstUITests.cs
```

To commit these changes, use:

```
git commit -m "Describe your changes here"
```

6. Push changes to the remote repository

After committing your changes locally, you need to push them to the remote repository so others can see and access them. Use the command:

```
git push origin my_automated_testing_getting_started
```

This pushes your changes to the `my_automated_testing_getting_started` on the remote repository.

1. Pull changes from the remote repository

If others have made changes to the repository and you want to update your local copy, use the command:

```
git pull origin master
```

This operation retrieves updates from the 'master' branch of the remote repository and incorporates them into the branch you're currently working on.

Remember, Git commands can be much more complex and nuanced, depending on the situation, but these examples should help you get started with basic operations.

GIT Tools

In most scenarios, you may not require the command line interface, as modern software development tools simplify the process. For instance, Visual Studio integrates built-in Git support. Besides, GitHub offers a user-friendly desktop client, named GitHub Desktop. Before delving into the integration with Visual Studio, let's quickly go over the key platforms based on Git:

- **GitHub** - founded in 2008, GitHub is the world's most prominent host of source code. GitHub is an online platform that leverages Git for version control. It encompasses all the distributed version control and source code management (SCM) capabilities of Git, complemented by additional features exclusive to the platform. You can collaborate on projects on GitHub, making it an excellent tool for open-source projects. It includes access control and several collaboration features, such as bug tracking, feature requests, task management, and wikis for every project.
- **Bitbucket** - created by Atlassian in 2008, Bitbucket is another web-based version control repository hosting service, but unlike GitHub, it offers both Git and Mercurial as version control systems. Bitbucket is famous for its robust integration with other Atlassian products, like Jira (for project management), Confluence (for collaboration), and Bamboo (for continuous integration and delivery). It also supports private repositories, making it suitable for businesses and developers, who want to keep their code private.
- **GitLab** - founded in 2011, GitLab is another web-based DevOps lifecycle tool that provides a Git-repository manager, offering wiki, issue-tracking, and continuous integration/continuous deployment pipeline features, using an open-source license. GitLab gives you a broader range of software development and deployment tools within a single platform compared to GitHub or Bitbucket. It has its continuous integration and deployment tools, which can be a big advantage for teams looking for such solutions.
- **Azure DevOps Git** - Azure DevOps, a Microsoft offering, includes Git as one of its version control options. Azure DevOps supports the complete development lifecycle, providing services from project tracking to testing, release, and more. It's fully integrated with other Microsoft services, making it particularly beneficial for teams using a Microsoft-centric development approach. The Git repositories in Azure DevOps are private by default, supporting small and large teams. Azure DevOps is notable for its comprehensive DevOps toolchain, including agile planning, CI/CD, and extensive automation capabilities.

GitHub Desktop

For example, if you open the books' GitHub repository and click on the **Code** button, a few integrations show up:

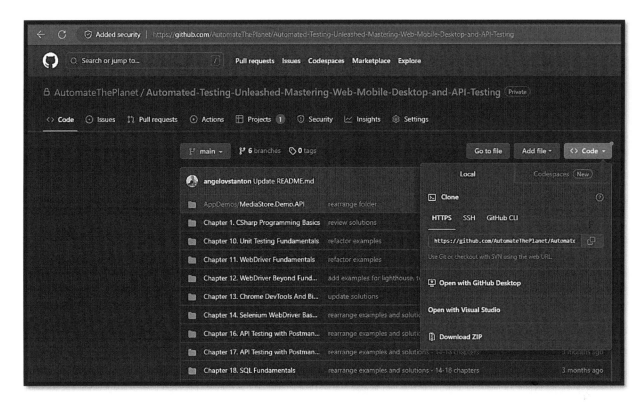

First, we have the CLI command to clone the repository. Then, we have the option to clone the repo via the GitHub desktop client, which I use on a daily basis. After that, we have a similar button for Visual Studio. Last, we can download the source code as a ZIP file without any connection with GIT.

Here is a quick view of GitHub Desktop:

This tool allows you effortlessly to observe changes in files that have been updated or newly created. You can perform important actions, such as committing changes, pushing them to the remote repository, fetching updates, pulling changes, and reverting files. While it may not provide advanced functionalities for code merging and similar tasks, it facilitates simple operations.

Visual Studio

Rather than providing a detailed walkthrough of each example, using the graphical user interface (GUI), the interface is highly intuitive. Furthermore, it undergoes frequent updates, so the appearance may differ when you consult the book. My primary objective is to ensure you grasp the fundamental workflow required to work with such source control systems.

Similar to GitHub Desktop, Visual Studio provides a dedicated Git window. To access it, navigate to the main menu and select "GIT." You can access various features from there, including branch management, pushing and pulling changes, cloning repositories, and many other capabilities:

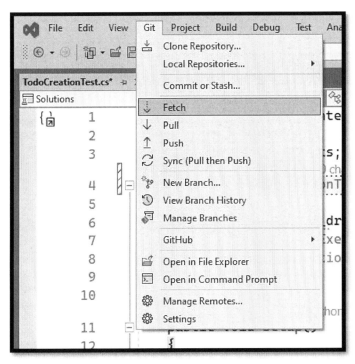

Below is a comprehensive view that allows us to observe any modifications, create commits, push changes to the remote repository, and generate pull requests:

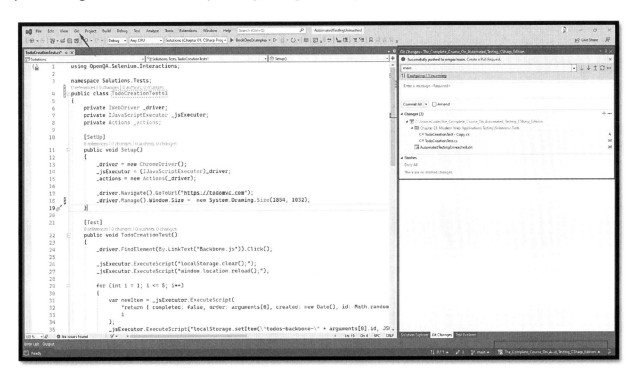

You'll find a convenient repository and branch-switching option in the bottom right corner of the screen.

For file history, simply open the right-click context menu and select "View History". From there, you can choose two commits and compare the versions.

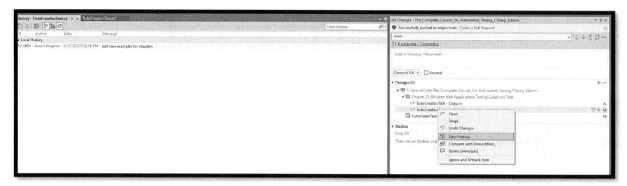

You will see the newly added statements in green and the deleted ones in red:

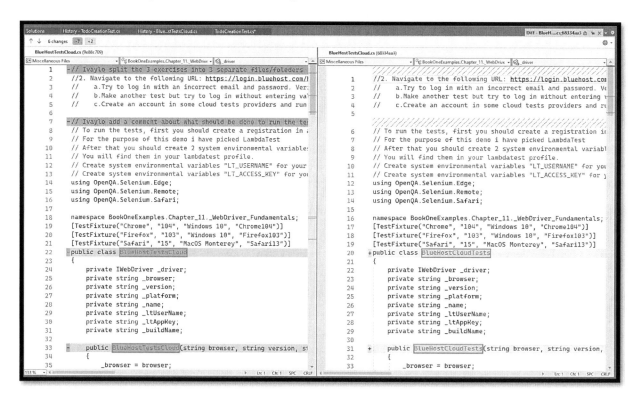

As mentioned, when merging two branches, not all changes may be compatible, necessitating the selection of the final version of statements to be included in the resulting file. The Visual

Studio merge window proves to be an excellent tool for assisting with this process.

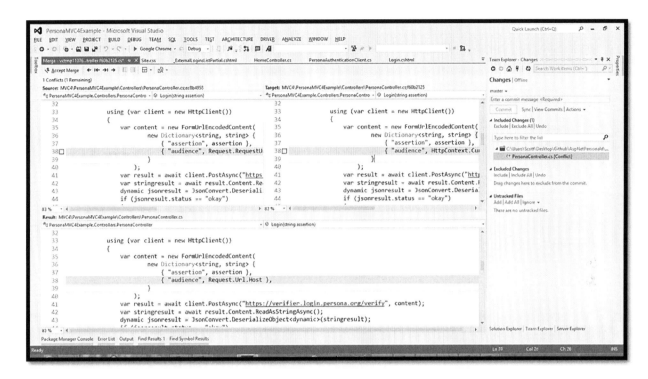

On the left side of the merge window, you will find the current version of your branch while, on the right side, you will see the incoming version. The resulting file is displayed at the bottom. All changes are marked, and using checkboxes, you can select each one to determine which version should be incorporated. While you can accept the entire file directly from one of the branches, there are instances where a thorough review of individual statements is necessary to decide which version should be selected.

Last, I'd like to demonstrate how to view the author of specific code changes. Open the context menu inside your code and select "Git Annotate." This action will provide a comprehensive view of the code, annotated with information about who made each change.

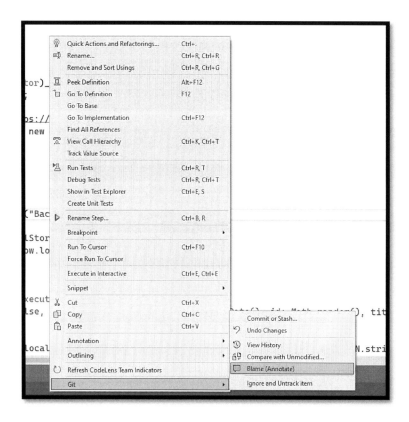

From the left, you will find information about the author and the specific commit:

```csharp
1 using OpenQA.Selenium.Interactions;
2
3 namespace Solutions.Tests;
4 public class TodoCreationTests
5 {
6     private IWebDriver _driver;
7     private IJavaScriptExecutor _jsExecutor;
8     private Actions _actions;
9
10    [SetUp]
11    public void Setup()
12    {
13        _driver = new ChromeDriver();
14        _jsExecutor = (IJavaScriptExecutor)_driver;
15        _actions = new Actions(_driver);
16
17        _driver.Navigate().GoToUrl("https://todomvc.com");
18        _driver.Manage().Window.Size = new System.Drawing.Size(1854, 1032);
19    }
20
21    [Test]
22    public void TodoCreationTest()
23    {
24        _driver.FindElement(By.LinkText("Backbone.js")).Click();
25
26        _jsExecutor.ExecuteScript("localStorage.clear();");
27        _jsExecutor.ExecuteScript("window.location.reload();");
28
29        for (int i = 1; i <= 5; i++)
30        {
31            var newItem = _jsExecutor.ExecuteScript(
32                "return { completed: false, order: arguments[0], created: new Date(), id: Math.random(), title: Math.rand
33                i
34            );
35            _jsExecutor.ExecuteScript("localStorage.setItem(\"todos-backbone-\" + arguments[0].id, JSON.stringify(argumen
36            var currentToDoValue = _jsExecutor.ExecuteScript("return localStorage.getItem('todos-backbone');");
37            _jsExecutor.ExecuteScript("localStorage.setItem(\"todos-backbone\", arguments[0] + \",\" + arguments[1].id)",
38        }
```

Automated Tests Development Source Control Best Practices

In this last part of the chapter, I want to discuss the source control best practices related to automated testing. However, to do that, we need a quick overview of the most commonly used software development methodologies. Depending on which one your team/company follows, how you use the GIT branches, pull requests, etc. might vary.

Definition: Waterfall Methodology

This is a linear approach to software development, where each phase is completed before moving to the next. Automated testing in waterfall occurs during the testing phase, with predefined test cases executed by dedicated testers based on predetermined requirements.

Definition: Agile Methodology

Agile is an iterative and flexible approach emphasizing collaboration, adaptability, and customer satisfaction. Agile methodologies, like Scrum or Kanban, involve cross-functional teams working collaboratively with continuous feedback. Automated testing is integral to Agile, performed continuously throughout sprints using test automation frameworks for early defect detection and rapid feedback. In sprint-based Agile, development is organized into time-boxed iterations, called sprints. Each sprint aims to deliver a working increment of software. In addition, automated testing plays a crucial role, enabling efficient regression testing and thorough testing within the sprint's timeframe.

Definition: Big Bang Methodology

The big bang methodology is a less structured approach, developing the entire software system at once, without specific phases or iterations. Testing in the big bang is challenging, as it occurs late, making defect identification and resolution difficult. Automated testing can still be applied to automate repetitive tasks, but the overall testing strategy may be less structured and more ad hoc.

The choice of testing strategy and automated testing integration depends on the development methodology. For example, agile methodologies provide a conducive environment for continuous integration, frequent testing, and test automation. On the other hand, waterfall and big bang methodologies may also employ automated testing but with a more concentrated and often later testing focus in the development lifecycle.

Throughout my career, I have primarily worked in agile software development environments. Therefore, my suggestions and recommendations will primarily focus on this type of development methodology. Agile methodologies have gained significant popularity and adoption in the industry due to their ability to adapt to the fast-paced and ever-changing realities of software development. It is expected that, in the near future, more companies will embrace and implement agile practices to stay competitive and effectively respond to market demands.

Automated Testing in the Agile Software Development

Let's discuss two more terms, Scrum and Lean.

Definition: Scrum

Scrum is a popular framework within Agile that provides a structured approach to project management. It divides work into time-boxed iterations, called sprints, typically lasting 1-4 weeks. Scrum teams have defined roles, such as Scrum Master, Product Owner, and Development Team. Daily stand-up meetings, sprint planning, sprint reviews, and retrospectives are key Scrum ceremonies. In addition, testing and quality assurance are integrated throughout the development process, ensuring regular feedback and continuous improvement.

Definition: Lean

Lean methodology, inspired by Lean Manufacturing, aims to eliminate waste, optimize efficiency, and improve value delivery. It focuses on identifying and reducing non-value-added activities. Lean principles include value stream mapping, continuous improvement, and respect for people. Lean software development emphasizes delivering value to the customer as early as possible, reducing waste in processes, and promoting collaboration among team members.

Automated testing is critical in Agile, Scrum, and Lean methodologies. It enables faster feedback, early defect detection, and continuous quality assurance. Test automation frameworks and tools are used to create and execute tests, allowing teams to validate software functionality, perform regression testing, and ensure consistent and reliable results. In addition, automated tests are typically integrated into the continuous integration and continuous delivery (CI/CD) pipelines, facilitating frequent and efficient testing throughout the development process.

I follow a specific process to facilitate collaboration and ensure smooth integration of automated tests within our development workflow:

In most projects I am involved in, we use sprint-based development, which uses 1 to 3-week-long release cycles. Thus, we have one MAIN branch storing the latest stable test code. All nightly or more frequent runs are executed against this branch. We merge code there only when we are sure the tests are stable and not flaky.

NOTE

I always emphasize to my co-workers the importance of running tests frequently, as individual tests may pass when executed in isolation but fail when run with other tests. This does not necessarily indicate poorly-written code or poor test quality, although those factors can contribute to test failures. Sometimes, the system's design under test can be a root cause.

Consider a scenario where the system is controlled by numerous global settings unrelated to specific user accounts. As tests interact with these settings, changes made by one test can impact the outcome of other tests. This can lead to random failures if tests are not adequately grouped and executed in parallel. We can identify and address such issues by running tests together more frequently and paying attention to new additions to the test suite.

Therefore, it is crucial to prioritize running tests together to detect potential problems arising from system settings or other factors that may affect test results. By doing so, we can enhance our test suite's overall reliability and quality.

For each sprint, we have a dedicated branch based on MAIN, for example, SPRINT_4 or SPRINT_10. All individual pull requests during the sprint are merged into this sprint branch. We can have separate runs of the tests developed in this branch and the rest to ensure they are stable.

When new tests are introduced, we mark them with a special category, called NEW_TEST. This allows us to track and distinguish these tests during development. Once we are confident the tests function correctly within the test suite, we remove the NEW_TEST category.

Software test engineers work on separate stories during each sprint, divided into smaller tasks with independent estimations. To streamline collaboration, each engineer works in their own sprint story branch. For example, the branch name may follow the format `SPRINT_4_Id123545_NewForumThreadsFilterSearch`.

Once the code and tests in the sprint story branch are ready, a pull request (PR) is submitted to merge the branch into the main sprint branch (e.g., `SPRINT_4`). A code review is conducted to ensure code quality and identify any potential issues. If there are comments or suggestions, they must be addressed before the merge is completed. If the story branch includes older code merged from other stories, the engineer needs to merge the main sprint branch into their story branch to resolve any conflicts before submitting the PR.

At the end of the sprint, the latest code from the `MAIN` branch is pulled and merged into the sprint story branch (e.g., `SPRINT_4`). Any conflicts that arise during the merge must be addressed and resolved. Once this is done, a second pull request is created, encompassing all updates from the sprint. A comprehensive code review is conducted, and all comments are resolved. The sprint branch is then successfully merged into the main branch, ensuring the integration of the sprint's work into the overall codebase.

By following this process, we maintain code quality, facilitate collaboration, and ensure the successful integration of automated tests within our development workflow.

Exercises

1. Create additional extension methods to the ADB commands library for working with backups. Find the proper commands in the provided cheat sheet. Install GitHub Desktop.
2. Create a GitHub Account.
3. Clone the books' source code repository.
4. Follow the GitHub repository for any future updates.
5. Create a separate working branch for the books' code challenges.

Summary

This chapter covered essential information for software engineers regarding effective teamwork and code integration. We explored the nature of source control, its significance in software development, and its advantages. Git, one of the popular tools in this field, was discussed, along with its integration into platforms like GitHub, AzureDevOps, and Bitbucket. We also examined key operations, such as code reviews, pull requests, merging code, and managing branches. Last, we highlighted best practices for creating automated test code and leveraging source control systems.

In the upcoming chapter, we plan to delve more into the nitty-gritty of HTML, the Hyper Text Markup Language that forms the basis of a web page. We'll uncover the elements that dictate how browsers present the content.

Chapter 8. HTML Crash Course

In the previous chapter, we discussed in short what HTML is. But now, let's discuss it in much more detail. It stands for Hyper Text Markup Language. It describes the structure of a web page and consists of a series of elements that instructs the browser on how to display the content. As a QA automation engineer, you need to understand everything related to web pages; otherwise, how will you automate them, right? It is possible, but you are doomed to be a mediocre tester.

We will first see a simple HTML web page and discuss the essential parts. Afterward, we will quickly review all essential HTML elements their attributes and see many examples.

Topics covered in this chapter:
- Building Your First Web page
- Basic HTML Elements
- Input HTML Elements

Building Your First Web Page

To work with HTML, you can use Visual Studio Code. First, create a new file and save it with the extension ".html". Afterward, you can locate the file and double-click it to view it in the browser or use Visual Studio Code shortcuts to load it faster. Below you can see the structure of a simple HTML document.

```
<!DOCTYPE html>
<html>
<head>
    <title>Page Title</title>
</head>
<body>
    <h1>This is your first web page!</h1>
    <p>Your first paragraph.</p>
</body>
</html>
```

`<!DOCTYPE html>` defines this document as an HTML5 document. It must only appear once, at the top of the page (before any HTML tags). `<html>` is the root element of the web page. The `<head>` element contains meta info about the page. `<title>` holds the title of the web page. It is displayed in the browser's title bar or page's tab. `<body>` is the document's body, a container for the visible contents such as paragraphs, hyperlinks, tables, headings, lists, etc. The `<h1>` element defines the main heading while the `<p>` element defines a paragraph. All HTML tags are not case sensitive. <H1> is the same as <h1>. Anyhow, W3C recommends using lowercase.

NOTE

Here is a short history of HTML versions:

1989 - Tim Berners-Lee invented www

1991 - Tim Berners-Lee invented HTML

1993 - Dave Raggett drafted HTML+

1995 - HTML Working Group defined HTML 2.0

1997 - W3C Recommendation: HTML 3.2

1999 - W3C Recommendation: HTML 4.01

2000 - W3C Recommendation: XHTML 1.0

2008 - WHATWG HTML5 First Public Draft

2012 - WHATWG HTML5 Living Standard

2014 - W3C Recommendation: HTML5

2016 - W3C Candidate Recommendation: HTML 5.1

2017 - W3C Recommendation: HTML5.1 2nd Edition

2017 - W3C Recommendation: HTML5.2

What is an HTML Element?

An HTML element is defined by a start tag, some content, and an end tag `<tagname>your content</tagname>` We call a web element for everything between the start tag to the end tag.

```
<h1>This is your first web page!</h1>
<p>Your first paragraph.</p>
```

Here we have two web elements one main heading `<h1>` and one paragraph `<p>`.
There are also empty elements that don't have content (like <br>) and don't have an end tag.
To add comments to your HTML code you can start it with `<!–` and after it end it with `-->`

```
<!-- Write your comments here -->
```

Pay special attention that the starting tag contains ! but the closing tag doesn't.

Basic HTML Elements

HTML <head> Tag

The <head> element holds metadata about the HTML document. (a data describing the data) It is placed between the <html> and <body> tags. Below you can find part of the head information of my website Automate The Planet.

```
<!DOCTYPE html>
<html lang="en">
<head>
    <head>
        <meta property="og:type" content="article">
        <meta property="og:url" content="https://www.automatetheplanet.com/">
        <meta name="twitter:card" content="summary_large_image">
        <meta property="og:site_name" content="Automate The Planet">
        <meta property="og:title" content="Automate The Planet">
        <meta name="twitter:title" content="Automate The Planet">
        <meta property="og:image" content="http://www.automatetheplanet.com/atp_logo.svg">
        <meta name="twitter:image:src"
content="http://www.automatetheplanet.com//atp_logo.svg">
        <meta property="og:description" content="Taking Software Quality to New Heights">
        <meta name="twitter:description" content="Taking Software Quality to New Heights">
        <meta name="twitter:creator" content="@https://twitter.com/angelovstanton">
        <meta name="twitter:site" content="@https://twitter.com/angelovstanton">
        <title>Homepage - Automate The Planet</title>
        <link rel="preload" as="font"
href="https://www.automatetheplanet.com/css/font/Lato.ttf">
        <meta name="viewport" content="width=device-width, initial-scale=1.0">
        <meta charset="UTF-8">
        <meta name="google-site-verification"
content="vJhe4TxEJRanmso899995maO4JTPJEiDLNKkBM">
        <meta name="msvalidate.01" content="7C6082CFD7EEDCE999B1FCF8A8BA9E">
        <meta name="yandex-verification" content="ce14b8ced19a0058">
        <link rel="canonical" href="https://www.automatetheplanet.com/">
        <meta property="og:locale" content="en_US">
        <meta property="og:type" content="website">
        <meta property="og:title" content="Homepage - Automate The Planet">
        <meta property="og:description" content="Taking Software Quality to New Heights">
        <meta property="og:url" content="https://www.automatetheplanet.com/">
        <meta property="og:site_name" content="Automate The Planet">
        <meta property="article:publisher"
content="https://www.facebook.com/automatetheplanet">
        <meta property="og:image" content="https://www.automatetheplanet.com/homepage-
img.svg">
        <meta name="twitter:site" content="@angelovstanton">
        <meta name="google-site-verification"
content="vJhe4TxEJRanmso8ZXMZA5zZQ5maO4JTPJEiDLNKkBM">
        <meta name="yandex-verification" content="ce14b8ced19a0058">
```

```
            <script type="text/javascript" src="https://www.automatetheplanet.com/wp-
includes/js/jquery/jquery.min.js"
                id="jquery-core-js"></script>

        <style type="text/css" id="thrive-default-styles">
            @media (min-width: 300px) {
                .tcb-style-wrap h3 {
                    color: rgb(0, 0, 0);
                    background-color: rgba(0, 0, 0, 0);
                    font-family: Lato, sans-serif;
                    font-size: 25.6px;
                    font-weight: 400;
                    font-style: normal;
                    margin: 18px 0px 9px;
                    padding-top: 0px;
                    padding-bottom: 0px;
                    text-decoration: none solid rgb(0, 0, 0);
                    text-transform: none;
                    border-left: 0px none rgb(0, 0, 0);
                    --tcb-applied-color: ;
                }
            }
        </style>
        <link rel="icon"
            href="https://www.automatetheplanet.com/cropped-atp-logo-site-icon-32x32.png"
            sizes="32x32">
        <link rel="icon"
            href="https://www.automatetheplanet.com/cropped-atp-logo-site-icon-192x192.png"
            sizes="192x192">
        <link rel="apple-touch-icon"
            href="https://www.automatetheplanet.com/cropped-atp-logo-site-icon-180x180.png">
    </head>
</head>
<body>

    <h1>This is a heading</h1>
    <p>This is a paragraph.</p>
</body>
</html>
```

The metadata is not displayed. It defines the title of the web page in this case "Homepage - Automate The Planet".

```
<title>Homepage - Automate The Planet</title>
```

Also, you can directly declare styles about the HTML document wrapped inside a <style> tag:

```
<style type="text/css" id="thrive-default-styles">
    @media (min-width: 300px) {
        .tcb-style-wrap h3 {
            color: rgb(0, 0, 0);
            background-color: rgba(0, 0, 0, 0);
            font-family: Lato, sans-serif;
            font-size: 25.6px;
```

```
                font-weight: 400;
                font-style: normal;
                margin: 18px 0px 9px;
                padding-top: 0px;
                padding-bottom: 0px;
                text-decoration: none solid rgb(0, 0, 0);
                text-transform: none;
                border-left: 0px none rgb(0, 0, 0);
                --tcb-applied-color: ;
        }
    }
</style>
```

However, on most web pages, instead of declaring the CSS styles like this to reuse them among many web pages, we link them through the `<link>` tag. So, you need to denote via the `rel` and `type` attributes that the link is CSS:

```
<link rel="stylesheet" type="text/css" href="styles.css">
```

Similarly, we can add a link to JavaScript files to reuse the JS code:

```
<script type="text/javascript" src=https://www.automatetheplanet.com/wp-
includes/js/jquery/jquery.min.js id="jquery-core-js"></script>
```

Like CSS you can define client-side JS code via the `<script>` tag:

```
<script>
    function setCodeDiv() {
        document.getElementById("codeDivId").innerHTML = "C# Rules!";
    }
</script>
```

Via the meta declaration about viewport, we make our website look good on all devices:

```
<meta name="viewport" content="width=device-width, initial-scale=1.0">
```

We use the <meta> tag to set page description, keywords, SEO related information or social media sharing meta data like:

```
<meta name="twitter:card" content="summary_large_image">
<meta property="og:site_name" content="Automate The Planet">
<meta property="og:title" content="Automate The Planet">
<meta name="twitter:title" content="Automate The Planet">
```

For example, we use the following meta tags to verify web analytics accounts and search engine master tools for popular platforms:

```
<meta name="google-site-verification" content="vJhe4TxEJRanmso899995maO4JTPJEiDLNKkBM">
<meta name="msvalidate.01" content="7C6082CFD7EEDCE999B1FCF8A8BA9E">
<meta name="yandex-verification" content="ce14b8ced19a0058">
```

Definition: SEO

Search engine optimization is the process of improving the quality and quantity of website traffic from search engines. SEO targets unpaid traffic rather than paid ad one.

Definition: Web Analytics

"Web analytics is the measurement, collection, analysis, and reporting of web data to understand and optimize web usage. Web analytics is not just a process for measuring web traffic but can be used as a tool for business and market research and assess and improve website effectiveness.", - Wikipedia

Definition: Search Consoles/Master Tools

Search consoles (master tools) of popular engines such as Google, Yahoo, Bing, Yandex allow website owners to check indexing status and optimize the visibility of their websites. They include tools such as - submitting/checking a sitemap, checking craw rate, view statistics, configuring rich cards, reviewing securing issues and many more.

HTML <h2> Tag

We already saw how to declare a mean heading of a web page through `<h1>`. To declare less important headings, you can use `<h2>` to `<h6>` tags. They should indicate what a section is or a paragraph is about. They are a critical part of SEO.

```
<h1>This is heading 1</h1>
<h2>This is heading 2</h2>
<h3>This is heading 3</h3>
```

HTML <a> Tag

To define a link, you need to use the `<a>` tag:

```
<a href="https://www.automatetheplanet.com/">Click here to navigate to Automate The Planet</a>
```

To set the link's destination we set the `href` attribute to the desired URL. The attributes are used to provide additional meta information about the HTML elements.

HTML <img> Tag

Relatively like links via `<img>` tag we can define images. To set the image's location we use the `src` attribute. We can also set alternative text to be displayed if the browser cannot visualize the image through the alt attribute. It is again something used in SEO, so it should be set. Also, you can set the width and the height.

```
<img src="atp-logo.png" alt="automatetheplanet.com" width="150" height="150">
```

HTML elements can contain other elements meaning they can be nested. Our first web page contained `<html>`, `<body>`, `<h1>` and `<p>`. The browsers can visualize the web pages even if there are problems with your HTML. However, you should be careful never to miss placing the end tag of the web elements. Most modern HTML IDEs are auto-completing them while typing. Also, you can use an online HTML markup checker to verify that your HTML is correct. For example: https://validator.w3.org/

HTML
 Tag

As I mentioned, there are tags without an end tag, such as `<br>`. The `<br>` tag defines a line break.

```
<p>This is a paragraph and <br> a line break.</p>
```

Let's quickly review other commonly used HTML tags that you will have to recognize while automating websites.

HTML <button> Tag

```
<button type="button">Buy Something Expensive!</button>
```

The `<button>` tag defines a button. You can also put inside of it other tags like images, info boxes, links, etc. This is the main difference compared to `<input>` buttons that we will discuss in a minute. You always need to specify the `type` of the button. There are three types - `submit`, `button`, and `reset`. Other important attributes are `disabled`, `autofocus`, `value`, and `name`. We will use four attributes quite often in automated tests. They are self-explanatory.

HTML <div> Tag

Another HTML tag that you will see many often is <div>. It is a bit weird at first because it doesn't display anything specific rather than we use it as a division or section in the HTML. It is a container that holds other web elements, and we often set its class or id attributes so that we can style the whole section through CSS. By there is always a line break before and after the <div> tag.

```
<html>
<head>
    <style>
        .roseDiv {
            border: 3px outset #0000ff;
            background-color: rosybrown;
```

```
            text-align: left;
        }
    </style>
</head>
<body>
    <div class="roseDiv">
        <h2>Some HTML Elements Explanations</h2>
        <p>Some awesome info about DIVs!</p>
    </div>
</body>
</html>
```

`.roseDiv` is a CSS class selector, meaning it selects all tags with class `attribute` = 'roseDiv', and it will change how they look based on the rules present in the following brackets' section. We will talk much more about CSS in the next section.

HTML <span> Tag

The <span> tag is like <div>. The difference is that <span> is used inline while <div> is used on a block level.

```
<html>
<head>
    <style>
        .boldSpan {
            color: #ff0000;
            font-weight: 1000;
        }
    </style>
</head>
<body>
    <p>Are you tired of <span class="boldSpan">"Hello World"</span> examples?
        Learn how to write automated tests through <span class="boldSpan">working real-
world</span> examples.</p>
</body>
</html>
```

This allows us to format only parts of the text. Here is how the text is visualized:

Are you tired of **"Hello World"** examples? Learn how to write automated tests through **working real-world** examples.

HTML <footer> Tag

```
<footer id="footer" class="blue padded-100">
    <p>Author: Anton Angelov</p>
    <a href="https://www.linkedin.com/in/angelovstanton/" target="_blank" title="Anton
Angelov LinkedIn" class="footer-social li"></a>
</footer>
```

To define a footer, you can use the <footer> tag. You can have a couple of them, and they usually contain info about the author, copyright, contact info, maps, and menu links.

HTML <ol> <ul> <li> Tags

In HTML, there are a couple of types of lists - ordered, unordered, and description. The ordered lists start with `<ol>` tag, and each item starts with the `<li>` tag. While the unordered lists start with the `<ul>` tag.

```
<h2>Your favorite drink:</h2>
<ol>
  <li>Coffee</li>
  <li>Green Tea</li>
  <li>Black Tea</li>
</ol>
<ul>
  <li>Coffee</li>
  <li>Green Tea</li>
  <li>Black Tea</li>
</ul>
```

Your favorite drink:

1. Coffee
2. Green Tea
3. Black Tea

- Coffee
- Green Tea
- Black Tea

HTML <table> Tag

To create a table representing tabular data, we use the `<table>` tag. Table rows start with <tr> tag while the columns start with `<th>`. The table headers are wrapped inside a `<thead>` tag. All data rows and columns are present inside `<tbody>` tag. Some tables contain a footer that begins with the `<tfoot>` tag.

```
<html>
<style>
    table,
    th,
    td {
        border: 1px solid black;
    }
</style>
<body>
    <p>Table of countries:</p>
```

```
<table>
    <tr>
        <th>Countries</th>
        <th>Capitals</th>
        <th>Population</th>
        <th>Language</th>
    </tr>
    <tr>
        <td>Bulgaria</td>
        <td>Sofia</td>
        <td>7 million</td>
        <td>Bulgaria</td>
    </tr>
    <tr>
        <td>Sweden</td>
        <td>Stockholm</td>
        <td>9 million</td>
        <td>Swedish</td>
    </tr>
    <tr>
        <td>Germany</td>
        <td>Berlin</td>
        <td>83 million</td>
        <td>German</td>
    </tr>
</table>
</body>
</html>
```

Countries	Capitals	Population	Language
Bulgaria	Sofia	7 million	Bulgaria
Sweden	Stockholm	9 million	Swedish
Germany	Berlin	83 million	German

To add a border, we use the CSS border property on the table, th, and td elements. To avoid having double borders like in the example above, set the CSS border-collapse property to `collapse`.

```
table, th, td {
  border: 1px solid black;
  border-collapse: collapse;
}
```

HTML <form> Tag

```
<form class="form login" method="post">
    <p class="form-row">
```

```
        <label for="username">Username or email address<span
class="required">*</span></label>
        <input type="text" class="Input " name="username" id="username" autocomplete="off">
    </p>
    <p class="form-row">
        <label for="password">Password<span class="required">*</span></label>
        <span class="password-input">
        <input class="Input" type="password" name="password" id="password"></span>
    </p>
    <p class="form-row">
        <label class="form__label">
            <input class="form__input-checkbox" name="rememberme" type="checkbox"
                id="rememberme" value="forever">
            <span>Remember me</span>
        </label>
        <input type="hidden" id="login-nonce" name="login-nonce" value="1de9eb4f8b">
        <input type="hidden" name="_wp_http_referer" value="/my-account/">
        <button type="submit" class="form-login__submit" name="login" value="Log in">Log
in</button>
    </p>
    <p class="LostPassword lost_password">
        <a href="https://demos.bellatrix.solutions/my-account/lost-password/">Lost your
password?</a>
    </p>
</form>
```

We use the <form> to define a form containing input elements such as inputs, selects, fields, buttons, etc. After filling in all of the required information, the form is usually used to submit the information to the server triggered by a button click. In the example, you can find a real login form that requires username, password and submits the info via a submit button. For protection from bots there are two hidden inputs that are not visible. The hidden fields allow us to include data that cannot be seen or modified by the users when the form is submitted. They often hold information which should be updated later into the database when the form is submitted. Let's review the other tags present in the form that we haven't yet discussed.

NOTE

Single or double quotes? As you can see in the examples, double quotes are the most common, but single quotes are OK too. When the attribute's value itself contains double quotes, then you need to use single quotes: `<p title="George' Coffee' Brandon">`

HTML <input> Tag

The <input> tags are used to allow user to enter data. They come in various types, the default one is text. Like the <button> tag you need to specify the type via the type attribute:

```
<input type="button">
<input type="checkbox">
<input type="color">
<input type="date">
<input type="datetime-local">
<input type="email">
<input type="file">
<input type="hidden">
<input type="image">
<input type="month">
<input type="number">
<input type="password">
<input type="radio">
<input type="range">
<input type="reset">
<input type="search">
<input type="submit">
<input type="tel">
<input type="text">
<input type="time">
<input type="url">
<input type="week">
```

As depicted in the image below, the input tags come in many forms, from checkboxes to color and date inputs. The <input> is the most crucial element of every form.

Various Input Types:

HTML <label> Tag

Keep in mind that we usually combine the <input> tags with <label> to define labels for the text, checkbox, radio, file, password and other inputs.

The for attribute of the <label> tag must be equal to the id attribute of the related input to bind them together. A label can be bound to an element by placing the element inside the label:

```
<label for="myButton">Providing default options Input Button</label>
<input type="button" id="myButton" name="start" value="Start">
<br>
<br>
<label for="myButton1">Test Hover Input Button</label>
<input type="button" id="myButton1" name="start" value="Start">
```

Let's review most of the input tags and discuss some of their essential attributes, especially those you will have to check in your automated test scripts.

HTML <progress>

The <progress> tag displays an indicator for completing a process, displayed as a progress bar.

The `value` attribute holds the current progress value.

```
<label for="file">File Download Progress:</label>
<progress value="82" max="100">
```

File Download Progress:

Input HTML Elements

HTML <input type="button">

This tag renders a simple push button. It is similar to <button> as we already discussed. <input> elements of type button are still perfectly valid HTML, the newer <button> element is now the favored way to create buttons. Given that a <button>'s label text is inserted between the opening and closing tags, you can include HTML in the label, even images.

```
<input class="cryptoStyle" type="button" value="Buy Me a Bitcoin" accesskey="b">
```

The `value` is used for text of the button.

Buy Me a Bitcoin

Through keyboard shortcuts, also know as access keys, you can allow the user to trigger the action via key or combination of keys on the keyboard. You can use the global attribute `accesskey`.

HTML <input type="submit">

The submit inputs are also rendered as buttons. The `click` event is triggered when clicked, and the browser submits the form to the server.

```
<form action="/buy_page.php" method="get" target="_blank">
    <div>
        <label for="full-name">Your name:</label>
        <input type="text" id="full-name" name="fname" tabindex="0" autofocus><br><br>
    </div>
    <div>
        <label for="bcount">Bitcoins Count:</label>
        <input type="number" id="bcount" name="bcount" tabindex="1"><br><br>
    </div>
    <div>
```

```
        <input type="submit" formmethod="post" value="Buy Bitcoins" accesskey="b"
tabindex="2">
    </div>
</form>
```

Purchase Bitcoins

Your name: [   ]

Bitcoins Count: [   ]

[Buy Bitcoins]

The `formmethod` attribute holds a string which represents the HTTP method to be used when submitting the form's data. It overrides the method attribute given on the owning form. The first input is marked as `autofocus` which means that it will automatically be focused on load. Afterward through the `tabindex` attributes we instruct the browser which should be the next focus element when we press TAB.

HTML <input type="image">

This tag is similar to the previous one but here we use images for creating a graphical submit buttons.

```
<form action="/buy_page.php" method="get" target="_blank">
  <label for="full-name">Your name:</label>
  <input type="text" id="full-name" name="fname" tabindex="0" autofocus><br><br>
  <label for="bcount">Bitcoins Count:</label>
  <input type="number" id="bcount" name="bcount" tabindex="1"><br><br>
 <input type="image" id="myImage3" src="https://interactive-
examples.mdn.mozilla.net/media/examples/login-button.png" alt="MDN" height="40" width="100"
formtarget="_blank">
```

`src` is the URL to the image. We can set the width and the height through the attributes with the same names. The `formtarget` attribute can hold the values `_self`, `_blank`, `_parent`, `_top`. In our case, `_blank` means to load the response in a new tab. This attribute can be used for buttons and submit inputs too.
For displaying images, we use the `<img>` tag.

HTML <input type="reset">

The reset inputs are rendered as buttons and clear all the information populated in the form that they are nested in.

```
<form action="/buy_page.php" method="get" target="_blank">
```

```
<div>
    <label for="full-name">Your name:</label>
    <input type="text" id="full-name" name="fname" tabindex="0" autofocus><br><br>
</div>
<div>
    <label for="bcount">Bitcoins Count:</label>
    <input type="number" id="bcount" name="bcount" tabindex="1"><br><br>
</div>
<div>
    <input type="submit" value="Buy Bitcoins" accesskey="b" tabindex="2">
    <input type="reset" value="Clear Data" accesskey="r" tabindex="3">
</div>
</form>
```

HTML <input type="checkbox">

The tag defines a checkbox which is displayed as a square box that is checked/ticked when clicked. They are used to allow user to select one or more options.

```
<input type="checkbox" id="coin1" name="coin1" value="Bitcoin">
<label for="coin1"> I own a Bitcoin</label><br>
<input type="checkbox" id="coin2" name="coin2" value="Ethereum" disabled>
<label for="coin2"> I own an Ethereum</label><br>
<input type="checkbox" id="coin3" name="coin3" value="Dogecoin">
<label for="coin3"> I own a Dogecoin</label><br>
```

The code is visualized as follow:

☐ I own a Bitcoin
☐ I own an Ethereum
☑ I own a Dogecoin

There are a few essential attributes. Through the `checked` attribute, you can configure whether the checkbox is ticked by default or not. Like many other attributes, we set the value for the element through the `value` attribute. Finally, through the `disabled` attribute, we disallow the users to check the input.

HTML <input type="radio">

Another widely used input type is the radio one. It is rendered as small circles, which are highlighted when selected.

Select a preferred cryptocurrency:

◉ Bitcoin
○ Dogecoin
○ Ethereum

```
<input type="radio" id="bitcoin" name="crypto" value="Bitcoin" checked>
<label for="bitcoin">Bitcoin</label>

<input type="radio" id="dogecoin" name="crypto" value="Dogecoin">
<label for="dogecoin">Dogecoin</label>

<input type="radio" id="ethereum" name="crypto" value="Ethereum">
<label for="ethereum">Ethereum</label>
```

Checkboxes are similar to radio buttons but are designed to select one value out of a set, whereas checkboxes let you turn individual values on and off. In addition, where multiple controls exist, radio buttons allow one to be selected, whereas checkboxes allow multiple values to be chosen.

To configure the radio buttons to be in the same radio group and thus only one to be selected, they all need to have the same name. In our example, "crypto". Suppose you don't add the value attribute and submit the form. The radio group's data won't be included in the form data. Then, the same happens if you don't select a radio button from the group and the required attribute is not present. If the checked attribute is present, it indicates that this is the default selected option.

HTML <input type="text">

As we discussed, the default input type is text:

```
<label for="myText">Placeholders</label>
<input id="myText" name="myText" type="Text" placeholder="your Text term goes here"
class="myTestClass">
<input id="myText2" type="Text" size="30" minlength="10" maxlength="80">
<input id="myText4" type="Text" autocomplete="on">
<input id="myText1" type="Text" size="30">
<input id="myText6" type="Text" readonly>
<input id="myText7" type="Text" required>
<input id="myText10" type="Text" disabled>
```

Placeholders	your Text term goes here
Physical input element size	
Element value length	
Autocomplete= ON	
Autocomplete= OFF	
Readonly Set	
Required Set	
Test Disabled	

As you probably noticed, some attributes are the same as the ones for checkboxes, like `disabled`, for example. The `placeholder` holds a short hint describing the expected value, displayed in light gray. Most of them can be used in most input types where it makes sense. For example, the `required` attribute defines that you cannot submit the form without filling in the data, while `readonly` means that you can read the info but are not allowed to change it. The `autocomplete` option specifies whether the tag enables autocomplete. The `size` attribute specifies the width in characters while `minlength` and `maxlength` are the minimum and the maximum number. We will discuss even more attributes with the following few examples.

HTML <input type="email">

Now let's investigate another popular input type - the email.

```
<input id="myEmail" name="myEmail" type="email" value="aangelov@automatetheplanet.com"
size="30" minlength="10" maxlength="80" placeholder="your email term goes here"
class="myTestClass" pattern=".+@globex\.com" autofocus required>
```

The `autofocus` specifies that the `<input>` should automatically get the focus when the page loads. As with all input tags, the `value` attribute holds what the user entered into the field, which is later sent to the server. Again, we can enforce automatic data validation through `size`, `minlength`, `maxlength`, and `required` attributes. You probably have noticed a new attribute called `pattern` with a regular expression that the value must match to pass constraint validation. It must be a valid JavaScript regular expression. You can use the `title` attribute to specify text most browsers will display as a tooltip to explain the requirements to match the pattern.

Your email address:

```
bob@
```

> Please enter an email address.

                                        and I have forgotten how to dance.

NOTE

While HTML form validation is easy to add, it is easy to bypass by only changing the HTML. Thus, in our tests, we need to ensure there is always another level of defense, such as additional validation scripts that guarantee that the entered data is in the proper format. This is sometimes referred to as client-side validation. However, even with these two layers of defense, it is still possible to submit data directly to your server; thus, you need to test that the website developers added server-side validations. This defensive layer makes sure that it validates the data before saving it into the DB. For example, we check whether the information is not too large, is of the wrong type, is in the expected format, and so on.

HTML <input type="password">

. The password inputs are often used in combination with the email ones. The difference is that they mask the value so it is not visible directly, displaying it via many '*' symbols. We can configure the type of the password, whether it only consists of numbers or various symbols, via the `inputmode` attribute. The `autocomplete` attribute can have two additional values - `new-password` and `current-password`. The first allows the browser to use the password manager to automatically enter a new website password. The latter instructs the browser to call the password manager to fill in the currently saved pass for the website.

```
<label for="userPass">Password:</label>
<input id="userPass" type="password" autocomplete="current-password">
<label for="pin">PIN:</label>
<input id="pin" type="password" inputmode="numeric" minlength="5" maxlength="10" size="10">
<label for="hexId">Hex ID: </label>
<input id="hexId" type="password" pattern="[0-9a-fA-F]{4,8}" title="Enter an ID consisting
of 4-8 hex digits" autocomplete="new-password">
```

Username:

Password (8 characters minimum):

••••••••••••••••

Sign in

HTML <input type="number">

For expecting numbers, we use `<input type="number">`.

Number of bitcoints (10-100):

11

```
<input type="number" placeholder="multiple of 10" step="10" min="0" max="100">
<input type="number" placeholder="1.0" step="0.01" min="0" max="10">
```

I added a few new attributes to the example. To specify the granularity, we use the `step` attribute, which is a number that the value must adhere to. In the first case, we can add only numbers with the step of 10, while in the second one, the up and down buttons allow us to enter decimal values with the step of 0.1. Next, we use the `min` and `max` attributes to specify a minimum and maximum value that the field can have.

We can offer the user a list of default options. We connect the input to the list via the list attribute that holds the datalist's id. The `<datalist>` tag has one `<option>` element per suggested value. Each option's value is the corresponding recommended value for the number entry box.

```
<input id="bitcoinsToSell" type="number" name="bitcointToSell" list="defaultBitocoinsCount">

<datalist id="defaultBitocoinsCount">
  <option value="10">
  <option value="20">
  <option value="50">
  <option value="100">
  <option value="500">
```

```
</datalist>
```

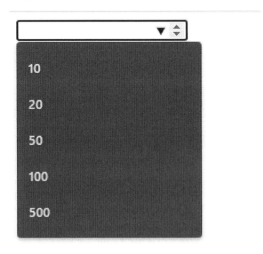

HTML <input type="date">

This type of input allows the user to enter dates. We can control the maximum, minimum, and step through the max, min, and step attributes.

```
<label for="bdate">When is your birthday?</label>
<input id="bdate" type="date" step="2" min="1900-01-01" max="2021-12-01" value="1985-08-07">
```

When is your birthday?

Also, we can set a default value via the `value` attribute. Finally, you can use an additional layer of protection using the `pattern` attribute to specify a regex expression for validating the date if it is entered via text and not using the selector.

```
<input type="date" name="bday" required pattern="\d{4}-\d{2}-\d{2}">
```

HTML <input type="time">

The time inputs are like the date ones but instead of dates the user can enter time like hours, minutes and optionally seconds.

```
<label for="taxi-time">Enter a time when the taxi driver to pick you up:</label>
<input type="time" id="taxi-time" min="09:00" max="21:00" required>
```

Enter a time when the taxi driver to pick you up: `10`: 17 AM 🕐

06	15	PM
07	16	**AM**
08	**17**	
09	18	
10	19	
11	20	
12	21	

The different browsers vary in how they handle the time inputs and render them a bit different, so you need to test the behavior accordingly. For example, the same control on Chrome for Android looks like this:

HTML <input type="url">

The URL inputs are used to accept URLs. For example, here you are asked to enter your favorite Automate The Planet blog's article URL:

```
<label for="url">Enter the URL of your favorite Automate the Planet article:</label>
<input type="url" id="url" placeholder="https://automatetheplanet.com/"
pattern="https://automatetheplanet.com/.*" size="100" spellcheck="true" maxlength="100"
minlength="20" required>
```

Enter the URL of your favorite Automate the Planet article:

https://www.automatetheplanet.com/

Submit

`spellcheck` is a global attribute which instructs the browser to turn on the spell check for the element.

NOTE

The HTML global attributes can be used with all HTML elements. We already saw a few of them - `accesskey`, `id`, `style`, `tabindex`, `title`, `class`, `hidden`. Other important global attributes are `lang`, `translate`, and `dir`. `lang` specifies the language of the content. For example, `lang="de"` - means the content is written in German. `translate` defines whether the content should be translated while `dir` specifies the text direction. For example, `dir="rtl"` displays the text right to left.

HTML <input type="color">

The color input allows you to specify a color via a picker or you can enter the color into a text field in hexadecimal format.

```
<p>Joker costume's colors:</p>
<div>
    <input type="color" id="top" value="#d93d3d">
    <label for="top">Top</label>
</div>
<div>
    <input type="color" id="bottom" value="#f29544">
    <label for="bottom">Bottom</label>
</div>
```

Joker costume's colors:

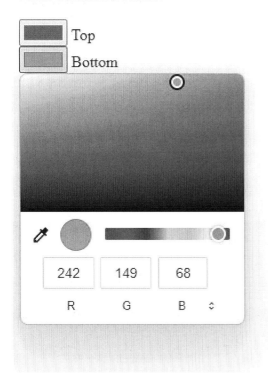

HTML <input type="range">

The range input gives you a slider or dial control to enter numeric values which must be no more than a given value.

```
<input type="range" id="volume" name="volume" min="0" max="20" step="2">
<label for="volume">Volume</label>
```

Audio settings:

 Volume

HTML <input type="tel">

This input type allows the user to enter or edit phone numbers. However, its value is not validated on form submission because the phone formats worldwide vary so much.

```
<label for="phone">Enter your phone number:</label>
```

```
<input type="tel" id="phone" name="phone" pattern="+359 [0-9]{2}-[0-9]{3}-[0-9]{3}"
required>
```

HTML <input type="file">

This HTML element allows user to choose one or more files from their device. Afterward, when the form is submitted the file can be uploaded to the server.

```
<label for="avatar">Choose a profile picture:</label>
<input type="file" id="avatar" name="avatar" accept="image/png, image/jpeg">
```

Choose a profile picture:

Choose File | No file chosen

You can add the `multiple` attribute to mention that you allow the selection of many files. The accept attribute takes a string that represents the unique file type specifiers. For example: `audio/*` (any audio file), `video/*`, `image/*` or specific file types such as `.jpg`, `.pdf`, `.doc`. You need to have this in mind when you test forms that contain file uploads. Check the requirements whether they mention what are the accepted file types and check the HTML.

HTML <textarea>

The text area represents a multi-line text editing control.

```
<label for="cover-letter">Tell us why you want to work for us:</label>
<textarea id="cover-letter" rows="10" cols="33" wrap="hard" spellcheck="true"
maxlength="6000" required>
The following are some Skills and highlights of my qualifications and experience:

- Working experience on Selenium WebDriver using Java for UI testing.
- Working Knowledge of tools like JIRA, Hp ALM, and Hp QC
- Experience in Maven, Jenkins
</textarea>
```

Tell us why you want to work for us:

```
The following are some Skills and highlights of my qualifications and
experience:

- Working experience on Selenium WebDriver using Java for UI testing.
- Working Knowledge of tools like JIRA, Hp ALM, and Hp QC
- Experience in Maven, Jenkins
```

The `cols` and `rows` attributes allow you to specify the control size. You can set the maximum number of characters via the `maxlength` attribute. The browser automatically inserts line breaks when you put the `hard` option for the `wrap` attribute.

HTML <output>

The output HTML element is a result calculation container. `for` attribute contains a space-separated list of the ids of the elements that contribute to the final result.

```
<form oninput="result.value = parseInt(a.value) + parseInt(b.value)">
    <input type="range" id="b" value="20" /> +
    <input type="number" id="a" value="5" /> =
    <output name="result" for="a b">25</output>
  </form>
```

The above form sums the numbers provided by the range and number inputs. The result is displayed automatically in the `<output>` tag. Notice the value of its `for` attribute.

Exercises

1. Write an HTML code for a login form. Do not create any actions. The form should have the appropriate labels, user/email input, password input, remember me checkbox, and buttons for login with social media. You should also add the proper labels and validations. Use the appropriate attributes to hint the user at the valid data that should be entered.

2. Create a new page simulating a registration form. It should require email, password, country (you need to provide a list of countries from a dropdown), zip, city, address, and, optionally phone number. Use the most appropriate HTML tags and add all the attributes you can think of to ease the page's usage and security.

Summary

In the chapter, we learned about the structure of every web page out there. We reviewed many of the essential HTML elements, and their most important attributes and saw them in action.

In the next shorter chapter, we review what the cascading style sheets are and how to use them to apply styles to the web pages.

Chapter 9. CSS Crash Course

In the previous chapter, we discussed the structure of every web page and the HTML elements. In many examples, we reviewed the essential ones and saw them plus their most important attributes. You must understand how they work since half of the job is to analyze the HTML elements when we automate websites.

Another vital component of every web page is CSS. It controls how the web pages look. Moreover, we use it extensively in automated testing to find elements using CSS selectors. The book aims to make you a great test automation QA, not a front-end developer. Thus, we won't spend much time discussing every nitty-gritty detail of styling websites, but it is crucial to understand how it works and how to use the CSS selectors.

Topics covered in this chapter:

- What Are Cascading Style Sheets CSS?
- CSS Syntax
- CSS Selectors
- CSS Colors, Fonts, and Sizes

What Are Cascading Style Sheets CSS?

We already talked a bit about CSS, but now let's investigate it in more detail. I cannot teach you CSS in 10 pages, which is not the book's goal. Instead, it is crucial for you to understand how websites work and to understand CSS as a whole. For automated testing, it is essential to use CSS selectors, mainly not so much knowing the thousands of CSS properties and nitty-gritty details.

CSS stands for Cascading Style Sheets and describes how the HTML is displayed. It can control the look of multiple web pages at once. We store the stylesheets in external CSS files linked to the HTML docs. CSS controls the font, color, spacing between elements, the size of the text, what background colors or images are to be used, how to look varies on various screen sizes, and much more. Probably, you are wondering why it is called "cascading"? A style applied to a parent element will also apply to all children within the parent. For example, if you change the background color of the body to red, all paragraphs, headings, and other text elements within the body will also be displayed in red.

CSS can be added in 3 ways: inline, internal, or external. You already saw all of them in the HTML examples. The inline way is using the `style` attribute. We use it to apply a unique style to a single HTML element:

```
<h1 style="color:red;">This will be displayed Blue</h1>
<p style="color:blue;">This paragraph will be red.</p>
```

The internal CSS is using `<style>` tag inside the `<head>`. This is how we added a border to the HTML table:

```
<html>
<style>
    table,
    th,
    td {
        border: 1px solid black;
    }
</style>
<body>
    <p>Table of countries:</p>
    <table>
        <tr>
            <th>Countries</th>
            <th>Capitals</th>
            <th>Population</th>
            <th>Language</th>
        </tr>
        <tr>
```

```
                <td>Bulgaria</td>
                <td>Sofia</td>
                <td>7 million</td>
                <td>Bulgaria</td>
            </tr>
            <tr>
                <td>Sweden</td>
                <td>Stockholm</td>
                <td>9 million</td>
                <td>Swedish</td>
            </tr>
            <tr>
                <td>Germany</td>
                <td>Berlin</td>
                <td>83 million</td>
                <td>German</td>
            </tr>
        </table>
    </body>
</html>
```

Internal CSS defines a style for a single web page. It can lead to duplication of markup, especially if your website is quite big. This leads to a maintenance problem when you must fix something or update the styles. Therefore, usually, we use the third approach of reusing the CSS by moving it to external files.

The last and most common way is the external one which uses `<link>` element to link to an external CSS file:

```
<link rel="stylesheet" type="text/css" href="styles.css">
```

The CSS files have the `.css` file extension and should contain CSS without HTML or JavaScript. With these external style sheet files, you can change the entire website's look by updating a single file.

CSS Syntax

A CSS rule consists of a selector and a declaration block. The selector locates the HTML element(s) the block will style. The block itself consists of one or more declarations separated by semicolons. Each declaration contains a CSS property and a value, separated by a colon. As stated, you can have multiple CSS declarations. We separate them with semicolons, and curly braces surround the declaration blocks.

<style>

```
p {
    color: blue;
    text-align: left;
}
h1 {
    color: blue;
    font-family: verdana;
    font-size: 300%;
}
```

</style>

CSS Selectors

We use the CSS selectors to specify the HTML element(s) we want to style. There are five categories of selectors - simple selectors (we locate the elements based on class, id, or name), combinator selectors (based on elements' relationship - child, parent, etc.), pseudo-class selectors (based on the elements' state), pseudo-elements selectors (we style only part of the element) and the last group are the attribute selectors (we find the elements based on their attributes). Let's discuss the most important of them.

Element Selectors

Selector	Explanation
ul#myId	<ul> element with @id= 'myId'
#myUniqueId	any element with @id='myId'
ul.myForm	<ul> element with @class = 'myForm'
.myForm.front	any element with @classes = 'myform' and 'front'

Contextual Selectors

Selector	Explanation
ul#myUniqueId > li	direct child element
ul#myUniqueId li	sub child element
div > p	elements that are a direct descendant of a <div> element
div + p	elements that are the next sibling of a <div> element (i.e., placed directly after)
div ~p	elements that follow and are siblings of <div> elements
form myForm.front + ul	next sibling
div.row *	selects all elements that are descendants (or children) of the elements with a div tag and 'row' class

Attribute Selectors

Selector	Explanation

ul[name = "automateName"][style = "style_name"]	\<ul\> element with attributes @name ='automateName' and @style= 'style name'
ul[@id]	elements with @id attribute
ul[id = "myId"]	\<ul\> element with @id='myId'
*[name='N'][value='v']	elements with name N and specified value 'v'
ul[id ^= "my"]	all elements with an attribute beginning with 'my'
ul[id$= "Id"]	all elements with an attribute ending with 'Id'
ul[id *= "unique"]	all elements with an attribute containing the substring 'unique'
ul[id ~= "unique"]	all elements with an attribute containing the word 'unique'
a[href='url']	anchor with target link 'url'

Useful n Values

- **odd or 2n+1** - every odd child or element
- **even or 2n** - every even child or element
- **n** - every nth child or element
- **3n** - every third child or element (3, 6, 9, ...)
- **3n+1** - every third child or element starting with 1 (1, 4, 7, ...)
- **n+6** - all but the first five children or elements (6, 7, 8, ...)
- **-n+5** - only the first five children or elements (1, 2, ..., 5)

Pseudo-class Selectors that Apply to Siblings

Selector	Explanation
ul#myUniqueId li:first-child	first child element
ul#myUniqueId li:nth-of-type(1)	first child element
ul#myUniqueId li:last-child	last child element
ul#myUniqueId li:nth-of-	last child element in case we have 3 elements

type(3)	
#TestTable tr:nth-child(3) td:nth-child(2)	cell by row and column (e.g., 3rd row, 2nd column)
p::first-letter	selects the first letter of the specified 'p'
p::first-line	selects the first line of the specified 'p'
p:first-of-type	selects any <p> that is the first element of its type among its siblings
p:last-of-type	selects any <p> that is the last element of its type among its siblings

Pseudo-class Selectors for Link and User States

Selector	Explanation
input:focus	the <input> element which has the focus
input:read-only	<input> elements with the 'readonly' attribute specified
input:required	<input> elements with the 'required' attribute specified
input:checked	checkbox (or radio button) that is checked
a:contains('Log Out')	anchor with inner text containing 'Log Out'
td:contains('t') ~td	cell immediately following the cell containing 't'
p:lang(language)	all <p> elements with a @lang attribute equal to 'language'
:not(p)	selects any element that is NOT a paragraph
p:not(.fancy)	<p> elements that are not in the class '.fancy'
p:not(.crazy, .fancy)	<p> elements that are not '.crazy' or '.fancy'
div:empty	returns all <div> elements that have no children
:root	selects the root element of the document
input:in-range	selects all elements with a value that is within a specified range
input:out-of-range	select all elements with a value that is outside a specified range

a:visited	all visited links
a:link	all unvisited links
a:hover	all links on the mouse hover
input:active	every active <input> element
input:disabled	every disabled <input> element
input:enabled	every enabled <input> element

CSS Colors, Fonts and Sizes

HTML colors are specified with predefined color names or RGB, HEX, HSL, RGBA, or HSLA values. You can set the background color, text color, and border color.
An RGB color value represents red, green, and blue light sources, while RGBA extends RGB, adding alpha channel or opacity.

```
rgb(red, green, blue)
```

Each parameter (red, green, and blue) defines the intensity of the color with a value between 0 and 255 which means that we have 256 x 256 x 256 = 16777216 possible colors. To display black, set all color parameters to 0, like this: `rgb(0, 0, 0)`. To display white, set all color parameters to 255, like this: `rgb(255, 255, 255)`. `rgb(255, 0, 0)` is red. The alpha parameter is between 0.0 and 1.0 (fully transparent to not transparent).

```
<h1 style="background-color:rgb(255, 0, 0);">rgb(255, 0, 0)</h1>
```

The second way of presenting colors is to use hexadecimal colors. It is specified with #RRGGBB, where the RR (red), GG (green), and BB (blue) hexadecimal integers identify the components of the color.

```
#rrggbb
```

rr (red), gg (green), and bb (blue) are hexadecimal values between 00 and ff (same as decimal 0-255).

- To display black, set all color parameters to 00: `#000000`
- To display white, set all color parameters to ff: `#ffffff`
- To display green, set all color parameters to ff: `#00ff00`

`#ff0000` is shown as red because red is set to its highest value `ff`, and the other two (green and blue) are set to `00`.

```
<h1 style="background-color:#ff0000;">#ff0000</h1>
```

Another essential aspect of the look of every website is the font. In CSS, we often change the font family and size. All the different font names belong to one of the generic font families. There are five generic font families:

- **Serif** fonts have a minor stroke at the edges of each letter
- **Sans-serif** fonts have clean lines
- **Monospace** fonts -all the letters have the same fixed width

- **Cursive** fonts mimic human handwriting
- **Fantasy** fonts are decorative fonts

We use the font-family property to specify the font of a text:

```
h1 {
  font-family: "Times New Roman", Times, serif;
}
h2 {
  font-family: Arial, Helvetica, sans-serif;
}
```

You must understand the CSS box model to visualize your HTML elements correctly and find the correct width and height in all major browsers. To calculate the total size of the HTML element, you must add its padding, borders, and margins. The box model is a "box" that wraps every HTML element and consists of margins, borders, padding, and content.

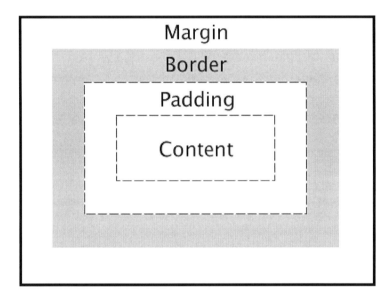

The content of the box, where text and images emerge. The padding is the area around the content, and it is transparent. The border goes around the padding and content. Lastly, the margin is the area outside the border which is also transparent. We use this model to add a border and define space between elements.

```
div {
  width: 150px;
  border: 18px solid blue;
  padding: 30px;
  margin: 10px;
}
```

The <div> element will have a total width of 266px. 150px (width) + 60px (left + right padding)

+ 36px (left + right border) + 20px (left + right margin) = 266px

Total element width = width + left padding + right padding + left border + right border + left margin + right margin

Total element height = height + top padding + bottom padding + top border + bottom border + top margin + bottom margin

The height and width properties may have the following values:

- **auto** - the default one. The browser calculates the height and width
- **length** - defines the height/width in px, cm, etc.
- **%** - defines the height/width in percent of the containing block
- **initial** - sets the height/width to its default value
- **inherit** - the height/width will be inherited from its parent value

```
div {
  height: 100px;
  width: 40%;
  background-color: red;
}
```

Now, let's discuss the CSS units. Many properties take length values, such as width, margin, padding, font-size, etc. A length is a number followed by a length unit, such as 20px, 3em, etc. Whitespace cannot appear between the number and the unit. There are two types of length units absolute and relative.

```
h2 {
 font-size: 30px;
}

div {
 font-size: 15px;
 line-height: 30px;
}
```

The absolute ones are fixed and are expressed in any of these will appear as precisely that size. The absolute length units are not recommended for use on-screen because screen sizes vary so much:

- **cm** - centimeters
- **mm** - millimeters
- **in** - inches (1in = 96px = 2.54cm)
- **px** * - pixels (1px = 1/96th of 1in)

- **pt** - points (1pt = 1/72 of 1in)
- **pc** - picas (1pc = 12 pt)

NOTE

Pixels (px) are relative to the viewing device. For low-dpi devices, 1px is one device pixel (dot) of the display. For printers and high-resolution screens, 1px implies multiple device pixels.

Relative length units establish a length close to another length property. The viewport is the browser window size. Here are all relative length units:

- **vmin** - relative to 1% of viewport's smaller dimension
- **vmax** - relative to 1% of viewport's larger dimension
- **vw** - relative to 1% of the width of the viewport
- **vh** - relative to 1% of the height of the viewport
- **%** - relative to the parent element
- **em** - relative to the font size of the element
- **ex** - relative to the x-height of the current font
- **ch** - relative to the width of the "0" (zero)
- **rem** - relative to font-size of the root element

`3em` means three times the size of the current font. If the viewport is 30cm wide, `1vw` = 0.3cm.

The `!important` rule in CSS is used to add more importance to a property/value than usual. If you set it, it will override all previous styling rules for that specific property on that element! However, it is recommended not to use it because it leads to unmaintainable and hard-to-debug CSS. Furthermore, it might not be obvious which style is considered most important because the only way to override an `!important` rule is to include another `!important` rule on a declaration with the same (or higher) specificity in the source code:

```
#myButton {
  background-color: blue !important;
}

.purchaseButton {
  background-color: gray !important;
}

button {
  background-color: red !important;
```

```
}
```

Before wrapping up, let's review a few examples:

```
.header {
  background-color: #f0f0f0;
  text-align: left;
  padding: 10px;
}
```

In the above example, we are changing the background color, visualizing the text left and adding a 10px padding the website's header which is usually located at the top of the website. Here is one more example but this time we are applying styles to the navigation bar which contains list of links to help visitors to navigate through the website:

```
/* links - change color on hover */
.topnav a:hover {
  background-color: #ddd;
  color: black;
}

/* navbar container */
.topnav {
  overflow: hidden;
  background-color: #222;
}

/* navbar links */
.topnav a {
  float: right;
  display: block;
  color: #f1f1f1;
  text-align: center;
  padding: 15px 18px;
  text-decoration: none;
}
```

Exercises

Create an HTML web page that looks like this:

Rockets Shop

Item Photo	Name	Price
	Falcon 9	$50
	Proton Rocket	$80
	Proton-M	3 for $80
	Saturn V	$120
	Falcon Heavy	NOT AVAILABLE

Summary

In the chapter, we learned how the styling of websites works through the help of CSS. Also, we learned extensively the CSS selectors that we will use later to locate elements that we will use in our automated tests.

In the next chapter, we will learn another core component of every web page that makes it interactable and moving - JavaScript. As you will see in the following chapters, we will often use JavaScript to handle complex automated testing problems where standard libraries don't have utilities.

Chapter 10. JavaScript Crash Course

In the previous chapter, we reviewed how the looks of the web pages are controlled via CSS. We discussed extensively the various CSS selectors that we will later use in the automated testing.

In the chapter, we will learn another core component of every web page that makes it interactable and moving - JavaScript. As you will see in the following chapters, we will often use JavaScript to handle complex automated testing problems where standard libraries don't have utilities. As you can see from the topics to be covered, it is a relatively long chapter, but basically, I will teach you to program on JavaScript. We will cover almost everything we did for C#. However, the tempo will be a bit faster because both C# and JavaScript are similar in many ways.

Topics covered in this chapter:
- Your First JavaScript Code
- HTML Events
- Variables and Data Types
- Operators and Conditions
- Collections and Loops
- Functions
- Objects
- JavaScript Classes
- JSON
- JavaScript HTML DOM
- Modifying HTML Elements
- DOM Navigation
- Browser Object Model BOM
- jQuery

Your First JavaScript Code

ECMAScript is the official name of the language. JavaScript was invented by Brendan Eich in 1995 and became an ECMA standard in 1997. ECMAScript versions have been abbreviated to ES1, ES2, ES3, ES5, and ES6. In addition, since 2016, new versions have been named by year (ECMAScript 2016 / 2017 / 2018). JavaScript is the programming language of the web, and it is the world's most popular programming language. It is used to program the behavior of web pages. It is free to use, and you don't have to get or download anything to use it since it is already running in your browsers.

Like with the CSS and HTML sections, my goal is not to teach you to become a front-end developer. Instead, I want you to understand the basics since we will use some JavaScript scripts later in our C# code, automating web pages via Selenium WebDriver.

Like CSS JavaScript has a special HTML tag where it is put inside <script>. You can create as many of these script section as you want. Usually, we place it inside the head, but it can be in the body too:

```
<script>
document.getElementById("divId").innerHTML = "Automating The Web";
</script>
```

As in C#, we can reuse code via methods in JavaScript. We call them functions. They can be executed when the user performs specific actions on HTML elements. These actions are called events. For example, when the user clicks a button or hovers it. First, we declared a JS function that finds a component by id in the following example. Then, through the property innerHTML we can set the inner HTML of the element to something else. For example, to "hook" the function to the button and trigger it when clicked, we set the onclick event equal to the JS function's name followed by (). onclick is called an HTML event, which the browser will rise once the button is clicked. There are many other events to which you can subscribe:

```
<!DOCTYPE html>
<html>
<head>
<script>
function hackLabel() {
  document.getElementById("label-to-be-updated-id").innerHTML = "You have been hacked!";
}
</script>
</head>
<body>

<h2>Demo JavaScript in Head</h2>
<label id="label-to-be-updated-id">A Paragraph.</label>
<button type="button" onclick="hackLabel()">Hack the Website</button>
</body>
```

```
</html>
```

When you click the "Hack the Website" button the label text will change from "A Paragraph" to "You have been hacked!". This is the text that we set to the inner HTML of the HTML element located by the id = "label-to-be-updated-id" in the JS function `hackLabel()` declared in the `<head>` section. As I shared, we can move the `<script>` section in `<body>` and it will continue to work as before:

```html
<!DOCTYPE html>
<html>
<head>
</head>
<body>
<h2>Demo JavaScript in Head</h2>
<label id="label-to-be-updated-id">A Paragraph.</label>
<button type="button" onclick="hackLabel()">Hack the Website</button>
<script>
function hackLabel() {
  document.getElementById("label-to-be-updated-id").innerHTML = "You have been hacked!";
}
</script>
</body>
</html>
```

The JavaScript code can be distributed and shared across many web pages through external `.js` files like with CSS. In addition, the web pages can be sped up by caching these JS files, among the other benefits such as code reuse and improved maintainability. You already saw such an example when we first discussed the HTML <head> tag:

```html
<script src="https://code.jquery.com/jquery-3.6.0.min.js" integrity="sha256-/xUj+3OJU5yExlq6GSYGSHk7tPXikynS7ogEvDej/m4=" crossorigin="anonymous"></script>
```

This is how the Automate The Planet website uses one of the most popular JavaScript libraries called jQuery. The JQuery and other widely used CSS and JavaScript libraries are distributed via CDN.

Definition: CDN

"A content delivery network (CDN) refers to a geographically distributed group of servers which work together to provide fast delivery of Internet content. A CDN allows for the quick transfer of assets needed for loading Internet content, including HTML pages, JavaScript files, stylesheets, images, and videos. A properly configured CDN may also help protect websites against some common malicious attacks, such as Distributed Denial of Service (DDOS) attacks.",- Cloudflare

---

Before discussing in more detail, the JavaScript syntax, let's first investigate more deeply the HTML events such as `onclick`.

HTML Events

As we saw in the previous sections' examples, HTML can trigger events on user action in a browser, like executing JS code when the user clicks a button. There are seven groups - window, form, keyboard, mouse, drag, clipboard, media, and misc. I will list just a few of the essential ones:

Window Events

Events that are triggered for the window object (`<body>`):

- `onload` - to be run after the page is finished loading
- `onresize` - to be run when the browser window is resized
- `onhashchange` - fires when there have been changes to the anchor part of the URL
- `onerror` - fires when an error occurs
- `onoffline` - fires when the browser starts to work offline
- `ononline` - fires when the browser starts to work online

Form Events

These are events that apply to most HTML elements:
- `onblur` - fires the moment that the element loses focus
- `onchange` - fires the moment when the value of the element is changed
- `oncontextmenu` - to be run when a context menu is triggered
- `onfocus` - to be run the moment when the element gets focus
- `oninput` - fires when an element gets user input
- `oninvalid` - fires when an element is invalid
- `onselect` - to be run after some text has been selected in an element
- `onsubmit` - to be run when a form is submitted

Keyboard Events
- `onkeydown` - to be run when a user is pressing a key
- `onkeypress` - to be run when a user presses a key
- `onkeyup` - to be run when a user releases a key

Mouse Events
- `onclick` - to be run on a mouse click on the element
- `ondblclick` - to be run on a mouse double-click on the element
- `onmouseover` - to be run when the mouse pointer moves over an element

Drag Events
- `ondrag` - to be run when an element is dragged
- `ondrop` - to be run when dragged element is being dropped
- `onscroll` - to be run when an element's scrollbar is being scrolled

Clipboard Events
- `oncopy` - to be run when the user copies the content of an element
- `oncut` - to be run when the user cuts the content of an element
- `onpaste` - to be run when the user pastes some content in an element

Media Events
Lastly, some events triggered by media like audio, video, and images:

- `onpause` - fires when the media is paused either by the user or programmatically
- `onplay` - fires when the media is ready to start playing
- `onplaying` - fires when the media has started playing
- `onprogress` - fires when the browser is in the process of getting the media data
- `onerror` - fires when an error occurs when the file is being loaded

Now when you know some basics, let's discuss the JS syntax in more detail. You already know how to program in C#, so everything should sound quite familiar. In some ways, it is much easier compared to C#.
We won't go into so many details as C# since it is not our primary goal to become JS programmers. Thus, I will go a bit faster.

Variables and Data Types

First, let's talk about variables and constants. You can declare them via 3 keywords `var`, `let`, and `const`. Nowadays, we use mainly `const` and `let`.

> **NOTE**
>
> The `var` keyword was used in all JavaScript code from 1995 to 2015, while the `let` and `const` keywords were introduced to JavaScript in 2015.

Like in C#, we use variables to store data that can be later updated:

```
let a = 8;
let b = 7;
let result = x + y;
```

We declare them via the `let` keyword. Later, you can update them if the variables are in the same scope:

```
a = 9;
b = 10;
window.alert(a + b);
```

You can use an alert box to display the result. If you want, you can skip the window keyword. Or, if you want to debug your code, you can use `console.log(a + b)` method in the browser to output the result. It will be displayed in the **Console Window**.

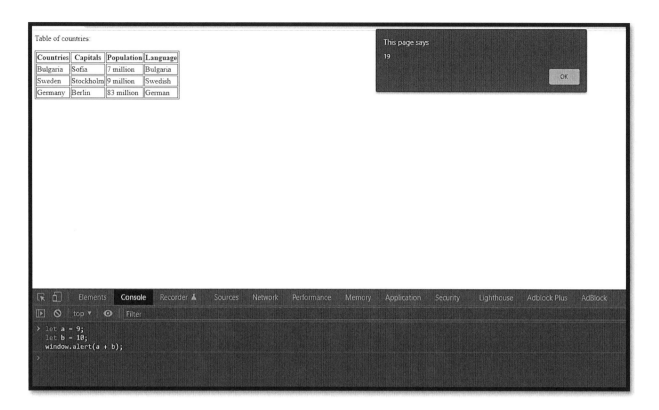

Similar to C#, you can use the const keyword to declare variables whose values cannot be changed.

```
const a = 7;
const b = 8;
let result = a + b;
```

NOTE

Please notice that in JS, we don't mention the data type. Probably you already saw the body of the previous JS function that it didn't contain any data types either.

All variables and functions should have unique names called identifiers. As with other OOP languages, it is better to use more descriptive names rather than a and b, which I use for readiness. I believe the rules for constructing the unique identifiers are more or less similar to those for C#, so you are good when you follow them.

var vs let

A few notes about the `var` keyword. As I said, it is advisable to use `let` instead. The `var` variables can be re-declared, leading to mistakes and buggy code. Also, once declared, they can be used anywhere and are not limited to the current scope.

```
var phoneProducer = "Samsung";
var phoneProducer = "Apple";
This won't work if you use let:
let phoneProducer = "Samsung";
let phoneProducer = "Apple";
```

Variables declared inside a { } block can be accessed only inside it:

```
{
  let a = 3;
}
// a can NOT be used here
```

If you use var, you can:

```
{
  var a = 3;
}
// a CAN be used here
```

If we don't assign a value when declaring the variables, their value will be equal to undefined:

```
let phoneProducer;
window.alert(phoneProducer);
```

Strings

Strings in JavaScript can be declared using double quotes or single quotes. This is useful when you need to use such quotes inside the string itself instead of escaping it:

```
let firstName = "My first name is  'Anton'";
let lastName = 'My last name is "Angelov"';
```

The string templates or string interpolation works similarly as in C#. It can help you to create complex strings using JS variables:

```
let firstName = "Anton";
let lastName = "Angelov";
let welcomeMessage = `Greetings ${firstName}, ${lastName}!`;
alert(welcomeMessage);
```

We start the string interpolation via ` and if you want to use JS variable or expression, you need to wrap it in ${ }.

NOTE

There is a lot else to be said about the work with strings like escape characters, string methods, string search, etc. I encourage you to search online if you need to work more with them. For automated testing using OOP languages like C# or Java, the info presented in this chapter should be sufficient.

Dates

JS uses the browser's time zone and displays dates as full-text string:

```
const currentDate = new Date(); // Fri Feb 04 2022 12:07:04 GMT+0200 (European Standard Time)
```

Like in C#, you have various constructors accepting a variable number of parameters to initialize the dates:

```
const d = new Date(2022, 11, 24);
console.log(d.toDateString()); // 'Sat Dec 24 2022'
console.log(d.toUTCString()); // Fri, 23 Dec 2022 22:00:00 GMT
```

In the example, we accept year, month, and day. We can get the UTC date and more readable string via the toDateString() method.

NOTE

JavaScript stores all dates as milliseconds' count since January 01, 1970, 00:00:00 UTC (Universal Time Coordinated). The start/zero time is January 01, 1970 00:00:00 UTC.

Type Conversion

You can convert strings to numbers via the Number() global function:

```
Number("5.19")    // returns 5.19
Number("")     // returns 0
Number("$")     // returns NaN (non a number)
Number("9 885")     // returns NaN.
```

Instead of Number you can use parseInt() or parseFloat() functions.

```
parseInt("15.66"); // 15
parseInt("17 6"); // 17
parseInt("-19.34"); // -19
parseFloat("15.66");  // 15.66
```

Vice versa to convert decimals to toPrecision() and toFixed(). The first returns a string with a number written with a specific length while `toFixed()` will round the results:

```
let x = 13.276;
x.toPrecision(2); // '13'
x.toPrecision(4); // '13.28'
x.toPrecision(6); // '13.2760'
x.toFixed(2); // '13.28'
x.toFixed(4); // '13.2760'
x.toFixed(6); // '13.276000'
```

To return a number as a `string`, you can use `valueOf()` function:

```
(999).valueOf(); // '999'
(257 + 23).valueOf(); // '280'
```

Exercises

1. Write JS code asking for your name and printing it.
2. Write JS code that prints the numbers 2, 202 and 2002.
3. Write JS code that prints the current date and time.
4. Write JS code that calculates and prints the square of the number 32346.
5. Declare two integer variables and assign them with 5 and 10 and after that exchange their values.

Operators and Conditions

All arithmetic rules for C# apply in JavaScript too:

```
let result = 10 + 5 + 3 - 2;
```

While the following we concatenate the strings:

```
let result = "Automate" + " The " + "Planet";
```

If you put a number in quotes, the rest of the numbers will be treated as strings, resulting in a concatenated string.

```
let x = "9" + 1 + 1;
```

You have the same assignment operators =, +=, -=, *=, /=, %= and **=. Only the ** operator is new to you. It means exponentiation:

```
2 ** 4 // 16
2 ** 3 // 8
3 ** 2.5 // 46.76537180435969
20 ** -1 // 0.5
```

And as for the rest, they are working the same way as in C#:

```
let a = 15;
a += 6; // 21
```

It is the same as:

```
a = a + 6;
```

Something else important that you need to remember JavaScript types are dynamic which means that the same variable can be used to hold different data types:

```
let a; // undefined
a = 9; // now it is an integer
a = "Anton"; // now it is a string
```

Comparison Operators

- ==   equal to
- ===   equal value and equal type
- !=   not equal
- !==   not equal value or not equal type
- >   greater than
- <   less than
- >=   greater than or equal to

- • <= less than or equal to
- • ? ternary operator

Logical Operators
- • && logical and
- • || logical or
- • ! logical not

Maybe the most confusing part is with the `===` and `==` and their counterparts `!=` and `!==`. The next few examples will make things clearer. Let's quickly review the conditional statements in JavaScript. Like in C#, we have - `if`, `else`, `else if` and `switch`. The way we use them is pretty much the same except the formatting that follows more Java-like syntax putting the opening bracket on the same line as the statement:

```
if (time < 9) {
  alert("Good morning");
} else if (time < 19) {
  alert("Good day");
} else {
  alert("Good evening");
}
```

Or we can use `switch` statement to select one of many code blocks to be executed based on `switch` expression evaluation:

```
switch (new Date().getDay()) {
  case 1:
  alert("Monday");
    break;
  case 2:
   alert("Tuesday");
    break;
  case 3:
  alert("Wednesday");
    break;
  case 4:
  alert("Thursday");
    break;
  case 5:
  alert("Friday");
    break;
  case 6:
   alert("Saturday");
  case 7:
   alert("Sunday");
    break;
  default:
   alert("Not a day of the week!");
}
```

The execution breaks out of the `switch` block when we reach a break keyword. The `default` keyword specifies the code to run if there is no case match. Switch cases use **strict** comparison `===`. **The values must be of the same type to match.** There won't be a match for the day variable in the following example since it is not an integer:

```
let day = "2";
switch (day) {
  case 1:
  alert("Monday");
    break;
  case 2:
   alert("Tuesday");
    break;
}
```

Then what do we use `==`? It is called a non-strict comparison, and JavaScript will ignore if the variable is a string. For example, x `==` "5" returns `true` while x `===` "5" returns false. The is valid for the non-equal operators: 6 `!=` 8 returns `true` while 6 `!=` "6" is `false` but 6 `!==` "6" returns `true`.

Like in C# in JavaScript, we have a short syntax for if-else statements called ternary.

```
let tempInCelsius = 21;
tempInCelsius < 20.0 ? alert("Cold.") : alert("Perfect!");
```

This is the same as:

```
if (tempInCelsius < 20.0) {
  alert("Cold.");
} else {
  alert("Perfect!");
}
```

Let's review a few examples if we compare different types. If we compare numbers with strings, JS will convert the strings to numbers when making the comparison. An empty string will result in 0. A non-numeric will be converted to NaN (not a number), which always leads to false.

```
5 < 15 // true
5 < "15" // true
9 < "Anton" //false
9 > "Anton" // false
9 == "Anton" // false
"9" < "15" // false
"9" > "15" // true
"9" == "15" // false
```

When comparing two strings, "5" will be greater than "15" because (alphabetically) 2 is less than 3. It is suggested to convert the variables to the proper data type before comparison:

```
age = Number(age);
```

```
if (isNaN(age)) {
  alert("the input is not a number!")
} else {
    age < 21 ? alert("too young to vote") : alert("old enough to vote");
}
```

Exercises

1. Write an expression that checks if given integer is odd or even.
2. Write an expression that calculates rectangle's area by given width and height.
3. Write an expression that checks if given positive integer number n (n ≤ 100) is prime. E.g. 37 is prime.
4. Write an expression that calculates trapezoid's area by given sides a and b and height h.
5. Write an IF statement that examines two integer variables and exchanges their values if the first one is greater than the second one.
6. Write a program that shows the sign of the product of three real numbers without calculating it. Use a sequence of if statements.

Collections and Loops

Working with arrays in JavaScript is easy:

```
const cities = ["Sofia", "Berlin", "London"];
```

NOTE

The keyword const is misleading because it does NOT define a constant array but rather defines a constant reference to it. Because of this, we can still change the elements of a constant array.

Two access the elements like in C#, we use the index operator []:

```
console.log(cities[1]); // prints Berlin
cities[1] = "Paris";
console.log(cities[1]); // prints Paris
```

The following code also create an array, but it is suggested to use the shorter version:

```
const cities = new Array("Sofia", "Berlin", "London");
```

The arrays provide some built-in methods and properties:

```
cities.length; // returns the number of elements
cities.sort(); // sorts the array
```

To go through all the array's items, we can use a for loop:

```
for (let i = 0; i < cities.length; i++) {
    console.log(cities[i]);
}
```

Another type of for look called **for...of**. It goes through the values of an iterable object such as arrays, strings, maps (dictionaries), etc.

```
for (city of cities) {
  console.log(city);
}
```

Or you can print each character of a string:

```
for (city of cities) {
    for (c of city) {
        console.log(c);
    }
}
```

```
> const cities = ["Sofia", "Berlin", "London"];
< undefined
> for (city of cities) {
      for (c of city) {
          console.log(c);
      }
  }
  S
  o
  f
  i
  a
  B
  e
  r
  l
  i
  n
  L
  o
  n
  d
  o
  n
```

Like in other popular programming languages, we have while and do-while loops. They follow the same rules as in C#:

```
let i = 0;
while (i < cities.length) {
    console.log(cities[i++]);
}
// or
let i = 0;
do {
  console.log(cities[i++]);
} while (i < cities.length);
```

If you want to break the loop prematurely, you can use the break operator.
You can also use the Array.forEach() function:

```
cities.forEach(console.log);
```

You can use the push function to add new items to the array. The JavaScript arrays act as C# lists:

```
cities.push("Rome");
```

The pop() function removes the last item from an array:

```
console.log(cities.pop()); // returns Rome
```

The shift() function removes the first array item and moves all other elements to a lower index:

```
let firstCity = cities.shift(); // assigns Sofia
```

While the unshift() function adds a new element at the beginning:

```
cities.unshift("Sofia");
```

You can also use the delete operator but be careful because it leaves undefined holes. It is suggested to use shift instead:

```
delete cities[0];
```

You can merge two arrays using the concat() function:

```
const asianCitities = ["Mumbai", "Tokyo", "Bangkok"];
const allCities = cities.concat(asianCitities);
```

To undo, you can use the slice() function, which will return a new array:

```
const europeanCities = allCities.slice(1, 3);
```

You can use the filter() function to create a new array with values that pass a specific predicate:

```
var filteredCities = cities.filter(c => c.startsWith("S")); // returns Sofia
```

Instead of passing a function, we pass an anonymous one using C# like lambda expression.

```
function filterArrayByFirstLetterEqualToS(value) {
  return value.startsWith("S");
}
cities.filter(filterArrayByFirstLetterEqualToS); // returns Sofia
```

You can get an items index using the indexOf() function.

```
let position = cities.indexOf("Sofia");
```

The lastIndexOf() is the same as indexOf() but returns the position of the last occurrence of the specified item.

I prepared a short comparison between C# and JavaScript array methods to ease your learning:

ForEach (C#) vs forEach (JS)

```
// C#
var numbers = new int[] {5, 6, 7, 8, 9};
numbers.ToList().ForEach(n => Console.WriteLine(n));

// JavaScript
const numbers = [5, 6, 7, 8, 9];
numbers.forEach(n => console.log(n));
```

Where (C#) vs filter (JS)

```
// C#
var numbers = new int[] {5, 6, 7, 8, 9};
var evenNumbers = numbers.ToList().Where(n => n % 2 == 0);

// JavaScript
const numbers = [5, 6, 7, 8, 9];
const evenNumbers = numbers.filter(n => n % 2 == 0); // return [6, 8]
```

Aggregate (C#) vs reduce (JS)

```
// C#
var numbers = new int[] {5, 6, 7, 8, 9};
var sumTotal = numbers.Aggregate(0, (total, currentItem)=> total + currentItem);
// returns 35

// JavaScript
const numbers = [5, 6, 7, 8, 9];
const sumTotal = numbers.reduce((accumulator, currentValue) => accumulator + currentValue,
0); // returns 35
```

OrderBy (C#) vs sort (JS)

```
// C#
var numbers = new int[] {5, 6, 7, 8, 9};
var numberSorted = listOfNumbers.OrderBy(p=> p);

// JavaScript
const numbers = [5, 6, 7, 8, 9];
numbers.sort();
```

Append (C#) vs push (JS)

```
// C#
var numbers = new int[] {5, 6, 7, 8, 9};
numbers.Append(10);

// JavaScript
const numbers = [5, 6, 7, 8, 9];
numbers.push(10);
```

FirstOrDefault (C#) vs find (JS)

```
// C#
var numbers = new int[] {5, 6, 7, 8, 9};
numbers.FirstOrDefault(n=> n == 8);
```

```
// JavaScript
const numbers = [5, 6, 7, 8, 9];
numbers.find(n=> n==8);
```

Any (C#) vs includes (JS)

Returns true or false whether the collection contains the specified item.

```
// C#
var numbers = new int[] {5, 6, 7, 8, 9};
numbers.Any(n=> n == 8); // true
```

```
// JavaScript
const numbers = [5, 6, 7, 8, 9];
numbers.includes(n=> n==8); // true
```

Reverse (C#) vs reverse (JS)

```
// C#
var numbers = new int[] {5, 6, 7, 8, 9};
numbers .Reverse();
```

```
// JavaScript
const numbers = [5, 6, 7, 8, 9];
numbers.reverse();
```

NOTE

This is not a complete reference for all array methods. Also, please check the documentation whether the functions are affecting the array or are returning a new one.

Now, let's investigate how to work with JavaScript functions.

Exercises

1. Write JS code that prints all the numbers from 1 to 30.
2. Write JS code that prints all the numbers from 1 to 30, that are not divisible by 3 and 7 simultaneously.
3. Write JS code that allocates an array of 20 integers and initializes each element by its index multiplied by 5. Print the obtained array on the console.

Functions

We already saw a function. As methods in C#, we use functions in JS to reuse code blocks. Once defined, later you can call it to perform some action like calculation.

```
function add(n1, n2) {
  return n1 + n2;
}
```

The function returns the sum of n1 and n2. To define a function, we use the `function` keyword, and afterward, we put the **name** followed by **parentheses** `()`. The name can contain letters, digits, underscores, and `$` sign. Commas separate the parameters. Please note that we don't specify a function return type nor a data type for parameters. Like C#, we return the result via the `return` keyword. The method parameters can be used inside the function as regular variables. To invoke the function, we use its name followed by `()` and pass the parameters separated by commas inside the `()`:

```
let result = add(5, 6); // result = 11;
```

You can define the same function using an expression:

```
const add = function (n1, n2) {return n1 + n2};
```

After the declaration, the `add` variable can be used as a function:

```
let result = add(5, 6); // result = 11;
```

This is called an anonymous function, as in a function without a name. You can declare the same thing using the arrow function (lambda expression):

```
const add = (n1, n2) => n1 + n2;
```

You may also need to use self-invoking functions in automated testing. These functions start automatically after being declared without being called:

```
(function () {
    alert("Automate The Planet!!");
})();
```

Interestingly, JS won't check whether you passed the correct number of parameters. Instead, if there is a number mismatch, the missing values will be passed as undefined. Also, it won't check the data type. As in C#, you can assign default values:

```
function add(n1 = 1, n2 = 2) {
  return n1 + n2;
}
```

> **NOTE**
>
> The arguments (what you pass to the function when you call it) are passed by value like in C#. This means that if you change them inside the function, their parameter's original value won't change. In the next section, we will talk about objects similar to C#. The objects are passed by reference, changing the originally passed variable since we give the function a pointer (reference) to its place in the memory.

Variables' Scope

The variables declared within a function are local to it and cannot be called outside of it - this is called the **Function** scope.

```
// code here can NOT use result
function add(a, b) {
  let result = a = b;
  // code here CAN use result
}
// code here can NOT use result
```

Variables with the same name can be used in other functions. These variables are created once the function starts and deleted on completion.

```
let result;
// code here can use result
function add(a, b) {
  result = a = b;
 // code here can also use result
}
```

A global variable is a variable declared outside a function. It can be used and changed in all functions; therefore, it has a **Global** scope. If you assign a value to a variable that has not been declared, it will automatically become a **Global** variable.

```
add(5, 6);
function add(a, b) {
  result = a = b;
}
```

JS Errors Try-Catch

Like other popular programming languages, you can catch errors (in JS we don't call them exceptions but "errors") via `try-catch` statements. The `finally` and `throw` keywords do the same thing as in C#. The returned error object has the `name` and `message` properties. Six different errors can be returned:

- **EvalError** - an error has appeared in the `eval()` function
- **RangeError** - a number "out of range" has appeared
- **ReferenceError** - an illegal reference has appeared
- **SyntaxError** - a syntax error has appeared
- **TypeError** - a type error has appeared
- **URIError** - an error in `encodeURI()` has appeared

Here is an example:

```
try {
   eval("alert('Automate The Planet)"); // Missing ' will produce an error
}
catch(err) {
   alert(err.name)
}
```

Exercises

1. Write a method `getMax()` with two parameters that returns the bigger of two integers.

Objects

In JavaScript almost everything, more or less, is an object. Therefore, it is essential to understand how to work with them. Moreover, there is always a global object. For example, when we declare global variables or functions outside of an object or class, they are part of this global object. In a web browser, the global object is the `window`.

```
var city = "Sofia";
city === window.city; // returns: true
```

Anyhow, you are allowed to skip the "`window`" part. The same is valid for the functions we looked at in the previous sections.

```
// add is part of the window global object
function add(n1, n2) {
    return n1 + n2;
}

window.add(5, 6);

// it is the same as:
add(5, 6);
```

In JavaScript, the primitive types are objects too. They can be declared with the `new` keyword:

```
let a = new Number(6);
```

NOTE

For performance optimizations and code readiness, it is suggested not to use `new` for primitive types but instead, use the literals.

Every variable is an object and can have many values:

```
let person = "Anton Angelov";
person = 5;
```

You can think of the JS objects as anonymous C# classes. You are declaring and initializing an instance at the same time:

```
const country = {name:"Germany", capital:"Berlin", gdp:3.806, population:83.2};
```

The object is a collection of key-value pairs. Like C# dictionary. With `name` : `value` syntax separated by a colon, we define the objects' properties. In the example, we have the object country with a `name`, `capital`, `gdp`, and `population` properties. It is common to declare them using the `const` keyword. This one statement declaration-creation process is called **object literal**. It is okay to use the following format too:

```
const country = {
  name:"Germany",
  capital:"Berlin",
  gdp:3.806,
  population:83.2
};
```

It is possible to add additional properties after the creation of the object. First, we create an empty object and afterward we add the same properties as before:

```
const country = {};
country.name:"Germany";
country.capital = "Berlin";
country.gdp = 3.806;
country.population = 83.2;
```

You can achieve the same using the `new Object()`:

```
const country = new Object();
country.name:"Germany";
country.capital = "Berlin";
country.gdp = 3.806;
country.population = 83.2;

console.log("Germany population: " + country.population); // we use the properties as in C#
```

Also, objects can have methods. An object method is an object property containing a function definition. Via the keyword `this`, you can access the current object and its variables. If you use this outside of an object, it will refer to the current global object.

```
const country = {
name:"Germany",
capital:"Berlin",
gdp:3.806, // trillion
population:83.2, // million
gdpPerCapita: function() {
    return (this.gdp * 1000000000000) / (this.population * 1000000);
  }
};
```

To call the `gdpPerCapita` method, we invoke it as a normal function but through the country object instance:

```
console.log(country.gdpPerCapita());
```

We could add it after the creation of the object:

```
const country = {};
country.name:"Germany";
country.capital = "Berlin";
```

```
country.gdp = 3.806;
country.population = 83.2;
country.gdpPerCapita = function() {
    return (this.gdp * 1000000000000) / (this.population * 1000000);
};
```

As stated before, the JS objects behave like C# dictionaries. This you can access the properties using the index `[]` operator providing the name of the property as a string:

```
console.log("Germany population: " + country["population"]);
// is same as
console.log("Germany population: " + country.population);
```

You can loop through the properties of an object via for...in statement.

```
for (let i in country) {
    console.log(country[i]);
}
```

Maps

We mentioned C# dictionaries a few times already. But does JS have something similar? Yes, it does, and it this type of collection is called `map`. We used it pretty much in a similar way:

```
const countries = new Map([
 ["Germany", 3.806],
 ["France", 2.603],
 ["United Kingdom", 2.708],
 ["Italy", 1.886],
]);
```

You can add elements to a map via the `set()` method:

```
countries.set("Spain", 1.281);
```

To return a value from the map we use the `get()` method and provide the key:

```
countries.get("France"); // return 2.603
```

You can use `has()` method to check whether a key exists in the dictionary or not:

```
countries.has("Portugal"); // return false
```

The following line deletes the entry:

```
countries.delete("United Kingdom");
```

To list all entries, you can use the `forEach` function:

```
countries.forEach (function(value, key) {
    console.log(`${key}'s GDP is ${value}`);
});
// the same as:
```

```
for (const c of countries.entries()) {
    console.log(`${c[0]}'s GDP is ${c[1]}`);
}
```

> **NOTE**
>
> You can read more about the Set collection that stores unique values as homework.

JavaScript Classes

After you know how to use objects, the next step is to reuse their declarations using classes. We use the keyword `class` to define a new class as in C#. However, in JS, to define a constructor, we don't use the name of the class, but we name this method - `constructor()`.

```javascript
class Country {
  constructor(name, capital, gdp, population) {
     this.name = name;
     this.capital = capital;
     this.gdp= gdp;
     this.population= population;
  }

  gdpPerCapita() {
    return (this.gdp * 1000000000000) / (this.population * 1000000);
  };
}
```

You need to initialize the properties inside the constructor, and you don't need to do anything else. As you can see in the example, I declared a class method. It follows all of the rules for JS functions except that we don't use the function keyword in front of the name.

To create a new class instance, we initialize it like in C# using the `new` keyword.

```javascript
let germany = new Country("Germany", "Berlin", 3.806, 83.2);
let bulgaria = new Country("Bulgaria", "Sofia", 0.069, 6.927);
console.log(germany.name); // this is how use properties
germany.gdpPerCapita(); // this is how we call methods
```

Inheritance

If you want to inherit the implementation code, you can inherit it from another class.

```javascript
class Rectangle {
    constructor(width, height) {
        this._width = width;
        this._height = height;
    }

    get area() {
        return this._height * this._width;
    }

    get width() {
        return this._width;
    }

    set width(x) {
        this._width = x;
```

```
    }

    get height() {
        return this._height;
    }

    set height(x) {
        this._height = x;
    }

    #somePrivateMethod() {
        console.log('You called me?');
    }
}
```

Like in Java, in JavaScript, we don't have such a thing as property, but instead, we have two separate methods called getters and setters. We prefix them with the keywords `get` and `set`. The difference between getters/setters and regular methods is that like C# properties, we call them without `()`, and their main purpose is to retrieve and initialize private fields. Also, notice the `#somePrivateMethod` method. It starts with the `#` symbol, this way, we mark it as private for the class. Here is how we use the getters and setters:

```
var rectangle = new Rectangle(5, 8);
rectangle.width = 10;
console.log(rectangle.width);
console.log(rectangle.height);
console.log(rectangle.area);
```

To distinguish the getters/setters from regular properties, adding the prefix "_" to the properties' names is OK.
Let's review how to reuse the code now with inheritance. Like in the OOP C# examples, we will create a child class called Square that will make the width and height equal to each other when initialized:

```
class Square extends Rectangle {
    constructor(width, height) {
        super(width, height);
        this.width = width;
        this.height = height;
    }

    get width() {
        return super.width;
    }

    get height() {
        return super.height;
    }
```

```
    set width(x) {
        super.width = x;
        super.height = x;
    }

    set height(x) {
        super.width = x;
        super.height = x;
    }
}
```

In the example, the Square class derives from the Rectangle class, e.g., it is reusing its code - the constructor, the properties, getters, and setters. To change the base implementation of a method or property, we define one with the same name. You can access base class getters and setters using the super keyword instead of this. This helps us to customize the behavior of the child classes. To properly initialize the base class data, you need to call the base class constructor and pass the required arguments via the super method inside the child class constructor.

Static Methods

It is possible to define static methods in JS too. Just add the static keyword in front of the method name.

```
class Country {
  constructor(name, capital, gdp, population) {
    this.name = name;
    this.capital = capital;
    this.gdp = gdp;
    this.population = population;
  }

  gdpPerCapita() {
    return (this.gdp * 1000000000000) / (this.population * 1000000);
  };

  static calculateGdpPerCapita(gdpInTrillions, populationInMillions) {
    return (gdp * 1000000000000) / (population * 1000000);
  };
}
```

To use it, we don't use the classes instances but the name of the class. gain the same as other popular OOP programming languages:

```
let result = Country.calculateGdpPerCapita(1.2, 45);
```

Exercises

1. You are asked to model an application for storing data about people. You should be able to have a person and a child. The child is derived of the person. The only constraints are:
   - People should not be able to have negative age
   - Children should not be able to have age more than 15
   - Person - represents the base class by which all others are implemented
   - Define a constructor that accepts name and age
2. You are working in a library. The task is simple - your program should have two classes - one for the ordinary books - `Book`, and another for the special ones - `GoldenEditionBook`.
   - `Book` - represents a book that holds title, author, and price. A book should offer information about itself in the format shown in the output below.
   - `GoldenEditionBook` - represents a special book holds the same properties as any Book, but its price is always 30% higher.
   - If the author's second name is starting with a digit - exception's message is: "*Author not valid!*"
   - If the title's length is less than 3 symbols - exception's message is: "*Title not valid!*"
   - If the price is zero or it is negative - exception's message is: "*Price not valid!*"
   - Price must be formatted to one symbol after the decimal separator

JSON

JavaScript Object Notation, called JSON for short, is the standard nowadays for exchanging data via the web. It is often used to send data from the server to a web page. JSON is a text-only format. Therefore, it is programming language independent. This is why in .NET, we use it extensively too. It is self-describing and easy to use-understand, and I guess this was the reason to displace XML as the primary data-transfer format. XML was the primary format for exchanging data in SOAP web services. At the same time, JSON is the primary data protocol used in REST web services.

Definition: SOAP

SOAP is the Simple Object Access Protocol, an XML-based protocol for accessing web services over HTTP. SOAP was developed as an intermediate language so that applications built on various programming languages could talk easily to each other.

Definition: REST

A REST API or RESTful API is an application programming interface API that follows the constraints of the REST architectural style and allows work with RESTful web services. Computer scientist Roy Fielding created it. The API favors stateless, client-server communication. The communication is managed through HTTP. In addition, some client-server interactions are eliminated via cacheable data. Finally, there is a uniform interface between components to transfer information in a standardized form instead of specific to an application's needs.

We have already learned about objects. You remember how we declare them. The JSON syntax is derived from JavaScript object notation syntax, but the JSON format is text only:

```
{
"countries":[
  {"name":"Germany", "capital":"Berlin"},
  {"name":"France", "capital":"Paris"},
  {"name":"Spain", "capital":"Madrid"}
 ]
}
```

The format is syntactically identical to the code for creating `country` JS objects. The data is represented via name-value pairs and separated by commas. We use curly braces { } to wrap objects and square brackets [ ] to mark arrays. All key-value pairs are separated by a colon : and are surrounded by double quotes "":

```
"name":"France"
```

We often use JSON to send data from the server to the website. We can represent the JSON as a JS string.

```
let textResponse = '{
"countries":[
  {"name":"Germany", "capital":"Berlin"},
  {"name":"France", "capital":"Paris"},
  {"name":"Spain", "capital":"Madrid"}
  ]
}';
```

We can convert this JSON string representation to JavaScript object via the JSON.parse() function:

```
const countries = JSON.parse(textResponse);
```

Vice versa, if you have the following JS object, you can convert it to JSON via JSON.stringify():

```
const country = {
  name:"Germany",
  capital:"Berlin",
  gdp:3.806,
  population:83.2
};
const germanyJSON = JSON.stringify(country);
// results in: '{"name":"Germany","capital":"Berlin","gdp":3.806,"population":83.2}'
```

Let's quickly review the JSON data types. As we discussed we can have arrays:

```
{
    "countries":["Bulgaria", "Germany", "France"]
}
```

Double quotes should not surround booleans:

```
{"eu-member":true}
```

Values can be null:

```
{"alternative-name":null}
```

Numbers are also directly used:

```
{"gdp":3.806}
```

JavaScript HTML DOM

When a web page loads, the browser creates page DOM (document object model). It is a tree structure of objects. In the case of HTML, all objects are HTML elements. It defines the properties of all HTML elements and gives us methods and events to access/work with them.

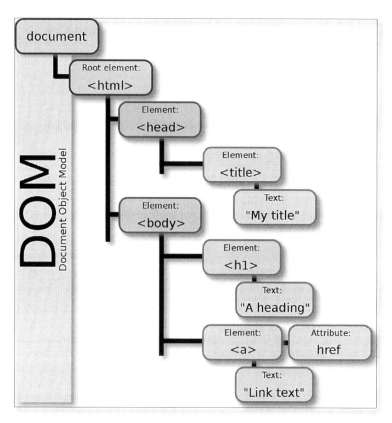

JavaScript can manipulate all HTML elements part of the DOM. For example, it can update its attributes, modify all CSS styles, add/remove HTML elements and attributes, create new HTML events or react on existing ones.

A DOM property is a value that you can get or set, for example, innerHTML, which changes the content of the <p> tag:

```html
<html>
<body>
    <p id="paragraphId"></p>
    <script>
        document.getElementById("paragraphId").innerHTML = "Automate The Planet!";
    </script>
</body>
</html>
```

In the above example, `getElementById()` is DOM element that finds an element by its `id`. You can use the `innerHTML` property to change the content of any web element. One more thing, in the example, we used the object document. The web page is represented as this document object. If you want to find elements in an HTML web page, we always start with the `document` object. Let's review some other methods that the `document` object provides us.

You can find elements by tag name or class name - `document.getElementsByTagName(name)` or `document.getElementsByClassName(name)`. `querySelectorAll()` searches elements by CSS selector. You have the same methods but in plural `getElementsByTagName()` that returns multiple elements. These methods return an `HTMLCollection` object which is an array-like list of the found HTML elements. If we have the following HTML:

```
<label for="myText">Placeholders</label>
<input id="myText" name="myText" type="Text" placeholder="your Text term goes here" class="myTestClass">
<input id="myText2" type="Text" size="30" minlength="10" maxlength="80">
<input id="myText4" type="Text" autocomplete="on">
```

You can use the following code to change the HTML elements:

```
document.getElementById("myText4").autocomplete = "off";
```

The code changes the `autocomplete` attribute, you can update any attribute like this or alternatively you can use `setAttribute()` method:

```
document.getElementById("myText4").setAttribute('autocomplete','off');
```

You can also change any CSS property via the `style` property:

```
document.getElementById("myText4").style.backgroundColor = ' #FDFF47';
```

As we reviewed before you can add event handlers via JavaScript:

```
<!DOCTYPE html>
<html>
<body>
    <h2>Demo JavaScript in Head</h2>
    <label id="label-to-be-updated-id">A Paragraph.</label>
    <button id="buttonId" type="button">Hack the Website</button>
    <script>
        document.getElementById("buttonId").onclick = function() {
        document.getElementById("label-to-be-updated-id").innerHTML = "You have been
hacked!";
        }
    </script>
</body>
</html>
```

You can use the `addEventListener()` method to attach an event handler to an element. It is different from the previous example since it won't overwrite the existing event handlers. You can add many event handlers to the same element using this method. Thus, when you click, all of them will be executed. Additionally, you can add event listeners to any DOM object, not only HTML elements, for example, the `window` object.

```
document.getElementById("buttonId").addEventListener("click", function() {
document.getElementById("label-to-be-updated-id").innerHTML = "You have been hacked!";});
```

NOTE

Please note that we don't use the "on" prefix as we do if we define the event through the HTML elements!

You can of course pass already defined functions too:

```
document.getElementById("buttonId").addEventListener("click", hackLabel);
function hackLabel() {
    document.getElementById("label-to-be-updated-id").innerHTML = "You have been hacked!";
}
```

In the following code we change the content of the `<p>` element when the window is resized:

```
window.addEventListener("resize", function(){
  document.getElementById("label-to-be-updated-id").innerHTML = "AUTOMATE THE PLANET";
});
```

You can use the `removeEventListener()` method to remove an event handler.

Modifying HTML Elements

Let's see some examples for adding new elements to HTML DOM. First, we create the new element via the `createElement()` method and then use the `appendChild()` to append it to an existing HTML component. Below, you can find a code that we will use to add debug capabilities to our automated tests in a later chapter:

```
var jqueryScript = document.createElement('script');
jqueryScript.type = 'text/javascript';
jqueryScript.src = 'https://cdnjs.cloudflare.com/ajax/libs/jquery/3.6.0/jquery.min.js';
document.getElementsByTagName('head')[0].appendChild(jqueryScript);
```

First, we create a new `<script>` element, we initialize some of its attributes. Afterward, we find the current head tag of the HTML docs via `document.getElementsByTagName('head')[0]` then we append the script to the head using the `appendChild()` method.
The `appendChild()` method appends the element as the last one of the parent. You can also use `element.insertBefore(parent ,child)`. If you need to delete an element, you can do so via the `remove()` method.

```
document.getElementByTagName("h1").remove();
```

You have also the methods `removeChild()` and `replaceChild()` that are also used to update HTML elements.

DOM Navigation

As we discussed at the beginning of the section, the HTML document is represented as a tree of objects (HTML nodes/elements). The top node is called root. Every node has a parent except the root. Every node can have children and siblings (the nodes on the same level, brothers and sisters sharing the same parent):

```
<html>
  <head>
    <title>DOM Navigation Explained</title>
  </head>
  <body>
    <h1>Automated Testing Fundamentals & Beyond</h1>
    <p>C# Edition!</p>
  </body>
</html>
```

Let's review the HTML nodes relations of this sample HTML doc:

- `<html>` is the root node
- `<html>` has no parents
- `<html>` is the parent of `<head>` and `<body>`
- `<head>` is the first child of `<html>`
- `<body>` is the last child of `<html>`
- `<head>` has one child `<title>`
- `<title>` has one child (a text node): "DOM Navigation Explained"
- `<body>` has two children: `<h1>` and `<p>`
- `<h1>` has one child: "Automated Testing Fundamentals & Beyond"
- `<p>` has one child: "C# Edition!"
- `<h1>` and `<p>` are siblings

JavaScript HTML DOM API gives us the following properties to navigate between the nodes:

- `parentNode`
- `childNodes[INDEX]`
- `firstChild`
- `lastChild`
- `nextSibling`
- `previousSibling`

```
document.getElementById("id").firstChild.nodeValue;
document.getElementById("id").childNodes[0].nodeValue;
```

You can retrieve the name of an element via the `nodeName` property:

```
<h1 id="id1">Automated Testing Fundamentals & Beyond</h1>
<p id="id2"></p>
console.log(document.getElementById("id1").nodeName); // returns h1
```

The node name is the same as the tag name and it is `readonly`. You have a similar property for retrieving the value called `nodeValue`. For text nodes in returns their inner text for the rest their `value` attribute.

Browser Object Model BOM

BOM stands for **Browser Object Model**. There isn't an official standard for it compared to DOM. Anyhow all modern browser supports it. They allow you to use the `window` object. As we mentioned previously, all globally declared objects, functions, and properties are members of the `window` object - even the `document` object is its property.

Let's review some of the major properties and methods this object provides. You can open a new window via the `window.open()` method, or you can close the current one via the `window.close()` or resize it - `window.resizeTo()`. You can get the current window's size (the browser window is also known as viewport) via the properties `innerWidth` and `innerHeight`, but keep in mind that they don't include the toolbars and scrollbars.

```
console.log(window.innerWidth);
console.log(window.innerHeight);
```

Additionally, via the window's property called `screen`, you can obtain even more info about the user's screen. Except for `colorDepth` the rest return results in pixels:

- `screen.width`
- `screen.height`
- `screen.availWidth`
- `screen.availHeight`
- `screen.colorDepth`
- `screen.pixelDepth`

`window.location` exposes other properties related to the current URL like `href`, `hostname` (domain name of the web host), `protocol` (http/https), `pathname` (path/filename of the current page), or `port` (like 80 or 443). `assign` can load a new page:

```
window.location.assign("https://www.automatetheplanet.com/blog/");
```

Via the `window.history` property, you can access the current's browser history, you have the `back()` and `forward()` method at your disposal.

Sometimes it is helpful to find more information about the user's browser. In this case, you can use the `window.navigator` property. Let's review what it provides us:

```
console.log("Are cookies enabled: " + navigator.cookieEnabled);
```

`navigator.appName` returns the name of the browser. It is not so helpful since it returns " *Netscape*" for IE11, Chrome, Firefox, and Safari.

NOTE

This is part of the reason browser detection is a bad practice and should be avoided. To change the behavior of a web page based on the browser, in rare cases, we can use the `userAgent`. Or the suggested approach is to use a strategy called "feature detecting". Lastly, when I checked the MDN Web Docs the property was even marked as deprecated.

Via `navigator.product` you can get the name of the browser engine but keep in mind that most browsers return "Gecko". `navigator.appVersion` returns the current browser's version while userAgent returns the user-agent header sent to the server. A few other properties are available, but I will leave it to you to find more info about them.

Lastly, the `window.cookie` object gives you an easy way to work with cookies. They are stored in small text files on your computer. Here is a quick way to create one:

```
document.cookie = "username=Anton Angelov";
```

By default, the cookies are deleted when you close the browser, but you can also set an expiry date:

```
document.cookie = "username=Anton Angelov; expires=Thu, 23 Nov 2011 12:00:00 UTC";
```

This is how you read a cookie:

```
let c = document.cookie;
```

You update a cookie the same way you created it:

```
document.cookie = "username=Anton Angelov; expires=Thu, 01 Nov 2015 18:00:00 UTC; path=/";
```

The old cookie is overwritten. To delete a cookie, you need to set its value to empty and set it to expire in the past:

```
document.cookie = "username=; expires=Thu, 01 Nov 2015 18:00:00 UTC; path=/";
```

NOTE

We will review further the rest of the JS Web APIs in the chapter "*Modern Web Application Testing.*"

Before finishing the chapter, let's quickly discuss jQuery, one of the most used JS libraries.

jQuery

John Resig created jQuery in 2006 to simplify HTML DOM manipulation, ajax, event handling, and other operations. For a decade, it was the most popular JS library globally. In 2009 JS Version 5 appeared, and most of jQuery's utilities could be solved with a few of vanilla JS (another term referring to regular JavaScript). Anyhow, jQuery is still heavily used, so we must examine it.

To use jQuery, you need to reference it in the head section of your web page. We usually include it from a CDN (content delivery network):

```
<script src="https://code.jquery.com/jquery-3.6.0.min.js" integrity="sha256-
/xUj+30JU5yExlq6GSYGSHk7tPXikynS7ogEvDej/m4=" crossorigin="anonymous"></script>
```

Let's first compare how we find elements with vanilla JS and compare it to jQuery selector alternatives:

```
var button = document.getElementById("buttonId"); // JS
var button = $("#buttonId"); // jQuery
```

Here is how we find elements by tag name:

```
var button = document.getElementsByTagName("button"); // JS
var button = $("button"); // jQuery
```

By class name:

```
var button = document.getElementsByClassName("login"); // JS
var button = $(".login"); // jQuery
```

And finally, by using CSS selectors:

```
var elements = document.querySelectorAll("div.intro"); // JS
var elements = $("div.intro"); // jQuery
```

We can agree that the jQuery ones are much shorter than their vanilla JS counterparts. So let's review some of the jQuery DOM and HTML element utilities.

Delete HTML element:

```
document.getElementById("button").remove(); // JS
$("#button").remove(); // jQuery
```

Get parent element:

```
var buttonParent = document.getElementById("button").parentNode.nodeName;
var buttonParent = $("#button").parent.prop("nodeName"); // jQuery
```

Set the inner text of elements:

```
textInput.textContent = "Automate The Planet"; // JS
textInput.text("Automate The Planet"); // jQuery
```

To get the inner text, we use the `text()` method:

```
var inputText = document.getElementById("inputId").textContent; // JS
var inputText = $("#inputId").text(); // jQuery
```

To get the value of an HTML element, you can use `val()`:

```
var inputValue = document.getElementById("inputId").value; // JS
var inputValue = $("#inputId").val(); // jQuery
```

If you want to access arbitrary attributes using jQuery, you can use the `attr()` method;

```
let loginUrl = $("#loginLink").attr("href"));
```

Set the HTML of an element:

```
div.innerHTML = "<p>Automate The Planet</p>"; // JS
div.html("<p>Automate The Planet</p>"); // jQuery
```

To get the HTML of an element, we use the `html()` method:

```
var content= document.getElementById("inputId").innerHTML; // JS
var content = $("#inputId").html(); // jQuery
```

To hide an HTML in JS, we set the display CSS property to "none" while in jQuery, we have the method `hide()`:

```
button.hide(); // jQuery
button.style.display = "none"; // JS
```

To show the button again, we use the `show()` method:

```
button.show(); // jQuery
button.style.display = ""; // JS
```

To set CSS properties in JS, we use the `style` object, while in jQuery, we need to use the method `css()`:

```
$("#button").css("background-color", "#FFFF00"); // jQuery
document.getElementById("button").style.background-color
= "#FFFF00"; // JS
```

jQuery Events

It is a good practice to wait for the document to be loaded entirely and then perform any JS operations. Thus, jQuery has a shortcut syntax:

```
$(document).ready(function(){
  // jQuery code goes here...
```

```
});
```

Or we can make it even shorter:

```
$(function(){
  // jQuery code goes here...
});
```

We already discussed JS events that help us execute logic when actions happen on HTML elements. jQuery eases the work with events, especially when assigning events' code to multiple elements. For example, here is a code for setting the click event on all the `divs` on a web page:

```
$("div").click(function(){
    $(this).text("Automate The Planet");
});
```

Via `$(this)`, we refer to the current clicked element.

```
$("div").dblclick(function(){
      $(this).hide();
});
```

When we double-click one of the `div` elements on the page in the above code, we hide it. Here are more examples where instead of passing the anonymous function, we use the arrow function syntax:

```
$("div").mouseenter(() => { $(this).hide(); });
$("div").mouseleave(() => { $(this).hide(); });
$("div").mousedown(() => { $(this).hide(); });
$("div").mouseup(() => { $(this).hide(); });
$("div").hover(() => { $(this).hide(); });
$("div").focus(() => { $(this).hide(); });
$("div").blur(() => { $(this).hide(); });
```

Or you can attach multiple event handlers to a `div` using the `on()` method:

```
$("div").on({
 mouseenter: function(){
    $(this).css("background-color", "blue");
  },
 mouseleave: function(){
    $(this).css("background-color", "red");
  },
  click: function(){
   $(this).css("background-color", "pink");
  }
});
```

NOTE

jQuery offers a rich set of methods for traversing the DOM tree. I will leave it to you to read more about them as homework.

Summary

In this chapter, we learned everything one automation QA should know about JavaScript, especially if it is not their primary programming language. Anyhow, it is essential to understand how it works and use it. It will be a tremendous help to us on many occasions, later, working on hard-to-automate otherwise test cases.

In the next chapter, we will learn everything you need to know about unit testing frameworks and tools that we will use later to write various types of automated tests.

Chapter 11. Unit Testing Fundamentals

In the following chapter, we will learn an essential tool that will later allow us to write complex UI tests - unit testing. Of course, I will not focus too much on component testing, mocking objects, etc., that backend developers should do to unit test their code. Instead, we will examine two popular unit testing frameworks in the .NET world and discuss how to use them for end-to-end testing. It is essential to understand them since libraries such as WebDriver for web automation and Appium for mobile testing don't provide any built-in assertions, test runners, or integrations in the IDEs. This is by design because it is expected to use them with a unit testing framework.

Topics covered in this chapter:

- Unit Testing Frameworks
- MSTest Unit Testing Framework
- Unit Testing Examples
- NUnit Unit Testing Framework
- Running Tests and Test Results

Unit Testing Frameworks

Doing tests and regression testing completely manually, repeating the same actions, is error-prone and time-consuming. These problems are mitigated by tooling. Unit testing frameworks assist developers in writing tests more quickly with a set of known APIs, run those tests automatically, and review the results easily. Unit tests are written as code using libraries from the unit testing framework. Then the tests are run from a separate unit testing tool or inside the IDE, and the results are analyzed. In short, you've been missing a framework for writing, running, and analyzing unit tests and their results. Unit testing frameworks are code libraries and modules that help developers unit-test their code. [Aut 14]

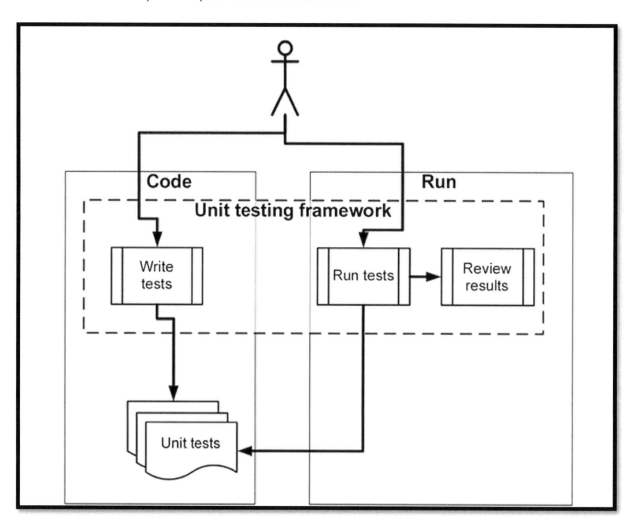

```
[TestClass]
public class GetTotalCost_Should
{
    [TestMethod]
    public void ReturnsUnchangedProductCost_When_RateIsZero()
    {
        var vatCalculator = new VatCalculator();

        double actualValue = vatCalculator.GetTotalCost(105, 0);

        Assert.AreEqual(105, actualValue, "The Total Cost was not as expected.");
    }
}
```

The unit testing frameworks give us attributes such as `[TestClass]` to specify tests and add other metadata. It also comes with tons of verification methods - `Assert.AreEqual()`. All major unit testing frameworks are fully integrated into the primary IDE tools so that you can review your tests, run, debug, and view their results directly in the IDE.

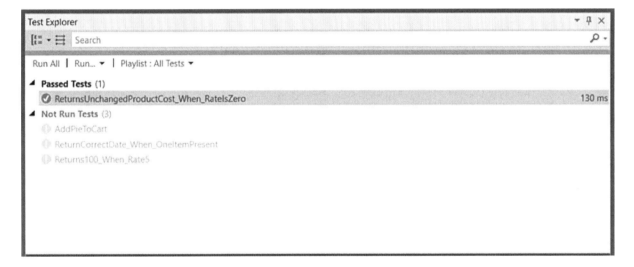

Also, as we will review at the end of the chapter, we can use CLI commands to filter and run tests thanks to these frameworks.

As we discussed, our primary goal is not to write unit testing, so we will just quickly go over the main features of the three primary unit testing frameworks in .NET. First, we will begin with MSTest.

NOTE

There are whole books about unit testing. If you want to dig deeper, I recommend reading *"The Art of Unit Testing with Examples in C#, Second Edition"* by Roy Osherove and *"Refactoring: Improving the Design of Existing Code"* by Martin Fowler.

MSTest Unit Testing Framework

MSTest stands for Microsoft Test Framework, which is now version 2. Version two made the framework open-sourced, and now it supports the latest .NET and thus, it is cross-platform. The easiest way to create an MSTest test project is using Visual Studio Wizard to create new projects. Just search for MSTest unit testing.

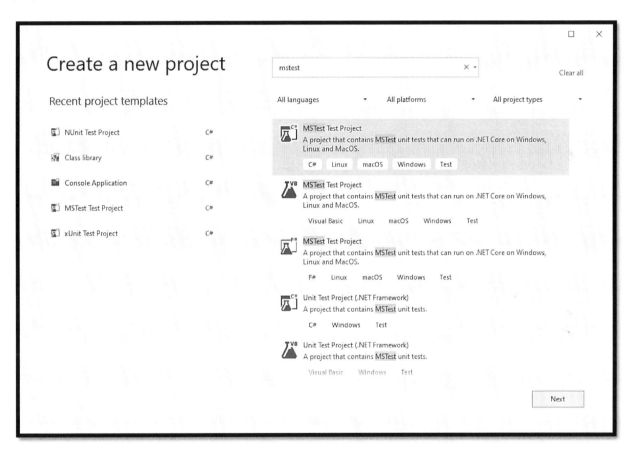

MSTest is delivered through a NuGet package: `MSTest.TestFramework`. However, if you need to create your project manually, you will need a few more NuGet packages to make it work. Two packages are required: `Microsoft.NET.Test.Sdk` and `MSTest.TestAdapter`. You can install them in a couple of ways. The easiest way is to use the **Visual Studio NuGet window** that you can open by right-clicking on your project and clicking on **Manage NuGet Packages**.

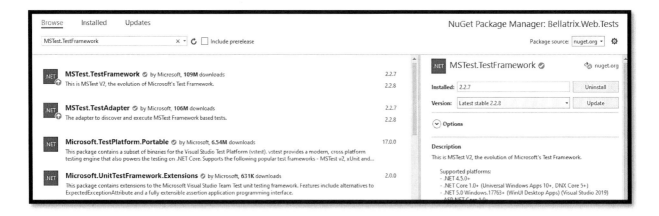

Or you can use the console:

```
Install-Package MSTest.TestFramework
Install-Package MSTest.TestAdapter
Install-Package Microsoft.NET.Test.Sdk
```

VSTest would call the test adapters based on your project configuration to discover or execute test cases. That is why NUnit/xUnit.net/MSTest all ask you to install a test adapter NuGet package to your unit testing projects). So MSTest.TestAdapter exists for that purpose.

MSTest.TestFramework itself implements the testing frameworks and their contracts. So you need to add a NuGet reference to it to write unit test cases and compile them. Only compiled projects along with the test adapter can then be consumed by Visual Studio.

MSTest Attributes

If we return to our example again.

```
[TestClass]
public class GetTotalCost_Should
{
    [TestMethod]
    public void ReturnsUnchangedProductCost_When_RateIsZero()
    {
        var vatCalculator = new VatCalculator();

        double actualValue = vatCalculator.GetTotalCost(105, 0);

        Assert.AreEqual(105, actualValue, "The Total Cost was not as expected.");
    }
}
```

The code is annotated using MSTest attributes. `[TestClass]` denotes a class holding unit tests.

[TestMethod] denotes a unit testing method. We can execute logic in various places of the test execution workflow. As you will see we will use this feature quite often in automated tests. So, let's review the text execution workflow.

```
[TestClass]
public class YourUnitTests
{
    [AssemblyInitialize]
    public static void AssemblyInit(TestContext context)
    {
        // Executes once before the test run. (Optional)
    }

    [ClassInitialize]
    public static void TestFixtureSetup(TestContext context)
    {
        // Executes once for the test class. (Optional)
    }

    [TestInitialize]
    public void Setup()
    {
        // Runs before each test. (Optional)
    }

    // Mark that this is a unit test method. (Required)
    [TestMethod]
    public void YourFirstTest()
    {
        // Your test code goes here.
    }

    [TestMethod]
    public void YourSecondTest()
    {
        // Your test code goes here.
    }

    [TestCleanup]
    public void TearDown()
    {
        // Runs after each test. (Optional)
    }

    [ClassCleanup]
    public static void TestFixtureTearDown()
    {
        // Runs once after all tests in this class are executed. (Optional)
        // Not guaranteed that it executes instantly after all tests from the class.
    }

    [AssemblyCleanup]
    public static void AssemblyCleanup()
```

```
    {
        // Executes once after the test run. (Optional)
    }
}
```

The methods are executed in the following order:

```
AssemblyInitialize (once per assembly)
    ClassInitialize (once per test class class)
        TestInitialize (before each test of the class)
            Test1
        TestCleanup (after each test of the class)
        TestInitialize
            Test2
        TestCleanup
...
    ClassCleanup (once per test class)
    ClassInitialize
...
    ClassCleanup
AssemblyCleanup (once per assembly)
```

You can define `AssemblyInitialize` and `AssemblyCleanup` only once per project and note that these methods are static. Also, `ClassInitialize` and `ClassCleanup` methods are marked as static, making the reuse through base test classes impossible. This is why I prefer the NUnit test framework because it solves this problem.

MSTest Assertions

Assertion is a predicate placed in a program code checking for some condition. We can safely say that assertions are making the test method a "real" test. Here we verify specifics of our code or applications.

```
Assert.AreEqual(42, actualValue, "This is not the answer of everything!");
```

We follow the so-called AAA pattern in most coded tests, which stands for Arrange Act Assert. We separate these three phases through white lines to make our tests more readable.

```
[TestMethod]
public void TestDeposit()
{
    BankAccount account = new BankAccount();
    account.Deposit(100.0);

    account.Deposit(25.0);

    Assert.AreEqual(125.0, account.Balance);
}
```

During the arrange phase, we set up the data for our test and perform the test case's arranges. Then we perform the actual actions we want to verify in the third assertion phase. Usually, in dev tests, the best practice is to have only one assert call per test, but in end-to-end/system-tests/UI tests, it is usually OK to have more since these tests take longer to execute, and we do this for optimization purposes. Of course, we should avoid one test being too long and cover more than one test case or requirement.

Now let's review the many assertion methods that come with MSTest test framework. It provides three big groups - regular assertions, string assertions and collection assertions.

Regular Assertions

```
Assert.AreEqual(28, _actualFuel);
```

Tests whether the specified values are equal.

```
Assert.AreNotEqual(28, _actualFuel);
```

Tests whether the specified values are unequal. Same as AreEqual for numeric values.

```
Assert.AreSame(_expectedRocket, _actualRocket);
```

Tests whether the specified objects both refer to the same object

```
Assert.AreNotSame(_expectedRocket, _actualRocket);
```

Tests whether the specified objects refer to different objects

```
Assert.IsTrue(_isThereEnoughFuel);
```

Tests whether the specified condition is true

```
Assert.IsFalse(_isThereEnoughFuel);
```

Tests whether the specified condition is false

```
Assert.IsNull(_actualRocket);
```

Tests whether the specified object is null

```
Assert.IsNotNull(_actualRocket);
```

Tests whether the specified object is non-null

```
Assert.IsInstanceOfType(_actualRocket, typeof(Falcon9Rocket));
```

Tests whether the specified object is an instance of the expected type

```
Assert.IsNotInstanceOfType(_actualRocket, typeof(Falcon9Rocket));
```

Tests whether the specified object is not an instance of type

```
Assert.ThrowsException<ArgumentNullException>(() => new Regex(null));
```

Tests whether the code specified by delegate throws exact given exception of type T

String Assertions

```
StringAssert.Contains(_expectedBellatrixTitle, "Bellatrix");
```

Tests whether the specified string contains the specified substring

```
StringAssert.StartsWith(_expectedBellatrixTitle, "Bellatrix");
```

Tests whether the specified string begins with the specified substring

```
StringAssert.Matches("(281)388-0388", @"(?d{3})?-? *d{3}-? *-?d{4}");
```

Tests whether the specified string matches a regular expression

```
StringAssert.DoesNotMatch("281)388-0388", @"(?d{3})?-? *d{3}-? *-?d{4}");
```

Tests whether the specified string does not match a regular expression

Collection Assertions

```
CollectionAssert.AreEqual(_expectedRockets, _actualRockets);
```

Tests whether the specified collections have the same elements in the same order and quantity.

```
CollectionAssert.AreNotEqual(_expectedRockets, _actualRockets);
```

Tests whether the specified collections does not have the same elements or the elements are in a different order and quantity.

```
CollectionAssert.AreEquivalent(_expectedRockets, _actualRockets);
```

Tests whether two collections contain the same elements.

```
CollectionAssert.AreNotEquivalent(_expectedRockets, _actualRockets);
```

Tests whether two collections contain different elements.

```
CollectionAssert.AllItemsAreInstancesOfType(_expectedRockets, _actualRockets);
```

Tests whether all elements in the specified collection are instances of the expected type

```
CollectionAssert.AllItemsAreNotNull(_expectedRockets);
```

Tests whether all items in the specified collection are non-null

```
CollectionAssert.AllItemsAreUnique(_expectedRockets);
```

Tests whether all items in the specified collection are unique

```
CollectionAssert.Contains(_actualRockets, falcon9);
```

Tests whether the specified collection contains the specified element

```
CollectionAssert.DoesNotContain(_actualRockets, falcon9);
```

Tests whether the specified collection does not contain the specified element

```
CollectionAssert.IsSubsetOf(_expectedRockets, _actualRockets);
```

Tests whether one collection is a subset of another collection

```
CollectionAssert.IsNotSubsetOf(_expectedRockets, _actualRockets);
```

Tests whether one collection is not a subset of another collection

Data Driven Tests

As a test automation engineer, you may avoid copy-pasting code. The idea is to create parameterized tests which means the test methods have parameters to parametrize the test. This way, one test method can be used to run N tests. MSTest v2 provides 3 ways to create parametrized tests.

The first one is to denote the test with the [DataTestMethod] instead of [TestMethod] and add [DataRow] attributes that hold each test case's data.

```
[DataRow(0, 0)]
[DataRow(1, 1)]
[DataRow(2, 1)]
[DataRow(80, 23416728348467685)]
[DataTestMethod]
public void GivenDataFibonacciReturnsResultsOk(int number, int result)
{
    var fib = new Fib();
    var actual = fib.Fibonacci(number);
    Assert.AreEqual(result, actual);
}
```

MSTest will generate one test per [DataRow] attribute passing the attribute's data to the test method's parameters.

The second way is to provide the data through a CSV file using the [DataSource] attribute. We can later access the data through the special class TestContext and its DataRow collection, where we need to provide the name of the column we want to access. Keep in mind that you need to convert the data yourself, which is inconvenient.

```
[DataSource("Microsoft.VisualStudio.TestTools.DataSource.CSV", "TestsData.csv",
"TestsData#csv", DataAccessMethod.Sequential)]
[TestMethod]
public void DataDrivenTest()
{
    int valueA = Convert.ToInt32(this.TestContext.DataRow["valueA"]);
    int valueB = Convert.ToInt32(this.TestContext.DataRow["valueB"]);
    int expected = Convert.ToInt32(this.TestContext.DataRow["expectedResult"]);
```

}

The third option is to use the `[DynamicData]` attribute that uses a special factory data method inside the test class. We need again to mark the method through the `[DataTestMethod]` attribute. The factory method should return each row of data through `yield return`.

```
[DataTestMethod]
[DynamicData(nameof(GetData), DynamicDataSourceType.Method)]
public void TestAddDynamicDataMethod(int a, int b, int expected)
{
    var actual = _calculator.Add(a, b);
    Assert.AreEqual(expected, actual);
}

public static IEnumerable<object[]> GetData()
{
    yield return new object[] { 1, 1, 2 };
    yield return new object[] { 12, 30, 42 };
    yield return new object[] { 14, 1, 15 };
}
```

> **NOTE**
>
> "The `yield` keyword signals to the compiler that the method in which it appears is an iterator block. The compiler generates a class to implement the behavior expressed in the iterator block. In the iterator block, the `yield` keyword is used with the `return` keyword to provide a value to the enumerator object. This is the value that is returned, for example, in each loop of a `foreach` statement. The `yield` keyword is also used with a `break` to signal the end of the iteration.", - MSDN

Execute Tests in Parallel

We will later in the chapter review how to execute the tests from CLI, but let's review what settings we need to execute the tests in parallel. Once in your project, you need to use the following attribute:

```
[assembly: Parallelize(Workers = 0, Scope = ExecutionScope.MethodLevel)]
```

Workers- the number of threads to run the tests. Set it to 0 to use the number of cores of your computer.
Scope- determine if the runner must parallelize tests at the method or class level. `MethodLevel` runs all tests in parallel. `ClassLevel` runs all test classes in parallel, but tests in a class are executed sequentially. You should use `ClassLevel` if the tests within classes have interdependencies.

If you have multiple test assemblies you want to parallelize, you can create a file named **.runsettings** at the root of the solution:

```xml
<?xml version="1.0" encoding="utf-8"?>
<RunSettings>
 <MSTest>
 <Parallelize>
 <Workers>8</Workers>
 <Scope>MethodLevel</Scope>
 </Parallelize>
 </MSTest>
</RunSettings>
```

Exercises

1. Write three classes: Student, Course, and School
   a. Students should have a name and a unique number (inside the entire School)
   b. Name cannot be empty; the unique number is between 10000 and 99999.
   c. Each course contains a set of students.
   d. Students in a course should be less than 30 and can join and leave courses.
2. Create an MSTest test project and create tests for the classes that created in Exercise 1.
   a. Use 2 class library projects in Visual Studio: `School.csproj` and `School.Tests.csproj`

Unit Testing Example

Before we proceed, let's see a full unit testing example. I found an awesome programming chrestomathy website called Rosetta Code. The chrestomathy website aims to present solutions to the same task in as many different languages as possible to demonstrate how languages are similar and different. So, the next code solution is got from there. Based on the algorithms I found - Shunting-yard and Reverse Polish Notation I created a C# calculator capable of calculating complex nested expressions with 5 operators - "^", "*", "/", "+", "-". The first algorithm parses/converts expressions such as "3 + 4 * 2 / (1 - 5) ^ 2 ^ 3" to reverse polish notation "3 4 2 * 1 5 - 2 3 ^ ^ / +" then using the RPN algorithm we perform the operations to find the final result. It is not important to understand how these algorithms work. I use the code to demonstrate how we can unit test such code. Again, in the simplest way possible.

Code Under Test

Here is the calculator's code. First, the Shunting-yard algorithm:

```
public static class ShuntingYard
{
    private static readonly Dictionary<string, (string symbol, int precedence, bool
rightAssociative)> operators
        = new (string symbol, int precedence, bool rightAssociative)[] {
        ("^", 4, true),
        ("*", 3, false),
        ("/", 3, false),
        ("+", 2, false),
        ("-", 2, false)
    }.ToDictionary(op => op.symbol);

    public static string ToPostfix(this string infix)
    {
        string[] tokens = infix.Split(' ');
        var stack = new Stack<string>();
        var output = new List<string>();
        foreach (string token in tokens)
        {
            if (int.TryParse(token, out _))
            {
                output.Add(token);
                Print(token);
            }
            else if (operators.TryGetValue(token, out var op1))
            {
                while (stack.Count > 0 && operators.TryGetValue(stack.Peek(), out var op2))
                {
                    int c = op1.precedence.CompareTo(op2.precedence);
```

```
                        if (c < 0 || !op1.rightAssociative && c <= 0)
                        {
                            output.Add(stack.Pop());
                        }
                        else
                        {
                            break;
                        }
                    }
                    stack.Push(token);
                    Print(token);
                }
                else if (token == "(")
                {
                    stack.Push(token);
                    Print(token);
                }
                else if (token == ")")
                {
                    string top = "";
                    while (stack.Count > 0 && (top = stack.Pop()) != "(")
                    {
                        output.Add(top);
                    }
                    if (top != "(")
                    {
                        throw new ArgumentException("No matching left parenthesis.");
                    }

                    Print(token);
                }
            }
            while (stack.Count > 0)
            {
                var top = stack.Pop();
                if (!operators.ContainsKey(top))
                {
                    throw new ArgumentException("No matching right parenthesis.");
                }

                output.Add(top);
            }
            Print("pop");
            return string.Join(" ", output);

            void Print(string action)
            {
                Console.WriteLine("{0,-4} {1,-18} {2}", action + ":", $"stack[ {string.Join(" ",
stack.Reverse())} ]", $"out[ {string.Join(" ", output)} ]");
            }
        }
    }
}
```

Here is the Reverse Polish Notation evaluator's code:

```csharp
public class RPNEvaluator
{
    public static decimal CalculateRPN(string rpn)
    {
        string[] rpnTokens = rpn.Split(' ');
        Stack<decimal> stack = new Stack<decimal>();
        decimal number = decimal.Zero;

        foreach (string token in rpnTokens)
        {
            if (decimal.TryParse(token, out number))
            {
                stack.Push(number);
            }
            else
            {
                switch (token)
                {
                    case "^":
                    case "pow":
                        {
                            number = stack.Pop();
                            stack.Push((decimal)Math.Pow((double)stack.Pop(),
(double)number));
                            break;
                        }
                    case "ln":
                        {
                            stack.Push((decimal)Math.Log((double)stack.Pop(), Math.E));
                            break;
                        }
                    case "sqrt":
                        {
                            stack.Push((decimal)Math.Sqrt((double)stack.Pop()));
                            break;
                        }
                    case "*":
                        {
                            stack.Push(stack.Pop() * stack.Pop());
                            break;
                        }
                    case "/":
                        {
                            number = stack.Pop();
                            stack.Push(stack.Pop() / number);
                            break;
                        }
                    case "+":
                        {
                            stack.Push(stack.Pop() + stack.Pop());
                            break;
                        }
                    case "-":
                        {
```

```
                    number = stack.Pop();
                    stack.Push(stack.Pop() - number);
                    break;
                }
            default:
                Console.WriteLine("Error in CalculateRPN(string) Method!");
                break;
            }
        }
        PrintState(stack);
    }

    return stack.Pop();
}

static void PrintState(Stack<decimal> stack)
{
    decimal[] arr = stack.ToArray();

    for (int i = arr.Length - 1; i >= 0; i--)
    {
        Console.Write("{0,-8:F3}", arr[i]);
    }

    Console.WriteLine();
}
}
```

The final class that utilizes both to calculate the result:

```
public class Calculator
{
    public decimal Calculate(string expression)
    {
        return RPNEvaluator.CalculateRPN(expression.ToPostfix());
    }
}
```

Naming Projects and Tests Conventions

Usually, the classes that we unit test are placed inside separate library projects, and we have separate unit test projects for each of these library projects:

1. Create a new unit testing project named: **[ProjectUnderTest].UnitTests**
2. Create a new folder for each class that you will unit test: **[ClassName]Tests**
3. Create separate classes for each class method under test: **[MethodName]_Should/_ShouldNot**
4. Name the tests using the following convention: **[DesiredResultOrOutcome]_When_[Conditions]**

Let's dig a bit deeper into automated test naming. Here is a convention we follow in Automate The Planet:

1. The first part of the Test name must contain the expected result of the test case *(for example, OrderDeleted in the test case OrderDeleted_When_ClickDeleteButton).*
2. The beginning of the test must be in the past tense *(OrderDeleted instead of DeletingOrder, or WillDeleteOrder).*
3. All parts of the test name should be separated with underscores *(for example OrderDeleted_When_ClickDeleteButton, or OrderNotDeleted_When_TryToDeleteOrder_And_DeletionReasonNotSet).*
4. Test actions should be separated by an underscore and "And" *(OrderDeleted_When_**ClickDeleteButton_And_ConfirmDeletion**).*
5. The test name's end should be in the present tense, starting with the action you are performing *(for example ClickButton, NavigateToPage, ConfirmDialog, DeleteRow).*
6. The test name's end should start with "Try" when the test case verifies a negative scenario *(for example, OrderNotDeleted_When_DeleteOrder_And_DeletionReasonNotSet).*

Test case design example questions:

1. What is the name of the feature that you are testing?

Invoice

2. In what conditions are you placing your feature under test?

There are existing orders attached.

3. What operation of the system are you verifying?

Deletion

4. What Action should the system perform in one word.

Deny

5. Is there a specific input parameter of the test case?

No

DeletionOfInvoiceDenied_*When*_ThereAreExistingOrdersAttached

1. What is the name of the feature that you are testing?

   Components

2. In what conditions are you placing your feature under test?

   Filter by component ID

3. What operation of the system are you verifying?

   Filtration

4. What is the Action that the system should perform in one word?

   List

5. Is there a specific input parameter of the test case?

   ID

FilteredComponentsListed_When_FilterByComponentId

1. What is the name of the feature that you are testing?

   Invoice

2. In what conditions are you placing your feature under test?

   Filter by invoice number

3. What operation of the system are you verifying?

   Filtration

4. What is the Action that the system should perform in one word?

   List

5. Is there a specific input parameter of the test case?

   Invoice Number

Invoice Type

FilteredInvoicesListed_When_FilterByInvoiceNumber_And_InvoiceType

1. What is the name of the feature that you are testing?

   Filter inputs

2. In what conditions are you placing your feature under test?

   Navigate to the Invoices Page

3. What operation of the system are you verifying?

   Filters Rendering

4. What is the Action that the system should perform in one word?

   Show

5. Is there a specific input parameter of the test case?

   No

AllFilterInputsShown_When_NavigateToInvoicesPage

1. What is the name of the feature that you are testing?

   Client Address Page Headers

2. In what conditions are you placing your feature under test?

   Client Address Mass Update Mode Use

3. What operation of the system are you verifying?

   Setting - Disabled

4. What is the Action that the system should perform in one word?

   Changed

5. Is there a specific input parameter of the test case?

No

**ClientAddressPageHeadersChanged_When_Setting_ClientrAddressMassUpdateModeUse_Di
sabled**

Unit Tests Project

Suppose we assume that the code under the test library is called **Calculator.Core** I would
name the unit testing project **Calculator.Core.UnitTests**. When we have only one class to be
tested, it doesn't make much sense to make folders, but if we must follow the convention we
listed, a new folder **CalculatorTests**, should be created. For the positive scenarios, we will
place them in a class named **Calculate_Should**. Here is the full source code:

```
[TestClass]
public class Calculate_Should
{
    [TestMethod]
    public void ExpressionCalculatedCorrectly_When_ContainsAllOperations()
    {
        // Arrange
        string expression = "3 + 4 * 2 / ( 1 - 5 ) ^ 2 ^ 3";
        var calculator = new Calculator();

        // Act
        decimal actualResult = calculator.Calculate(expression);

        // Assert
        Assert.AreEqual(3.0001220703125, actualResult);
    }

    [TestMethod]
    public void
ExpressionCalculatedCorrectly_When_ContainsOnlyAdditionTwoSingleNumberedOperands()
    {
        // Arrange
        string expression = "5 + 4";
        var calculator = new Calculator();

        // Act
        decimal actualResult = calculator.Calculate(expression);

        // Assert
        Assert.AreEqual(9, actualResult);
    }

    [TestMethod]
    public void
ExpressionCalculatedCorrectly_When_ContainsOnlyAdditionTwoMultipleNumberedOperands()
    {
```

```
    // Arrange
    string expression = "51 + 489";
    var calculator = new Calculator();

    // Act
    decimal actualResult = calculator.Calculate(expression);

    // Assert
    Assert.AreEqual(540, actualResult);
    }
}
```

We can add more test cases to verify the many test cases we have for the calculator. However, I believe this code is enough to see a complete unit testing example. Notice the test names and how I separated the arrange-act-assert phases with white lines to make the tests more readable.

NUnit Unit Testing Framework

Maybe the most popular unit testing framework in the .NET world is NUnit. It is also my favorite because it is quite extensible and provides many additional attributes that ease automated testing. The easiest way to create an NUnit test project is to use Visual Studio wizard for creating new projects; just search for NUnit unit testing.

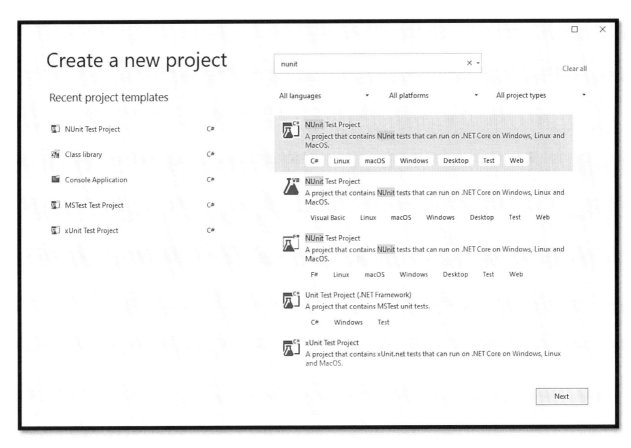

NUnit is delivered through a NuGet package: NUnit. However, if you need to create your project manually, you will need a few more NuGet packages to make it work. Two packages are required: Microsoft.NET.Test.Sdk and NUnit.TestAdapter. You can install them in a couple of ways. The easiest way is to use the **Visual Studio NuGet window** that you can open by right clicking on your project and clicking on **Manage NuGet Packages**.

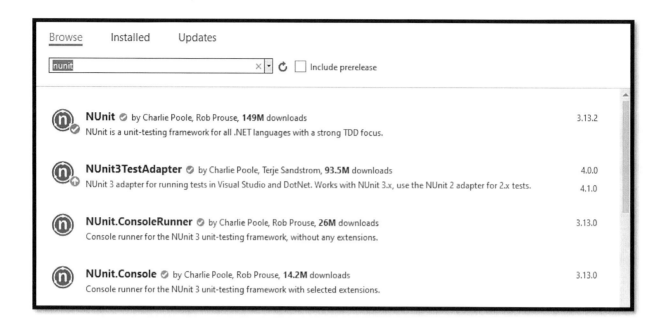

Or you can use the console:

```
Install-Package NUnit
Install-Package NUnit.TestAdapter
Install-Package Microsoft.NET.Test.Sdk
```

To discover or execute test cases, VSTest would call the test adapters based on your project configuration. That is why NUnit/xUnit/MSTest all ask you to install a test adapter NuGet package to your unit testing projects). So, NUnit.TestAdapter exists for those purposes.

NUnit itself implements the testing frameworks and its contracts. So, you need to add a NuGet reference to it to write unit test cases and have them compiled. Only compiled projects along with the test adapter can then be consumed by Visual Studio.

NUnit Attributes

If we return to our example:

```
[TestFixture]
public class GetTotalCost_Should
{
    [Test]
    public void ReturnsUnchangedProductCost_When_RateIsZero()
    {
        var vatCalculator = new VatCalculator();
```

```
        double actualValue = vatCalculator.GetTotalCost(105, 0);

        Assert.AreEqual(105, actualValue, "The Total Cost was not as expected.");
    }
}
```

The code is annotated using MSTest attributes. [TestFixture] denotes a class holding unit tests. [Test] denotes a unit testing method. We can execute logic in various parts of the test execution workflow. As you will see we use this feature often in automated tests. So, let's review the text execution workflow.

```
// A class that contains NUnit unit tests. (Required)
[TestFixture]
public class NonBellatrixTests
{
    [OneTimeSetUp]
    public void ClassInit()
    {
        // Executes once for the test class. (Optional)
    }

    [SetUp]
    public void TestInit()
    {
        // Runs before each test. (Optional)
    }

    [Test]
    public void YourFirstTestMethod()
    {
    }

    [Test]
    public void YourSecondTestMethod()
    {
    }

    [TearDown]
    public void TestCleanup()
    {
    // Runs after each test. (Optional)
    }

    [OneTimeTearDown]
    public void ClassCleanup()
    {
    // Runs once after all tests in this class are executed. (Optional)
    // Not guaranteed that it executes instantly after all tests from the class.
    }
}

// A SetUpFixture outside of any namespace provides SetUp and TearDown for the entire
assembly.
```

```
[SetUpFixture]
public class MySetUpClass
{
    [OneTimeSetUp]
    public void RunBeforeAnyTests()
    {
        // Executes once before the test run. (Optional)
    }

    [OneTimeTearDown]
    public void RunAfterAnyTests()
    {
        // Executes once after the test run. (Optional)
    }
}
```

The methods are executed in the following order:

```
OneTimeSetUp from SetUpFixture (once per assembly)
    OneTimeSetUp from TestFixture (once per test class class)
        SetUp (before each test of the class)
            Test1
        TearDown (after each test of the class)
        SetUp
            Test2
        TearDown
...
    OneTimeTearDown from TestFixture (once per test class)
    OneTimeSetUp from TestFixture
...
    OneTimeTearDown from TestFixture
OneTimeTearDown from SetUpFixture (once per assembly)
```

There are two big differences compared to MSTest. These are not static methods which means that we can reuse them through inheritance. Additionally, the assembly, initialize, and cleanup methods must be placed inside a separate class.

NUnit Assertions

Now let's review the many assertion methods that come with the NUnit test framework. It provides three big groups - regular, string, and collection assertions. NUnit has two different assertion syntaxes - the classic and constraint models. It is a matter of preference which one you will use. Some people believe that the constraint model makes the code more readable; some don't. It is crucial to pick one of them and stick to it.

Regular Assertions Classic Model

```
Assert.AreEqual(28, _actualFuel);
```

Tests whether the specified values are equal.

```
Assert.AreNotEqual(28, _actualFuel);
```

Tests whether the specified values are unequal. Same as AreEqual for numeric values.

```
Assert.AreSame(_expectedRocket, _actualRocket);
```

Tests whether the specified objects both refer to the same object.

```
Assert.AreNotSame(_expectedRocket, _actualRocket);
```

Tests whether the specified objects refer to different objects.

```
Assert.IsTrue(_isThereEnoughFuel);
```

Tests whether the specified condition is true.

```
Assert.IsFalse(_isThereEnoughFuel);
```

Tests whether the specified condition is false.

```
Assert.IsNull(_actualRocket);
```

Tests whether the specified object is null.

```
Assert.IsNotNull(_actualRocket);
```

Tests whether the specified object is non-null.

```
Assert.IsInstanceOf(_actualRocket, typeof(Falcon9Rocket));
```

Tests whether the specified object is an instance of the expected type.

```
Assert.IsNotInstanceOf(_actualRocket, typeof(Falcon9Rocket));
```

Tests whether the specified object is not an instance of type.

```
Assert.Throws<ArgumentNullException>(() => new Regex(null));
```

Tests whether the code specified by delegate throws exact given exception of type T.

String Assertions Classic Model

```
StringAssert.AreEqualIgnoringCase(_expectedBellatrixTitle, "Bellatrix");
```

Tests whether the specified strings are equal ignoring their casing.

```
StringAssert.Contains(_expectedBellatrixTitle, "Bellatrix");
```

Tests whether the specified string contains the specified substring.

```
StringAssert.DoesNotContain(_expectedBellatrixTitle, "Bellatrix");
```

Tests whether the specified string doesn't contain the specified substring.

```
StringAssert.StartsWith(_expectedBellatrixTitle, "Bellatrix");
```

Tests whether the specified string begins with the specified substring.

```
StringAssert.StartsWith(_expectedBellatrixTitle, "Bellatrix");
```

Tests whether the specified string begins with the specified substring.

```
StringAssert.IsMatch("(281)388-0388", @"(?d{3})?-? *d{3}-? *-?d{4}");
```

Tests whether the specified string matches a regular expression.

```
StringAssert.DoesNotMatch("281)388-0388", @"(?d{3})?-? *d{3}-? *-?d{4}");
```

Tests whether the specified string does not match a regular expression.

Collection Assertions Classic Model

```
CollectionAssert.AreEqual(_expectedRockets, _actualRockets);
```

Tests whether the specified collections have the same elements in the same order and quantity.

```
CollectionAssert.AreNotEqual(_expectedRockets, _actualRockets);
```

Tests whether the specified collections do not have the same elements, or the elements are in a different order and quantity.

```
CollectionAssert.AreEquivalent(_expectedRockets, _actualRockets);
```

Tests whether two collections contain the same elements.

```
CollectionAssert.AreNotEquivalent(_expectedRockets, _actualRockets);
```

Tests whether two collections contain different elements.

```
CollectionAssert.AllItemsAreInstancesOfType(_expectedRockets, _actualRockets);
```

Tests whether all elements in the specified collection are instances of the expected type.

```
CollectionAssert.AllItemsAreNotNull(_expectedRockets);
```

Tests whether all items in the specified collection are non-null.

```
CollectionAssert.AllItemsAreUnique(_expectedRockets);
```

Tests whether all items in the specified collection are unique.

```
CollectionAssert.Contains(_actualRockets, falcon9);
```

Tests whether the specified collection contains the specified element.

```
CollectionAssert.DoesNotContain(_actualRockets, falcon9);
```

Tests whether the specified collection does not contain the specified element.

```
CollectionAssert.IsSubsetOf(_expectedRockets, _actualRockets);
```

Tests whether one collection is a subset of another collection.

```
CollectionAssert.IsNotSubsetOf(_expectedRockets, _actualRockets);
```

Tests whether one collection is not a subset of another collection.

Constraint Model Assertions

The constraint-based assert model uses a single method of the `Assert` class for all assertions. The logic necessary to carry out each assertion is embedded in the constraint object passed as the second parameter to that method. The second argument in this assertion uses one of NUnit's syntax helpers to create an `EqualConstraint`.

```
Assert.That(28, Is.EqualTo(_actualFuel));
```

Tests whether the specified values are equal.

```
Assert.That(28, Is.Not.EqualTo(_actualFuel));
```

Tests whether the specified values are unequal. Same as AreEqual for numeric values.

```
Assert.That(_expectedRocket, Is.SameAs(_actualRocket));
```

Tests whether the specified objects both refer to the same object.

```
Assert.That(_expectedRocket, Is.Not.SameAs(_actualRocket));
```

Tests whether the specified objects refer to different objects.

```
Assert.That(_isThereEnoughFuel, Is.True);
```

Tests whether the specified condition is true.

```
Assert.That(_isThereEnoughFuel, Is.False);
```

Tests whether the specified condition is false.

```
Assert.That(_actualRocket, Is.Null);
```

Tests whether the specified object is null.

```
Assert.That(_actualRocket, Is.Not.Null);
```

Tests whether the specified object is non-null.

```
Assert.That(_actualRocket, Is.InstanceOf<Falcon9Rocket>());
```

Tests whether the specified object is an instance of the expected type.

```
Assert.That(_actualRocket, Is.Not.InstanceOf<Falcon9Rocket>());
```

Tests whether the specified object is not an instance of type.

```
Assert.That(_actualFuel, Is.GreaterThan(20));
```

Tests whether the specified object greater than the specified value.

```
Assert.That(28, Is.EqualTo(_actualFuel).Within(0.50));
```

Tests whether the specified values are nearly equal within the specified tolerance.

```
Assert.That(28, Is.EqualTo(_actualFuel).Within(2).Percent);
```

Tests whether the specified values are nearly equal within the specified % tolerance.

```
Assert.That(_actualRocketParts, Has.Exactly(10).Items);
```

Tests whether the specified collection has exactly the stated number of items in it.

```
Assert.That(_actualRocketParts, Is.Unique);
```

Tests whether the items in the specified collections are unique.

```
Assert.That(_actualRocketParts, Does.Contain(_expectedRocketPart));
```

Tests whether a given items is present in the specified list of items.

```
Assert.That(_actualRocketParts, Has.Exactly(1).Matches<RocketPart>(part => part.Name ==
"Door" && part.Height == "200"));
```

Tests whether the specified collection has exactly the stated item in it.

Advanced Attributes

As I said my favorite unit testing framework for .NET is NUnit because of the many additional attributes it gives to its users. So, let's review them.

The [Author] attribute adds information about the author of the tests. It can be applied to test fixtures and to tests.

```
[TestFixture]
[Author("Joro Doev", "joro.doev@bellatrix.solutions")]
public class RocketFuelTests
{
    [Test]
    public void RocketFuelMeassuredCorrectly_When_Landing() { /* ... */ }

    [Test]
    [Author("Ivan Penchev")]
    public void RocketFuelMeassuredCorrectly_When_Flying() { /* ... */ }
}
```

The `[Repeat]` attribute is used on a test method to specify that it should be executed multiple times. If any repetition fails, the remaining ones are not run, and a failure is reported.

```
[Test]
[Repeat(10)]
public void RocketFuelMeassuredCorrectly_When_Flying() { /* ... */ }
```

The `[Combinatorial]` attribute is used on a test to specify that NUnit should generate test cases for all possible combinations of the individual data items provided for the parameters of a test.

```
[Test]
[Combinatorial]
public void CorrectFuelMeassured_When_X_Site(
[Values(1,2,3)] int x,
[Values("A","B")] string s)
{
    //...
}
```

Generated tests:

```
CorrectFuelMeassured_When_X_Site(1, "A")
CorrectFuelMeassured_When_X_Site(1, "B")
CorrectFuelMeassured_When_X_Site(2, "A")
CorrectFuelMeassured_When_X_Site(2, "B")
CorrectFuelMeassured_When_X_Site(3, "A")
CorrectFuelMeassured_When_X_Site(3, "B")
```

The `[Pairwise]` attribute is used on a test to specify that NUnit should generate test cases in such a way that all possible pairs of values are used.

```
[Test]
[Pairwise]
public void ValidateLandingSiteOfRover_When_GoingToMars([Values("a", "b", "c")] string a,
[Values("+", "-")] string b, [Values("x", "y")] string c)
{
    Debug.WriteLine("{0} {1} {2}", a, b, c);
}
```

Resulted pairs:

a + y

a - x

b - y

b + x

c - x

c + y

The `[Random]` attribute is used to specify a set of random values to be provided for an individual numeric parameter of a parameterized test method. The following test will be executed fifteen times, three times for each value of x, each combined with 5 random doubles from -1.0 to +1.0.

```
[Test]
public void GenerateRandomLandingSiteOnMoon([Values(1,2,3)] int x, [Random(-1.0, 1.0, 5)]
double d)
{
    //...
}
```

The [Range] attribute is used to specify a range of values to be provided for an individual parameter of a parameterized test method. NUnit creates test cases from all possible combinations of the provided parameters - the combinatorial approach.

```
[Test]
public void CalculateJupiterBaseLandingPoint([Values(1,2,3)] int x,
[Range(0.2, 0.6)] double y)
{
    //...
}
```

Generated tests:

```
CalculateJupiterBaseLandingPoint(1, 0.2)
CalculateJupiterBaseLandingPoint(1, 0.4)
CalculateJupiterBaseLandingPoint(1, 0.6)
CalculateJupiterBaseLandingPoint(2, 0.2)
CalculateJupiterBaseLandingPoint(2, 0.4)
CalculateJupiterBaseLandingPoint(2, 0.6)
CalculateJupiterBaseLandingPoint(3, 0.2)
CalculateJupiterBaseLandingPoint(3, 0.4)
CalculateJupiterBaseLandingPoint(3, 0.6)
```

The [Retry] attribute is used on a test method to specify that it should be rerun if it fails, up to a maximum number of times.

```
[Test]
[Retry(3)]
public void CalculateJupiterBaseLandingPoint([Values(1,2,3)] int x,
[Range(0.2,0.6)] double y)
{
    //...
}
```

The [Timeout] attribute is used to specify a timeout value in milliseconds for a test case. If the test case runs longer than the time specified it is immediately cancelled and reported as a failure, with a message indicating that the timeout was exceeded.

```
[Test]
[Timeout(2000)]
public void FireRocketToProximaCentauri()
```

```
{
    //...
}
```

Execute Tests in Parallel

Parallel execution of methods within a class is supported starting with NUnit 3.7. In earlier releases, parallel execution only applies down to the `TestFixture` level, `ParallelScope.Children` works as `ParallelScope.Fixtures` and any `[Parallelizable]` attribute placed on a method is ignored.

```
[assembly: Parallelizable(ParallelScope.Fixtures)]
[assembly:LevelOfParallelism(3)]
```

The `[Parallelizable]` attribute may be specified on multiple levels of the tests. Settings at a higher level may affect lower-level tests, unless those lower-level tests override the inherited settings.

```
[TestFixture]
[Parallelizable(ParallelScope.Fixtures)]
public class TestFalcon9EngineLevels
{
    // ...
}
```

Exercises

1. Write three classes: Student, Course and School
   a. Students should have name and unique number (inside the entire School)
   b. Name cannot be empty, and the unique number is between 10000 and 99999.
   c. Each course contains a set of students.
   d. Students in a course should be less than 30 and can join and leave courses.
2. Create an NUnit test project and create tests for the classes that you created in 1.
   a. Use 2 class library projects in Visual Studio: `School.csproj` and `School.Tests.csproj`

Running Tests and Test Results

The easiest way to execute your tests is to use Visual Studio. Open Test Explorer. You can search by test name, test class or apply filters by category, project, namespace, etc.

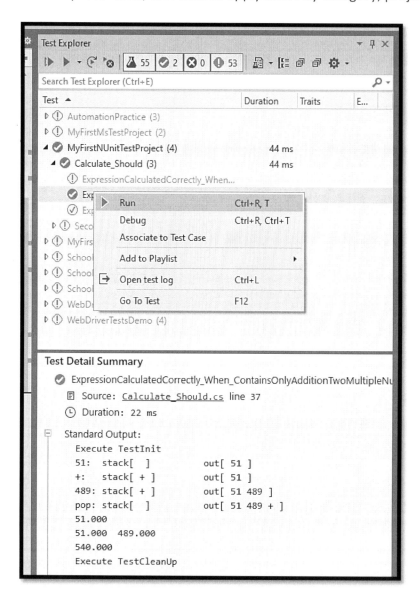

You can configure whether to run the tests in parallel or rerun only the failures. It is very convenient to debug the tests. You have one more option inside Visual Studio by clicking on the test name and opening the context menu.

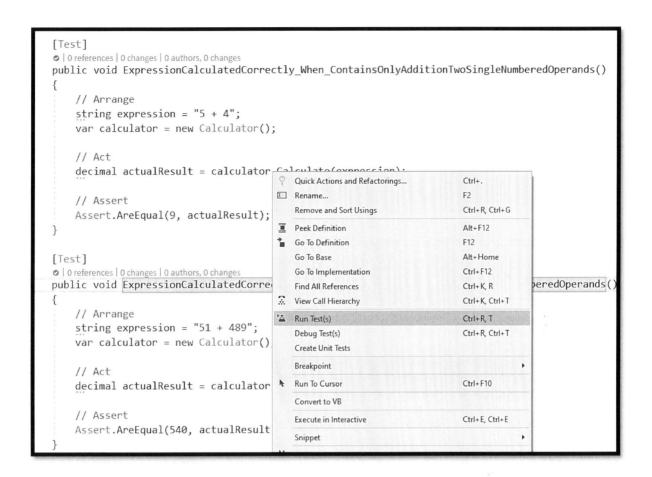

```
[Test]
  ⊘ | 0 references | 0 changes | 0 authors, 0 changes
public void ExpressionCalculatedCorrectly_When_ContainsOnlyAdditionTwoSingleNumberedOperands()
{
    // Arrange
    string expression = "5 + 4";
    var calculator = new Calculator();

    // Act
    decimal actualResult = calculator.Calculate(expression);

    // Assert
    Assert.AreEqual(9, actualResult);
}

[Test]
  ⊘ | 0 references | 0 changes | 0 authors, 0 changes
public void ExpressionCalculatedCorre                                      beredOperands()
{
    // Arrange
    string expression = "51 + 489";
    var calculator = new Calculator();

    // Act
    decimal actualResult = calculator

    // Assert
    Assert.AreEqual(540, actualResult
}
```

Context menu options:

💡	Quick Actions and Refactorings...	Ctrl+.
▭	Rename...	F2
	Remove and Sort Usings	Ctrl+R, Ctrl+G
⊠	Peek Definition	Alt+F12
➚	Go To Definition	F12
	Go To Base	Alt+Home
	Go To Implementation	Ctrl+F12
	Find All References	Ctrl+K, R
	View Call Hierarchy	Ctrl+K, Ctrl+T
	Run Test(s)	Ctrl+R, T
	Debug Test(s)	Ctrl+R, Ctrl+T
	Create Unit Tests	
	Breakpoint	▸
▸	Run To Cursor	Ctrl+F10
	Convert to VB	
	Execute in Interactive	Ctrl+E, Ctrl+E
	Snippet	▸

To run the test from command line you can use the **dotnet test** command that comes with the installation of the latest version of .NET. The **dotnet test** command executes unit tests in a given solution. The dotnet test command builds the solution and runs a test host application for each test project in the solution. Then, the test host executes tests in the given project using a test framework, for example, MSTest, NUnit, or xUnit, and reports the success or failure of each test. If all tests are successful, the test runner returns 0 as an exit code; otherwise, if any test fails, it returns 1. The information here is acquired from the official MSDN documentation about dotnet test, since it is not a book, I haven't quoted it. Check it for more detailed explanations.

Run the tests in the project in the current directory:
dotnet test

Run the tests in the Calculator.Core.UnitTests project and generate a test results file in the **trx** format:

dotnet test ~/projects/Calculator.Core.UnitTests.csproj -logger trx

You can filter your tests using **-filter <expression>.** <expression> has the format **<property><operator><value>[|&<Expression>]**. <property> is an attribute of the Test Case. The following are the properties supported by popular unit test frameworks:

MSTest:
- FullyQualifiedName
- Name
- ClassName
- Priority
- TestCategory

NUnit:
- FullyQualifiedName
- Name
- TestCategory
- Priority

The <operator> describes the relationship between the property and the value:

=	Exact match
!=	Not exact match
~	Contains
!~	Not contains

<value> is a string. All the lookups are case insensitive.

An expression without an **<operator>** is automatically considered as a contains on **FullyQualifiedName** property (for example, **dotnet test --filter xyz** is same as **dotnet test -- filter FullyQualifiedName~xyz**). Expressions can be joined with conditional operators:

|	OR
&	AND

You can enclose expressions in parenthesis when using conditional operators (for example, (Name~TestMethod1) | (Name~TestMethod2)).

Run the CI tests in the Calculator.Core.UnitTests project:
dotnet test ~/projects/Calculator.Core.UnitTests.csproj -filter Category=CI

To run tests that have either FullyQualifiedName containing **Calculator** and have a Trait with a key of "Category" and value of "NightlyRun" or have a Trait with a key of "Priority" and value of 1.

dotnet test ~/projects/Calculator.Core.UnitTests.csproj --filter "(FullyQualifiedName~Calculator&Category=NightlyRun)|Priority=1"

Summary

In the chapter, we learned an essential tool that will allow later to write complex UI tests - unit testing. Then, we investigated two popular unit testing frameworks in the .NET world and discussed how to use them for end-to-end testing. Also, we saw a detailed example of how to test production like code from scratch. In this part, we discussed various naming conventions and practices for applying unit testing frameworks in end-to-end testing. Lastly, we reviewed a few ways to run, filter, execute and view test results.

In the upcoming appendix chapter, we will talk about coding standards - naming the action and assertion methods right, as well as variables and parameters. At the end of the appendix, we will discuss various tools to help us enforce all coding guidelines we agreed to use. **After that, you will find information about the next series book focusing on entirely writing automated web tests.**

Appendix 1. High-quality Code

Meaningful Names

A big part of the role of readable code is to communicate its intent to the reader without the need for huge comments. In the following section, we will talk about various guidelines that you can follow while naming various parts of your code, and by doing so, make your code much easier to understand and comprehend.

General Naming Guidelines

Always use English. Avoid abbreviations:

- `buttonsCnt` vs `butonsCount`
- `usrLt` vs `usersList`
- `cdCrdsNums` vs `creditCardNumbers`
- `dtenRegExPtrn` vs `dateTimeEnglishRegExPattern`

Always prefer names that are meaningful to short ones. It is more critical for your names to be readable than brief. Do not use words that most of your code users won't know. Their meaning should come off the top of your head, instead of making people ask colleagues or searching in specialized dictionaries. The names should answer a couple of questions:

What does this class do?
What is the intent of this variable?
What is this variable used for?
What would this method return?

Correct

`DiscountsCalculator, buttonsCount, Math.PI, fileNames, GenerateInvoice`

Incorrect

`d, d8, d6, u33, HCJ, anchor3, variable, temp, tmp, temp__var, something, someValue`

Whether a name is meaningful or not depends on the context where you are using it. Let's look at a few examples below.

Correct

- `Generate()` in the class `DiscountsGenerator`
- `Find(string item)` in the class `ItemFinder`
- `CreateInvoice(decimal amount)` in the class `Account`

Incorrect
- `CreateInvoice()` in the class `Program`
- `Search(string item)` in the class `DiscountsGenerator`

Naming Classes

Class names are written in UpperCamelCase. Class names are typically nouns or noun phrases.

Do not use Hungarian notation. Do not use underscores, hyphens, or any other non-alphanumeric characters. Avoid using names that conflict with keywords such as **new**, **class**, and so on.

NOTE

Hungarian notation is a naming convention in programming, in which the name of a variable or method indicates its intention and type—for example, `bBusy` for `boolean` or `iSize` for `integer`.

Do not use abbreviations or acronyms as part of the names, especially if they are not widely accepted. Even if they are, use them only when necessary - for example, `GetWindow()` rather than `GetWin()`.

Correct

```
SalesOrdersInvoiceCreator salesOrdersInvoiceCreator;
SuggestedOrdersInvoiceCreator suggestedOrdersInvoiceCreator;
```

Incorrect

```
InvoiceCreator1 creator1;
InvoiceCreator2 creator2;
```

Classes are named starting with the name of the class they are testing and end with Test(s) if we are talking about unit tests.

Correct: `OrderCalculatorTests`, `InvoiceCreatorTests`

Incorrect: `Orders`, `ScreenshotCapture`

With UI, system, API, and similar test classes, you can start the class's name with a short description of the context they cover.

Correct: `ProductPurchaseWithoutPagesObjectsTests`, `SearchEngineTests`

Incorrect: `PerformSearches`, `MakeOrders`

If you create an exception class, its name should end with the suffix 'Exception'.

Correct: `NumberFormatException`, `StaleElementException`

Incorrect: `ElementNotFound`, `StaleElement`

How long can the name be? As long as required. Do not abbreviate names. As mentioned, opt for readability over brevity. The modern programming IDEs have features easing the work with long names.

Correct: `CreateOrderWithActiveCustomerViaShoppingCart()`, `ClientSupportInvoiceService`
Incorrect: `CreateOrdActiveCustViaSC()`, `CustSprInvSrvc`

Naming New Versions of Existing API

Sometimes adding new behavior to an existing class is not possible, and a new version should be created. This means that a new type should be introduced that will live together with the original class. In this situation you need to find a proper new name.

It is better to use names close to the existing API. Prefer using a suffix than a prefix to differentiate both types. Previously, we mentioned that it is not good practice to use numbers in class names. However, sometimes no other meaningful suffix can be used for the new version of the API than just adding a numeric suffix. In such cases, it is OK to use a numeric suffix. For example, `X509Certificate` and `X509Certificate2`.

It is good practice not to delete the old versions of the API immediately. Instead, give your users time to migrate their code to the new versions by marking the old API with the `ObsoleteAttribute` and providing explanations of why the code is deprecated and what should be used instead.

Here is an example from the official WebDriver C# bindings GitHub repository:

```
public interface ITimeouts
{
    TimeSpan ImplicitWait { get; set; }
```

```
    [Obsolete("This method will be removed in a future version. Please set the ImplicitWait
property instead.")]
    ITimeouts ImplicitlyWait(TimeSpan timeToWait);
}
```

Naming the Methods - The Right Way

Another essential step in the quest for readable code is naming your methods the right way.

General Naming Guidelines

Like classes, they should answer a specific question, in this case- "**What does this method do?**". If you cannot answer it, this usually means that the method does more than one thing and should be refactored. Since methods perform actions, their names should include **verbs** or **verb phrases.**

Correct: `FindItem()`, `LoadPage()`, `PlacePurchase()`, `CreateInvoice()`

Incorrect: `method1()`, `doSomething()`, `handleStuff()`, `sampleMethod()`, `somewhere()`

Follow the formats **[Verb], [Verb] + [Noun],[Verb] + [Adjective] + [Noun]**.

NOTE

The suggested "case" may vary based on which programming language you use. The examples in this book are for C#.

Correct: `Generate()`, `LoadConfigurationFile()`, `FindItemByPattern()`, `ToString()`, `PrintItemsList()`

Incorrect: `Student()`, `Creator()`, `Counter()`, `Black()`, `MathUtilities()`

Just as in other parts of the code, do not use underscores in the names of methods (except for the names of tests).

Correct

```
public PerformActionKeys(IKeyboard keyboard, string keysToSend)
{
    //...
}
```

Incorrect

```
public Perform_Action_Keys(IKeyboard keyboard, string keysToSend)
{
    //...
}
```

Using Meaningful Method Names

If you cannot answer the question "**What does this method do?**", then your method most probably has more than one purpose. Therefore, it doesn't follow the **Single Responsibility principle**. It should be refactored and divided into multiple methods.

Correct

```
int count = GetCountByItemId(client, itemId);
```

Incorrect

```
GetAllByItemCount(client, itemCount);
```

The rules about the length of method names are applicable here. They should not be abbreviated and should be as long as they need to be. Otherwise, the code can become much harder to understand.

Correct

```
LoadClientSupportInvoiceService(), CreateAnnualDiscountsReport()
```

Incorrect

```
LoadClnSuppInvSrvc(), CreateMonthDiscReport()
```

Best Practices for Method Parameters

Use a short list of method parameters. The more parameters you add, the harder it will be for the library's users to understand your code. If you need to pass more than 4 parameters to your method, you should think about grouping them in a separate class and using it as a single parameter.

Correct

```
public void CreateInvoiceReport(
    DateTime startDate,
    DateTime endDate, int limit,
    bool isForExistingClients)
{
    //..
}
```

Incorrect

```
public void CreateInvoiceReport(
    DateTime startDate,
    DateTime endDate, int limit,
    bool isForExistingClients,
    bool isForMonthlyBucket,
    out double requestedAmount,
    out double dependentClientAmount,
    out double futureCustomerDemand,
    out double upperClientLevelAmount,
    out double dependentClusterAmount)
{
    //..
}
```

As with method names, there is a preferable format for naming parameters- **[Noun] or [Adjective] + [Noun]**. They should be in camelCase, and the parameter's unit should be visible from the name, as shown.

Correct: lastName, reportName, supportTicket, recurringBillingOrder, timeInSeconds

Incorrect: d, d1, d2, generate, FirstName, first_name, convertFormat

We discussed some of the best practices for naming identifiers, methods, and parameters. In the next section, we will talk about automatically enforcing these guidelines to your code.

Follow Coding Standards - Tools

Depending on which programming language and IDE you use, the tools for enforcing coding standards may be different. Here, I will mention two of the most popular ones in the .NET world, but you can find similar alternatives for all popular programming languages. The way these tools work is almost identical.

NOTE

Coding standards are a set of guidelines, best practices, programming styles, and conventions that developers adhere to when writing the source code for a project.

Enforcing Coding Standards Using EditorConfig

EditorConfig helps programmers define shared coding styles between different editors. The project consists of a file format for determining coding styles that will be followed, and a collection of text editor plugins that enable IDEs to read the file format. After that, warning messages are displayed in cases of non-adherence.

The tool is integrated into the newest versions of Visual Studio. If you open C# **Code Style** settings, you can configure it.

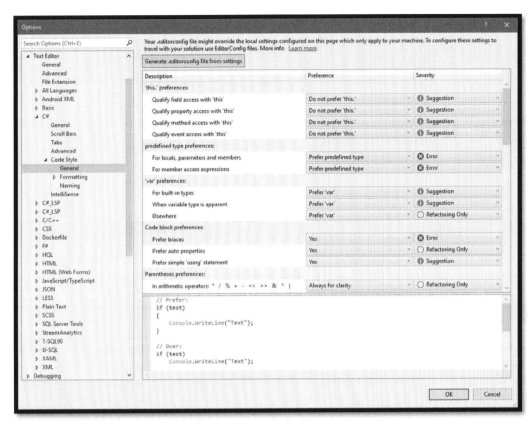

You can override the global settings through a **.editorconfig** file placed on the solution level.

When some of the users of your library don't follow some of the defined rules, the editor displays warnings.

For .NET projects, you can change the project's settings so that all warnings are treated as errors; by doing so all users will be forced to fix the errors immediately instead of ignoring the warnings for years.

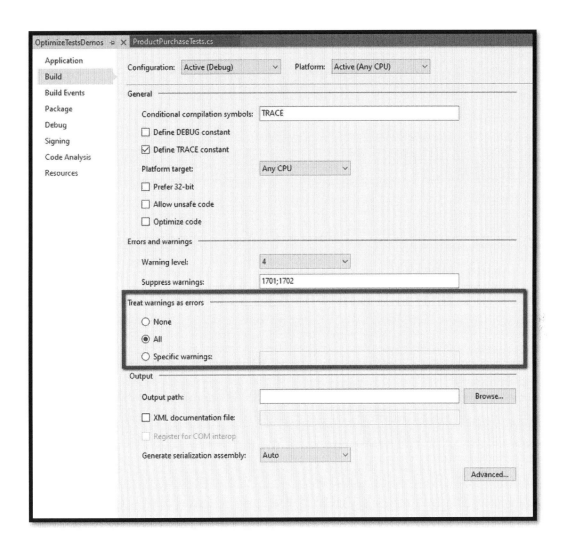

Some other popular solutions for applying coding standards in the .NET world are StyleCop and ReSharper. You can check their documentation to find the corresponding settings and how to configure them.

This concludes the first installment of the Automated Testing Unleashed Series. Please proceed to the following page to learn more about what's coming next. More insightful content awaits you!

What Is Next?

Source Code & Excluse LinkedIn Group

You can grasp its central concepts by perusing the code snippets in the book. Yet, to get hands-on experience, it's advised to execute the solutions firsthand. To begin, clone the book's GitHub repository via this link: https://bit.ly/3YUCLuq

To gain access and confirm your book purchase, send me a screenshot of the book order or the Kindle via LinkedIn, along with your GitHub username.

As an added perk, I've initiated an exclusive LinkedIn group for the book's readers. There, I'll share supplementary resources and videos tailored for those who own any book series volume. This includes insights for career advancement, interview preparation, checklists, and in-depth videos on topics that couldn't fit within the book's pages. **To join, provide proof of purchase by sending a screenshot of your book order or the Kindle version via a LinkedIn message.** Exclusive group's link - https://bit.ly/3qPnBtP

At the end of every chapter, you'll encounter a set of exercises. Their solutions are housed in **"Automated Testing Unleashed: The Complete Handbook - Automated Testing Practice - Solving Real-World Challenges Volume 5."** This volume offers exhaustive solutions to most exercises from the initial four editions of the "Automated Testing Unleashed" collection. Furthermore, it elucidates vital code sections to deepen your comprehension. A dedicated GitHub repository accompanies it.

Automated Testing Unleashed: Web Automated Testing Volume 2

What this book covers?

Chapter 1. WebDriver Fundamentals

Chapter 2. WebDriver Beyond Fundamentals

Chapter 3. Chrome DevTools & BiDirectional APIs

Chapter 4. Selenium WebDriver-Based Tools

Chapter 5. Defining High-Quality Test Attributes

Chapter 6. Layout, Style, and Responsive Testing with Selenium

This comprehensive guide to Selenium WebDriver navigates from foundational to advanced aspects of web test automation (over 300 pages). Readers will gain skills in executing JavaScript, managing cookies, leveraging the Actions API, and utilizing Selenium 4's revolutionary features, such as Chrome DevTools and BiDirectional API.

The book expands on an array of WebDriver-based tools that boost Selenium's potential, spotlighting cutting-edge automated testing types like layout, style, and responsive tests. Moreover, the book illuminates vital principles of high-quality test attributes and the SOLID principles, which are critical for every test engineer. It also clarifies often misunderstood terms in test automation, improving your comprehension and command of the technical language.

In essence, this book is a reliable companion for anyone keen on enhancing their skills in Selenium WebDriver and web test automation, delivering expert knowledge in an easy-to-understand manner.

Note to My Readers

If you've found value in this book and enjoyed its content, please take a moment to rate and review it. Your feedback helps other readers discover this book and provides valuable insights for future publications. Your voice can make a difference, and I genuinely appreciate your support in sharing your thoughts!

Thank you for being a part of this journey with me.

Warm regards,
Anton Angelov

Bibliography

[Sgt 18] "Standard Glossary of Terms used in Software Testing Version 3.2", ISTQB, Feb 2018

[Sdp 14] "Selenium Design Patterns and Best Practices", Dima Kovalenko, Sep 2014

[Isg 19] "ISTQB Glossary", International Software Testing Qualification Board, Dec 2019

[Rid 18] "Refactoring: Improving the Design of Existing Code", Martin Fowler, Nov 2018

[Caa 17] "Clean Architecture: A Craftsman's Guide to Software Structure and Design", Robert C. Martin, Sep 2017

[Cgt 18] "Complete Guide to Test Automation: Techniques, Practices, and Patterns for Building and Maintaining Effective Software Projects", Arnon Axelrod, Sep 2018

[Hfd 04] "Head First Design Patterns: A Brain-Friendly Guide", Eric Freeman, Elisabeth Freeman, Kathy Sierra, Bert Bates, Oct 2004

[Sfd 18] "Selenium Framework Design in Data-Driven Testing: Build data-driven test frameworks using Selenium WebDriver, AppiumDriver, Java, and TestNG", Carl Cocchiaro, Jan 2018

[Fdg 08] "Framework Design Guidelines: Conventions, Idioms, and Patterns for Reusable .NET Libraries (Microsoft Windows Development Series), 2nd Edition", Krzysztof Cwalina, Oct 2008

[Dpe 94] "Design Patterns: Elements of Reusable Object-Oriented Software", John Vlissides, Richard Helm, Ralph Johnson, Erich Gamma, Nov 1994

[Ast 22] "Advanced Software Testing - Vol. 3, 2nd Edition: Guide to the ISTQB Advanced Certification as an Advanced Technical Test Analyst", Jamie L Mitchell, Rex Black, Mar 2015

[Cid 19] "C# in Depth: Fourth Edition", Jon Skeet, Mar 2019

[Pcn 21] "Professional C# and .NET", Christian Nagel, Sep 2021

[Clr 12] "CLR via C# (Developer Reference)", Jeffrey Richter, Nov 2012

[Wcc 14] "What Is Clean Code and Why Should You Care?", Carl Vuorinen, Apr 2014

[Aut 14] "The Art of Unit Testing with Examples in C#, Second Edition", Roy Osherove, Nov 2014

[Hos 22] "Hands-On Selenium WebDriver with Java: A Deep Dive into the Development of End-to-End Tests", Boni García, May 2022

[Mta 22] "Mobile Test Automation with Appium: Mobile application testing made easy", Nishant Verma, June 2017

[Ctd 18] "Continuous Testing for DevOps Professionals: A Practical Guide From Industry Experts", Eran Kinsbruner, Sep 2018

Printed in Great Britain
by Amazon

37152856R00202